Daily Feast

MEDITATIONS FROM
FEASTING ON THE WORD®

❧ YEAR A ❧

ALSO AVAILABLE IN THIS SERIES

*Daily Feast: Meditations from
Feasting on the Word®, Year B*

*Daily Feast: Meditations from
Feasting on the Word®, Year C*

Daily Feast

MEDITATIONS FROM
FEASTING ON THE WORD®

❧ YEAR A ❧

EDITED BY

Kathleen Long Bostrom
Elizabeth F. Caldwell
Jana K. Riess

WJK WESTMINSTER
JOHN KNOX PRESS
LOUISVILLE · KENTUCKY

First edition
Published by Westminster John Knox Press
Louisville, Kentucky

13 14 15 16 17 18 19 20 21 22 —10 9 8 7 6 5 4 3 2 1

Book design by Drew Stevens
Cover design by Dilu Nicholas

Library of Congress Cataloging-in-Publication Data

Daily feast : meditations from Feasting on the Word / Kathleen Long
Bostrom and Elizabeth Caldwell, editors. — 1st ed.
    p. cm. — (Daily feast)
Includes index.
ISBN 978-0-664-23796-7 (Year A : alk. paper)
ISBN 978-0-664-23798-1 (Year C : alk. paper)
ISBN 978-0-664-23797-4 (Year B : alk. paper) 1. Bible—Meditations. 2.
Devotional calendars. 3. Common lectionary (1992) I. Bostrom, Kathleen
Long. II. Caldwell, Elizabeth, 1948- III. Feasting on the Word.
BS491.5.D35 2011
242'.2—dc23

                                                              2011023555

PRINTED IN THE UNITED STATES OF AMERICA

♾ The paper used in this publication meets the minimum requirements of
the American National Standard for Information Sciences—
Permanence of Paper for Printed Library Materials, ANSI Z39.48-1992.

Contents

Introduction

When we opened the first volume of Feasting on the Word: Preaching the Revised Common Lectionary and began reading, we knew that the contents were consistent with the title. As teachers and preachers, to have four perspectives on the lectionary in one volume truly satisfied our hunger for rich engagement with biblical texts. With the publication of each additional volume in the twelve-volume series, we became excited about the possibilities for the ways these essays could be resources for other spiritual practices.

This book is designed to give you a chance to step back and focus on a smaller piece from some of essays from the Feasting on the Word commentaries. Whether you are a pastor, educator, church member, or lay leader, let these reflections on biblical texts be a daily feast for your continuing formation in the life of the Christian faith.

Consider the ways that *Daily Feast* might be used:

- → **Daily meditation:** Begin or end your day with a reading and reflection on one of the texts for the week.
- → **Journaling:** As you read, think, and pray, journal in response to the thoughts that are evoked for you. Some find that journaling with words works best. Others find that using markers, crayons, or water colors invites a different kind of imaging in response to text.
- → **Preparing for preaching or worship leadership:** Have a copy of this available to give to liturgists and choir directors, all those involved in worship leadership. As staff or worship teams work on liturgy and prepare for worship leadership, this book can become a resource for meditation and prayer, and may even be adapted for use in worship.
- → **Preparing for teaching:** Use in your own meditation during the week as you prepare your heart and mind to teach all ages of God's children.

- → **Reaching out beyond the church:** Use in a variety of settings where a pastoral presence is invited to participate, such as social agencies, health-care facilities, hospitals, prisons, and mission trips.
- → **In committee meetings or staff meetings:** Use a *Daily* Feast selection as an opening meditation.

Note that portions of the texts for each Sunday are presented, beginning on the previous Monday, so that you can spend the week reflecting on the Scripture passages for the coming Sunday. Each weekday and Saturday will feature reflections on one of the four passages—Old Testament, Psalm, Epistle, and Gospel—along with a response and a prayer. Sundays and special days such as Christmas Eve and Holy Week will contain reflections on all four of the texts. (See "A Note from the Publisher" for more information about the Revised Common Lectionary and an explanation of how Feasting on the Word follows the lections during Ordinary Time.)

Included here are brief excerpts from each of the Scripture readings, but we encourage you to have a Bible handy so you can read the complete passage.

As we have read texts and the reflections on these texts from the four perspectives, we found ourselves slowing down, taking time to read Scripture, and connecting with these essays in new ways. We anticipate that the variety and depth of the perspectives on biblical texts of the authors of the essays will enrich your own spiritual practices.

We hope that our experience will be yours. So take some time. Read the text. Read the reflection. Consider your response, and be in prayer. May this resource be a daily feast for you.

Kathleen Bostrom, Elizabeth Caldwell, and Jana Riess

A Note from the Publisher

This devotional is a part of the series Feasting on the Word: Preaching the Revised Common Lectionary, a twelve-volume commentary series for preaching and teaching. The uniqueness of the approach in the Feasting commentaries is in providing four perspectives on each preaching occasion from the Revised Common Lectionary. The theological, pastoral, exegetical, and homiletical dimensions of each biblical passage are explored with the hope that preachers will find much to inform and stimulate their preparations for preaching from this rich "feast" of materials.

Feasting on the Word follows the readings in the Revised Common Lectionary (RCL) as developed by the Consultation on Common Texts, an ecumenical consultation of liturgical scholars and denominational representatives from the United States and Canada. The RCL provides a collection of readings from Scripture to be used during worship in a schedule that follows the seasons of the church year. In addition, it provides for a uniform set of readings to be used across denominations or other church bodies.

The RCL provides a reading from the Old Testament, a Psalm response to that reading, a Gospel, and an Epistle for each preaching occasion of the year. It is presented in a three-year cycle, with each year centered around one of the Synoptic Gospels. Year A is the year of Matthew, Year B is the year of Mark, and Year C is the year of Luke. John is read each year, especially during Advent, Lent, and Easter. The RCL offers two tracks of Old Testament texts for the Season after Pentecost or Ordinary Time: a semicontinuous track, which moves through stories and characters in the Old Testament, and a complementary track, which ties the Old Testament texts to the theme of the Gospel texts for that day. Some denominational traditions favor one over the other. For instance, Presbyterians and Methodists generally follow the semicontinuous track, while Lutherans and Episcopalians generally follow the complementary track. To appeal to an ecumenical audience, the readings in this devotional follow the complementary track for Year A, are split between the complementary and semicontinuous tracks for Year B, and cover the semicontinuous stream for Year C.

Because not all lectionary days are used in a given year, depending on how the calendar falls, you may not need some of the readings here until a subsequent lectionary cycle. Check the official RCL Web site at http://lectionary.library.vanderbilt.edu for a list of readings for the current year.

Originally designed to be a twelve-volume set of preaching commentaries, the series has now grown to include several other related projects in addition to this devotional. A full church school curriculum program is now available at www.feastingontheword.net/curriculum. A six-volume set of worship resources to complement the commentaries is now being published, and a guide to children's sermons will soon follow. And a major new undertaking using the four-perspective approach, Feasting on the Gospels, a seven-volume series of commentaries on the entirety of the Gospels, began publishing in fall 2013. Information about these projects can be found on the Feasting on the Word Web site, www.feastingontheword.net.

Finally, we would like to thank all who were involved in the original Feasting on the Word series, including our partner, Columbia Theological Seminary; general editors David L. Bartlett and Barbara Brown Taylor; editorial board members Charles L. Campbell, Carlos Cardoza-Orlandi, Gary W. Charles, Allen Hilton, Cynthia A. Jarvis, E. Elizabeth Johnson, Thomas G. Long, Kathleen M. O'Connor, Marcia Y. Riggs, George W. Stroup, Emilie M. Townes, and Richard F. Ward; project manager Joan Murchison; and project compiler Mary Lynn Darden.

❧ *First Sunday of Advent* ❧

Isaiah 2:1–5

In days to come
   the mountain of the LORD's house
shall be established as the highest of the mountains,
   and shall be raised above the hills;
all the nations shall stream to it.
   Many peoples shall come and say,
"Come, let us go up to the mountain of the LORD,
   to the house of the God of Jacob;
that he may teach us his ways
   and that we may walk in his paths." (vv. 2–3)

Psalm 122

Pray for the peace of Jerusalem:
   "May they prosper who love you.
Peace be within your walls,
   and security within your towers." (vv. 6–7)

Romans 13:11–14

Let us then lay aside the works of darkness
and put on the armor of light; let us live honorably
as in the day, not in reveling and drunkenness, not in
debauchery and licentiousness, not in quarreling
and jealousy. (vv. 12b–13)

Matthew 24:36–44

"Keep awake therefore, for you do not know
on what day your Lord is coming." (v. 42)

✦ MONDAY ✦

Isaiah 2:1–5

REFLECTION

Consumerist visions of the good life may seem to prevail in
our culture at this time of year, but Isaiah's prophecy will stand
up to any of them. This picture of unity, of justice, of shared
openness to the divine way, and of peace speaks to some of our
deepest hopes. The preacher would do well to find ways to build
bridges between the listeners' culturally driven anticipation and
the deeper yearnings that lie beneath. How might the many
pictures of happy families and yuletide gatherings actually
speak to something real, like the desire for harmony across
many divisions? How might the nostalgia for Christmases past
and the idolization of childhood wonder represent our desire
to believe again in things that seem impossible to us as adults—
like peace on earth and goodwill for all?

STACEY SIMPSON DUKE

RESPONSE

Which part of Isaiah's vision do you long for the most?

PRAYER

At the start of this Advent season, O God, teach me to see
beyond the cultural pleasures of Christmas to the deeper joys of
your justice and mercy. Amen.

✦ TUESDAY ✦

Psalm 122

REFLECTION

Our purpose, then, is to become the peace with which we have been gifted and to return it to the world. When the psalmist writes that the people said, "Let us go to the house of the LORD," it reminds us that the first act of the psalm is an act of worship—an act of going to the temple to encounter the Lord, pray, and give praise. We can see then how, when one praises God, one begins to care about others, pray for them, and work on their behalf. That work becomes the work of peace, work that will shape the world into the hope God has for it.

Each time we approach our Advent pilgrimage anew, we are different. The end of one journey positions us to begin the next. Our yearly pilgrimage gives us once again an opportunity to reconsider the way we are living our lives. Through pilgrimage, praise, prayer, and purpose, the psalmist reminds us that we are always waiting in hope, always called to be light in the world and to work on behalf of God's reign of justice and peace. We are forever engaged in an act of new creation.

CAROL L. WADE

RESPONSE

How can Advent be for you a pilgrimage to the house of the Lord?

PRAYER

Let me be glad and rejoice in your presence, God. Amen.

✣ WEDNESDAY ✣

Psalm 122

REFLECTION

"I was glad when they said to me, 'Let us go to the house of the LORD!'" I almost detect some ambivalence, here; the image is of people encouraging each other to go to worship, and the psalmist proclaims gladness at this—as opposed to some other prevalent emotions, perhaps? In my own context, people who proclaim an affinity for the church and for Christianity stay away from worship in droves. In the minds of some, it appears that "going to church" is indeed something that has been "decreed" (v. 4), an obligation that has been laid on us. We go to church not because we want to, but because we think we should. In the minds of many, also, are the images of a judgmental God and a judgmental church. Church can be the place where "thrones for judgment [are] set up" (v. 5)—where we expect to be judged and made to feel guilty.

Why would anyone be *glad* to worship? In what way could those "thrones for judgment" be positive and life-giving for us?

DAVID HOLMES

RESPONSE

When you were last in church, were you there because of joy, habit, or a sense of obligation?

PRAYER

Renew my sense of passion for you, God, and ignite my eagerness to serve your people. Amen.

✢ THURSDAY ✢

Romans 13:11–14

REFLECTION

In the early years of the Christian movement, believers lived with a sense of real anticipation. The promises they read in the Hebrew Scriptures seemed tangible; the reign of God and all that it meant for cosmic "regime change" seemed close at hand. When they prayed (daily), "Thy kingdom come . . . on earth as it is in heaven," they were looking forward to that happening within their own lifetimes.

Two thousand years later, the sense of anticipation has diminished. . . . To the extent that this is so, we may be the poorer for having lost this vision, because for Paul, this anticipation is not so much about circling a date on the calendar as it is about *hope*. Paul really believes that the birth, death, and resurrection of Jesus is God's sign that all of those promises about life and wholeness prevailing over brokenness and death are true, and that God can be trusted to do what God has promised. Paul *knows* what time it is: it is time to wake up and look forward to what God will do in the future and what God is beginning to do now in your life and mine.

CYNTHIA M. CAMPBELL

RESPONSE

Remember a moment when you felt that the kingdom of heaven was very near. What would it require to live in that state of constant anticipation?

PRAYER

O God of the now and the not yet, when I am caught up in the things of this world, keep my vision always focused on your divine future. Amen.

→ FRIDAY ←

Matthew 24:36–44

REFLECTION

The season of Advent usually begins with an eschatological text, as a way of framing Advent as the end of an old order and the birth of a new era. . . .

The theme of this section of Matthew's discourse is the necessity for watchfulness in light of the uncertainty surrounding the coming (Parousia) of Jesus. Verse 36 makes a startling claim: "neither the angels of heaven nor the Son" know when "that day" will occur. It is remarkable how many interpreters seem to believe that they can accomplish what the Son confesses he cannot do.

WILLIAM R. HERZOG II

RESPONSE

How do you respond when a fellow Christian claims to know the precise timing of Christ's return?

PRAYER

May I keep awake, Lord, and be watchful of your return even while understanding that I know neither the day nor the hour. Amen.

✦ SATURDAY ✦

Matthew 24:36–44

REFLECTION

Our text presents a splendid opportunity to show . . . that uncertainty is a condition of even the best biblical faith. This does not solve any of the unanswered questions, of course, but it may begin to bring our people a kind of rapture of relief because it takes the pressure off. It is a relief to know Christ does not expect us to know everything.

We are not expected to know everything, but we are expected to do something. The Jesus of the verses before us calls persons to a life of work in a spirit of wakefulness. Work in this sense means activity here and now. Biblical faith as Jesus envisions it is not so concerned with otherworldly matters that it neglects this world's affairs. Matthew's Jesus has an eye on what is to come and believes something decisive is going to happen in the future, but he keeps attention focused on the present day and the needs of the hour. We find this in the manner in which he directs people to the field, the mill, the daily grind, the ordinary places of human endeavor where life is lived. This region of the mundane is where faithfulness happens, and it is not to be neglected. Biblical faith knows it does not know everything, but it does know it is called to do something here and now.

MARK E. YURS

RESPONSE

What lingering questions do you have about faith and God? Right now, allow those questions to simply exist without requiring immediate answers.

PRAYER

God, I know you do not expect me to know everything there is to know about my beliefs. Help me to walk by faith and not by sight. Amen.

Isaiah 2:1–5

REFLECTION

Light is a strong image in the prophecies of Isaiah. . . . Light is also, of course, one of the primary symbols of Advent. This First Sunday finds the Advent community brimming with confidence. The light of the world is coming in Jesus Christ, and the world will be transformed. We light the candles of Advent as a foretaste of the light that is to come in the Christ child. The darkness of the world will not prevail. Conflict is replaced by community, and those who would oppose the advent of God's reign will be judged and overcome. God's light will not be denied. The reign of God will come.

BRUCE C. BIRCH

Psalm 122

REFLECTION

Advent, the beginning of the church year, is a time to begin our journey of faith afresh. Today's psalm captures in miniature the movement in the life of faith, that all of life should be one continual act of praise for God and service of neighbor. The psalmist creates a roadmap for peace that begins and ends in God (vv. 1, 9). This divine cartography propels the pilgrim's journey in acts of praise and prayer and purpose. When we journey to the heart of God, we become God's peace in the world.

CAROL L. WADE

Romans 13:11–14

REFLECTION

During the Advent season, the church prepares for the coming of Christ. Even as we make ready for the baby to be born in

Bethlehem, the lectionary this First Sunday of Advent takes us beyond the birth, life, death, and resurrection of Jesus to a new moment of expectancy as the Day of Christ approaches and the reign of God is made fully manifest.

JOANNA M. ADAMS

Matthew 24:36–44

REFLECTION

The season of Advent invites us to consider again the character of Christian existence "between the times." On the one hand, Advent reminds us of God's promises to Israel of Immanuel. God comes in human flesh to deliver God's people from sin and evil. On the other hand, Advent calls us to anticipate the day on which this Immanuel will return as King of kings and Lord of lords. He will put all that resists him, even death itself, under his feet. Living between the times, we give thanks to God for the Christ child, even as we plead with God to realize, once and for all, the kingdom that Jesus declared to be at hand.

JOHN P. BURGESS

RESPONSE

As the first Advent candle is lit today, imagine its light overcoming the darkness that surrounds it. How can you be a part of what God is doing to call the world toward the light?

PRAYER

Holy God, teach me to walk in the light of your love and to open my eyes to the promise of Immanuel—the good news that you are with us. Amen.

✤ *Second Sunday of Advent* ✤

Isaiah 11:1–10

A shoot shall come out from the stump of Jesse,
  and a branch shall grow out of his roots.
The spirit of the LORD shall rest on him,
  the spirit of wisdom and understanding,
  the spirit of counsel and might,
  the spirit of knowledge and the fear of the LORD. (vv. 1–2)

Psalm 72:1–7, 18–19

May he defend the cause of the poor of the people,
  give deliverance to the needy,
  and crush the oppressor.
May he live while the sun endures,
  and as long as the moon, throughout all generations.
                                                                (vv. 4–5)

Romans 15:4–13

For whatever was written in former days was written
for our instruction, so that by steadfastness and by the
encouragement of the scriptures we might have hope. May the
God of steadfastness and encouragement grant you to live in
harmony with one another, in accordance with Christ Jesus,
so that together you may with one voice glorify the God
and Father of our Lord Jesus Christ. (vv. 4–6)

Matthew 3:1–12

In those days John the Baptist appeared in the
wilderness of Judea, proclaiming, "Repent, for the
kingdom of heaven has come near." (vv. 1–2)

⇢ MONDAY ⇠

Isaiah 11:1–10

REFLECTION

According to Isaiah, the transformation from a culture of fear to a world at peace begins with a stump. Out of something that appears finished, lifeless, left behind, comes the sign of new life—a green sprig.

This is how hope gets its start—it emerges as a tiny tendril in an unexpected place. Listeners might be asked to examine where the stumps are in their own lives; where do they feel cut off? Can they imagine or believe that even now God might be nurturing the growth of something new and good from their old, dead dreams? They might consider what areas of their lives most need the promise of new life, and how they might become open to such newness. Isaiah's promise is not just a future one; even now there are tiny signs of hope and life in places that look dead and discarded.

Of course Isaiah's promise is not meant as a merely personal one. He proclaims the coming reign of God, which we read through our Christian lens as the coming of Christ. The little shoot will rise to be a new kind of king, one who judges with righteousness and brings justice for the poor and the meek. He manifests a power unlike any other, and his power is for the weak.

STACEY SIMPSON DUKE

RESPONSE

What is the "stump of Jesse" in your life—something that appears lifeless and finished? What would it mean for that stump to bring forth light and life?

PRAYER

Lord, you never abandon hope. Help me to envision your possibilities even when I have given up hope. Amen.

⇢ TUESDAY ⇠

Isaiah 11:1–10

REFLECTION

With or without us, God will accomplish a new creation.
Having raised up the righteous leader, the Creator will make a
new paradise of the earth. Enter the animals. Imagine—baby
goats are best friends with grizzlies; a lamb and a wolf enjoy
conversing over a breakfast of clover. Imagining such unlikely
friendships between ex-predators and prey invites a little fun,
but we should guard against getting too cute. The text has its
eye on the deadly aggressions and fears that sicken the world,
the ending of which can be envisioned only in a far-future
tense. A thoroughly healed creation is imagined, nothing
less than Eden remade. We notice that there is not much of a
human presence in it—only a few little children are there.

PAUL SIMPSON DUKE

RESPONSE

Take a moment to visualize something you fear. Then imagine
the Christ child removing your aggression and dread as the
object of your fear is tamed.

PRAYER

You have not granted us a spirit of timidity, O God, but one of
power and love. Amen.

⤏ WEDNESDAY ⤎

Psalm 72:1–7, 18–19

REFLECTION

Carefully looking at the world as it is, while praying this psalm during the season of Advent, suggests a number of directions for Christians today. First, while acknowledging the psalm's vision of the kind of leadership that God desires for us and that we hope for ourselves, we can and ought to pray for rulers today: good, bad, and ugly. After all, if we take Jesus at his word in Matthew 5, God rains blessings on the nice and the nasty, and we are called to love and bless like God. How then can we pray only for those political leaders who hold the views and enact the policies with which we agree?

Second, it is finally one, and one alone, upon whom we can fully pray this prayer. He is the one hoped for in Isaiah's words about a shoot from the stump of Jesse (Isa. 11:1), the one whose life and death and resurrection have already begun a reign that embodies God's very life, transforming the life of the world. In him we finally find a "king" whose spirit is of the Lord, who will rule with justice and righteousness for all the earth.

CHRISTIAN SCHAREN

RESPONSE

Pray now for your nation's leaders, whether you approve of them or not (and perhaps especially if you don't).

PRAYER

Give our leaders justice and righteousness, O God, that they may care for the health and well-being of the most vulnerable members of our society. Amen.

✦ THURSDAY ✦

Romans 15:4–13

REFLECTION

Paul's exhortation to hope comes in a particular context that turns this from a well-meaning bromide into a critically important word for the church today. Paul is writing to a community of believers in Rome made up of both Jews and pagans or Gentiles. They are together because Paul and others have been preaching a gospel whose message is that the promises that God made long ago to God's people Israel are now open to all because of the life, death, and resurrection of Jesus.

The summary of all he has said in chapters 12–14 comes in 15:7: "Welcome one another, therefore, just as Christ has welcomed you, for the glory of God." In order to give glory and praise to God, Paul says, Christ extended his welcome to all— Jew and Gentile alike. In order to fulfill God's promises, Christ embodied God's intention to widen the circle of divine love. *Therefore* (Paul's favorite word for making the transition from theology to ethics), if God has welcomed you—*all of you*—you are to be imitators of God. Life in Christian community is to be shaped by the practice of extending a welcome, of opening one's home and life, of giving hospitality to the "other." Each side is to welcome *the other*. There is no longer insider and outsider. Now all are hosts and all are guests, because all have been welcomed by the infinite expanse of divine love.

CYNTHIA M. CAMPBELL

RESPONSE

To whom should you be extending Christ's welcome right now?

PRAYER

God, I will welcome others even as you have welcomed me, knowing that your mercy is for all people. Amen.

✣ FRIDAY ✣

Romans 15:4–13

REFLECTION

The twentieth-century theologian Paul Tillich claims that *faith is the courage to accept acceptance.* I am accepted by God as I am, not as I should be. However, this requires an act of faith. It requires the courage to embrace Acceptance, that is, God's very self. God absolutely, fully accepts me and intimately knows my name: "See, I have inscribed you on the palms of my hands" (Isa. 49:16).

It is one thing to know I am accepted and quite another to embrace it. It takes a long time to believe that I am accepted by God as I am. The basic faith is that I know myself to be accepted by God. Self-acceptance can never be based on my own self, my own qualities, or my own herculean efforts. Such a foundation would collapse. Self-acceptance is an act of faith. When God loves me, I must accept myself as well. I cannot be more demanding than God, can I?

Our reading proclaims that *Christ accepted you for the glorification of God* (vv. 7, 9). The glorification of God will be possible only if the acceptance enacted by Christ flows through to mutual acceptance of one another, in particular those "weak in faith." Whatever one has received from God is bound to spread to others.

PATRICK J. HOWELL

RESPONSE

Do you believe, at the core of your being, that God accepts you without reservation?

PRAYER

In grace you saved me while I was yet a sinner. I believe this good news, but . . . help my unbelief. Amen.

✢ SATURDAY ✢

Matthew 3:1–12

REFLECTION

The promises of God that are coming to fulfillment in Christ should compel people to confess their sins. John asks us to examine ourselves, rather than bask in holiday wonder. We should bear good fruit, rather than worry about material things to get or give. John is almost a comical figure, dressed in camel's hair and eating locusts and wild honey, but his message is hard-hitting: "Repent, for the kingdom of heaven is at hand."

Repentance is a confusing concept to many Christians today. Does it mean feeling sorry for our mistakes? Is it a matter of trying to be a better person? Is repentance something that we even need to do, if our lives are now hidden with Christ, our Savior? . . .

What John—and Advent—remind us is that repentance is not primarily about our standards of moral worthiness, but rather about God's desire to realign us to accord with Christ's life. Repentance is not so much about our guilt feelings as about God's power to transform us into Christ's image. For Matthew, John's strange clothes and harsh sayings are necessary aspects of communicating the full meaning of the gospel. While warm and fuzzy feelings at Christmastime are not all wrong, they fail to capture the full picture of what God has done for us in becoming human flesh.

JOHN P. BURGESS

RESPONSE

Where are your priorities out of alignment with God's?

PRAYER

Turn me back to you, O God, and transform me in the image of your Son. Amen.

⊰ SUNDAY ⊱

Isaiah 11:1–10

REFLECTION

Advent is a good time for reexamining our old assumptions
and definitions, including how we think of and use power.
In Christ, power has been reinterpreted. How might our
own lives be reinterpreted in his light? How might our own
lives be remade—so that the wolf and the lamb within us live
together in a new kind of harmony? Our own lives can become
peaceable kingdoms when subjected to the judgment and
transformation of Christ.

STACEY SIMPSON DUKE

Psalm 72:1–7, 18–19

REFLECTION

On this Second Sunday of Advent the church is invited to
consider the political ramifications of the coming of the
Lord—both as the child Jesus and as the returning Lord. What
implications does the coming of Christ have for the way we
order our society?

DAVID HOLMES

Romans 15:4–13

REFLECTION

"Peace on earth, goodwill among those whom God favors":
this is the message the angels will sing, come Christmas Eve.
Until then, may the church be the demonstration project of the
peaceable kingdom God intends.

In *Seasons of Celebration*, Thomas Merton wrote, "The
Advent mystery is the beginning of the end of all in us that is

not yet Christ."* Until then, may harmony mark our holidays, and may the peace of Christ calm and correct our divided world.

JOANNA M. ADAMS

Matthew 3:1–12

REFLECTION

"Advent is about looking ahead," we pray and preach and teach, "waiting expectantly for what is to come."

Then here comes John the Baptist, dressed up in such a way as to remind us of old Elijah and speaking words taken directly from old Isaiah. "The voice of one crying out in the wilderness: 'Prepare the way of the Lord, make his paths straight.'"

Here comes John the Baptist to remind us that in the odd economy of God's grace—as we find it in Scripture—we look forward only by looking back. The Jesus we wait for in our future was already planned for in God's past.

Maybe our people are not as hopeless as we thought. Looking back on Advent past they find the courage to trust in Advent present and wait for Advent to come. Those ghosts who made Scrooge look back before he could look ahead had a point.

DAVID L. BARTLETT

RESPONSE

As the second candle is lit today, think back to Advent last year and what you were hoping for then. What happened with that hope? What are you hoping for now?

PRAYER

God of the past and the future, help me to abide in your time this Advent season. Amen.

---

*Thomas Merton, *Seasons of Celebration: Meditations on the Cycle of Liturgical Feasts* (Notre Dame, IN: Ave Maria Press, 2009), 77.

THE WEEK LEADING UP TO THE

❧ *Third Sunday of Advent* ❧

Isaiah 35:1–10

And the ransomed of the LORD shall return,
    and come to Zion with singing;
everlasting joy shall be upon their heads;
    they shall obtain joy and gladness,
        and sorrow and sighing shall flee away. (v. 10)

Psalm 146:5–10

The LORD sets the prisoners free;
    the LORD opens the eyes of the blind.
The LORD lifts up those who are bowed down;
    the LORD loves the righteous. (vv. 7b–8)

James 5:7–10

Be patient, therefore, beloved, until the coming
of the Lord. The farmer waits for the precious crop from
the earth, being patient with it until it receives the early and
the late rains. You also must be patient. Strengthen your
hearts, for the coming of the Lord is near. (vv. 7–8)

Matthew 11:2–11

When John heard in prison what the Messiah was doing, he
sent word by his disciples and said to him, "Are you the one who is
to come, or are we to wait for another?" Jesus answered them, "Go
and tell John what you hear and see: the blind receive their sight,
the lame walk, the lepers are cleansed, the deaf hear, the dead are
raised, and the poor have good news brought to them. And
blessed is anyone who takes no offense at me." (vv. 2–6)

✦ MONDAY ✦

Isaiah 35:1–10

REFLECTION

In some churches, each Sunday of Advent is represented with a particular word: Hope for the first Sunday, then Peace, Joy, and finally Love. Whether or not we are in churches that observe these themes explicitly, it is worth noting that this text from Isaiah is an extraordinary match to the traditional theme of Gaudete (Rejoice) Sunday, the Third Sunday of Advent. Joy pulses through Isaiah 35 from the first line, with its glad lands and blossoming deserts, to the last, when a ransomed people come home singing.

The transformation promised in the previous Isaiah texts for Advent glistens here in every line; redemptive reversals will be dramatic and complete. What kind of changes do worshipers in Advent seek? What do they sigh for, what sorrows have brought them to tears? We may not know what haunts each heart in the room, but we can take a cue from Isaiah, who speaks in detail of how the world looks now, and what it will be when God has saved it. Just as the prophet wrote for a scattered people, we too speak to people living fragmented lives in a fractured world, with torn-apart families and broken hearts.

STACEY SIMPSON DUKE

RESPONSE

Where can you find God's joy this week, despite difficult circumstances?

PRAYER

Thank you, God, for joy that transcends time and circumstance, and for redeeming your people. I will rejoice! Amen.

✣ TUESDAY ✣

Isaiah 35:1–10

REFLECTION

The final words are poignant. "Sorrow and sighing shall flee away" (v. 10b). We are not surprised to hear that sorrow will vanish, but sighing? Beyond sorrow, we sigh with weariness and regret; we sigh for beauty we cannot reach and for understanding beyond our grasp; we sigh in our aching desire for union and love, and in our longing for what we do not even know how to name.

Perhaps in the end it is all a sighing for home. Perhaps it is the sighing of the earth itself—and if biblical faith is true, it is the sighing of God. It will not always be so. The Lord will come and save. The ransomed will come home singing with gladness; and sorrow and sighing, all sighing, will flee away.

PAUL SIMPSON DUKE

RESPONSE

Let out a deep, satisfying sigh as you think about your heavenly home.

PRAYER

One day, God, I shall obtain joy and gladness in your Zion. Thank you for this redemption! Amen.

❖ WEDNESDAY ❖

Psalm 146:5–10

REFLECTION

Psalm 146 is a powerful lead-in to the great surprise of Christmas, the birth of the Messiah in a stable, into poverty and oppression. It confronts us with the conflict and contradiction in our images of God. It forces us to look honestly and deeply for the grace of God, the true ways in which God is trustworthy, just, and compassionate. It asks us, as the gospel so often does, to be the change we hope to see in the world. It prepares us for the surprise that God's grace will find us in the places where we are least deserving, and most in need.

DAVID HOLMES

RESPONSE

How is God calling you to "be the change" you hope to see in the world?

PRAYER

You who open the eyes of the blind, open my eyes, for I have been blind to the needs of those around me. Amen.

✦ THURSDAY ✦

James 5:7–10

REFLECTION

Many of us grew up with the adage "Patience is a virtue." It comes to mind as we read the opening words of the text from James: "Be patient, therefore, beloved, until the coming of the Lord." The author compares the patience he encourages to the patience of the farmer who waits for "the early and the late rains." Then, as the passage ends at verse 10, the author connects patience with suffering: "As an example of suffering and patience, beloved, take the prophets who spoke in the name of the Lord." What do patience, suffering, and farming have to do with one another and with the season of Advent?

Patience can also be a virtue in situations where waiting is required and where one is essentially powerless to change the circumstances: sitting in the car on the freeway during rush hour, standing in the seemingly interminable security line at the airport, waiting in the checkout line at the grocery store at 5:00 p.m. with a checker who is learning how to run the cash register. In these situations, there is an unavoidable delay. Try as we may, we can exert no control over some important factors in our lives. You can either get angry and fret and feel your blood pressure rise, or you can be patient. This aggravating wait will be familiar to everyone as well.

CYNTHIA M. CAMPBELL

RESPONSE

In this season of waiting, what tries your patience most?

PRAYER

Teach me the patience that comes from recognizing how many things are simply out of my control. Help me to surrender those things to you. Amen.

⇥ FRIDAY ⇤

James 5:7–10

REFLECTION

One way you strengthen your heart is to avoid "grumbling against one another." What an odd and yet appropriate exhortation. Survival over the long haul requires patience, not only with the Lord who will return in God's own good time, but with each other, lest you destroy the community that holds you up during the waiting.

Another reason not to grumble is that others will judge you and, in you, the Christ whom you claim to serve. In these between times, how do people know what Christ is like, if not through you? There is only the body of Christ to witness to his lordship and his love.

The most important reason not to grumble, however, is that God will judge you for it. As a matter of fact, "the Judge is standing at the doors!" (v. 9). If you do not want to be judged by the Judge, you had best leave judgment of others to the Judge as well. The day of salvation is near, and when that day comes, the Lord will take care of everything and everybody. Until then, the thing for you to do is to attend to the sinner who lives under your own hat.

JOANNA M. ADAMS

RESPONSE

The next time you are tempted to grumble or to judge another person, say a prayer for patience.

PRAYER

Keep me in patience and good humor, O God, and may the words of my mouth be acceptable in your sight. Amen.

✦ SATURDAY ✦

Matthew 11:2–11

REFLECTION

One reason we try to encourage simple Christmases in our homes and in our congregations is because the event we are awaiting has its own simplicity. John the Baptist foreshadows the poverty of Christ by the simplicity of his own life. The only rich people to show up for Christmas in Matthew's Gospel are the magi, and they bow down and then give up their gifts.

Here is a thought: could we try a simple Christmas in church as a model for a simple Christmas at home? What about not paying $200 for the brass choir and giving the money to the local food pantry instead? What about doing what many churches already do, asking members to send one card to the church to be displayed for the entire congregation, and sending the money that otherwise would have gone to Hallmark to the Salvation Army? We love soft robes and palaces, especially at this season, but the kingdom is about something else.

DAVID L. BARTLETT

RESPONSE

Today, give more than a token donation to charity. Imagine you are bringing that gift directly to the Christ child.

PRAYER

In this month of abundance, even excess, help me to find and cherish your simplicity. Amen.

⁂ SUNDAY ⁂

Isaiah 35:1–10

REFLECTION

This text does what Advent does: it points backward to old promises, which point forward to a fuller, future joy. We still live in the in-between time, as this prophet's people did. We are asked to take heart. God will come and save; we will find our Holy Way toward home, and our mouths will be filled with no more sighing, only song.

STACEY SIMPSON DUKE

Psalm 146:5–10

REFLECTION

The Third Sunday of Advent is traditionally called Gaudete Sunday or Joy Sunday, the day when we turn from preparation and judgment toward expectations of joy and fulfillment. That expectation will only continue to grow as we approach the celebration of the Christ's birth, and today's psalm captures that ebullient spirit.

The psalm reveals how joy is found through reliance on God. The psalmist's words are flung aloft in high hopes for the help that God brings, and we see this demonstrated in swelling praises of God's shalom. The exalted words of happiness and the ensuing divine deeds are surely a testament that the psalmist's hope is well founded.

CAROL L. WADE

James 5:7–10

REFLECTION

The contrast between the first and second readings on this Third Sunday of Advent could not be stronger. Isaiah paints a picture of the parched land exulting, the desert land blooming, and the whole earth rejoicing. In counterpoint, James encourages the early Christians, probably Jewish Christians, to stand firm, not to judge one another, but to bear each other's faults and failings with patience. Isaiah has a theology of exuberance, James a theology of patient endurance.

As Christians, we are invited to live fully into both these realities. We are invited into the paradoxical place of joy and sorrow, of a grace-filled vocation and the daily grind of duty; of the earth bursting with abundance and the dry-as-dust times when the farmer can barely eke out a living.

PATRICK J. HOWELL

Matthew 11:2–11

REFLECTION

"Who am I?" asked Dietrich Bonhoeffer, Barth's contemporary, in a poem from prison only a few months before the Nazis hanged him. Despite all his efforts to live faithfully, he wondered whether he was just a hypocrite or a weakling. "Who am I?" every Christian sometimes asks. In John the Baptist, we find an answer: to be a disciple is no longer to look at oneself, but rather to look at Christ. In pointing to him alone, the disciple's own identity finally becomes clear: "Whoever I am, thou knowest, O God, I am thine."

JOHN P. BURGESS

RESPONSE

As you look at the light of the third Advent candle today, rejoice! God's light is coming soon into the world, piercing the darkness.

PRAYER

Light of God, illumine my darkness and chase the shadows away. Come quickly, Lord Jesus. Amen.

❧ *Fourth Sunday of Advent* ❦

Isaiah 7:10–16

Then Isaiah said: "Hear then, O house of David!
Is it too little for you to weary mortals, that you weary my
God also? Therefore the Lord himself will give you a sign.
Look, the young woman is with child and shall bear a
son, and shall name him Immanuel." (vv. 13–14)

Psalm 80:1–7, 17–19

Restore us, O LORD God of hosts;
   let your face shine, that we may be saved. (v. 19)

Romans 1:1–7

To all God's beloved in Rome, who are called to be saints:
Grace to you and peace from God our Father and the
Lord Jesus Christ. (v. 7)

Matthew 1:18–25

But just when he had resolved to do this, an angel
of the Lord appeared to him in a dream and said, "Joseph,
son of David, do not be afraid to take Mary as your wife, for
the child conceived in her is from the Holy Spirit. She will bear
a son, and you are to name him Jesus, for he will save his
people from their sins." All this took place to fulfill what
had been spoken by the Lord through the prophet:

"Look, the virgin shall conceive and bear a son,
   and they shall name him Emmanuel,"
which means, "God is with us." (vv. 20–23)

✦ MONDAY ✦

Isaiah 7:10–16

REFLECTION

The four Sundays of Advent are like great tympani beats sounding a prophetic word of yearning and hope. In the Fourth Sunday, Isaiah brings us round to the great sign of God's promise: a young woman will give birth to a son whose name will be Immanuel, "God with us." The church's overfamiliarity with words about a virgin conceiving and bearing a son may lead many to take this claim for granted. Theologically speaking, we expect this in Advent. Yet others, outside the church and unfamiliar with the language of Zion, may be mystified. What can keep us from either presumption or incredulity about the prophet's Advent proclamation of this sign?

DON E. SALIERS

RESPONSE

When did you last feel truly surprised by the miracles of the Christmas story?

PRAYER

O God of mystery and incarnation, renew my spirit with your nearness. Prepare my heart for the unexpected gift of Christmas—not a warrior king but an infant. Amen.

✦ TUESDAY ✦

Isaiah 7:10–16

REFLECTION

When God instructs Ahaz to ask for a sign, Ahaz responds: "I will not ask and I will not put the LORD to the test" (v. 12). At first, it seems that Ahaz is piously following the law of God, but, as Isaiah makes clear, the king is missing the point of God's offer entirely. Ahaz does not test God if he accepts God's free offer; rather God is testing Ahaz. When Ahaz refuses the sign, he is actually refusing to trust in the living God who is speaking to him.

This is an opportunity . . . to reflect on your own encounters with and responses to the living God. How does God meet you in unexpected ways, with unexpected grace? Can you think of pieties that sound righteous but are actually refusals of God's grace? Even more to the point, consider the challenge that God presents to Ahaz: How do you respond with trust to the living God—to God with us?

PATRICK W. T. JOHNSON

RESPONSE

How do you respond with trust to the gracious and unexpected presence of the living God with us?

PRAYER

Immanuel God, open my heart to receive you. Amen.

✦ WEDNESDAY ✦

Psalm 80:1–7, 17–19

REFLECTION

In this psalm the community laments the absence of God,
petitioning God to "stir up your might" (v. 2). The psalmist
describes the community as a beautiful vine ravaged by wild
animals (vv. 8–13, sadly not included in the lectionary). They
see no signs of God's presence in the midst of this disaster,
which appears to be the demise of the northern kingdom (v.
2). To the worshipers, God appears distant or inactive. As the
psalmist and this community gather to worship, they do not
shirk from exposing the whole range of raw emotions they
feel, including hurt, anger, and grief (vv. 4–6). When injustice
prevails, God's people lament. Corporate worship is too
important to pretend that God is in heaven and all is right with
the world when it is not.

DAVE BLAND

RESPONSE

Since Christmas is a joyful time, Psalm 80 seems a dark text for
the season. But how does its raw honesty speak to your heart
right now? Do you ever feel that God has fed you with the
"bread of tears"?

PRAYER

Restore me, O Lord God of hosts, and let your face shine, that I
may be saved. Amen.

✢ THURSDAY ✢

Romans 1:1–7

REFLECTION

"Called"—Paul makes it sound so simple and straightforward! Three times in the space of his letter's *long* first sentence, Paul tosses off the term without hesitation, qualification, or seeming awareness of how debatable his claim might be. Especially since this "call" is supposedly from *God*, and asserted to apply to his *listeners* as well, anyone within the reach of Paul's voice might be pardoned for raising an eyebrow! . . . .

Amid all the pitches that are pressed upon us at this time of the year (Buy this! Give to that!); amid all the internal impulses that surge to consciousness during the days before Christmas (I must have this! I should do that!)—how do we discern to what we are "called," and by whom?

DAVID J. SCHLAFER

RESPONSE

To what are you being "called" right now? How can you discern that calling?

PRAYER

Amid the noise of the busy Christmas season, may the God of peace make my path clear through the still, small voice of the Spirit. Amen.

✢ FRIDAY ✦

Matthew 1:18–25

REFLECTION

In today's story of Mary and Joseph, God's work often upsets comfortable social expectations and conventions. The first Christmas was not produced by a flawless lead-up and elaborate preparations dictated by convention. Certainly most people would not expect the incarnation to happen through the life of the young virgin girl, Mary. Many in our congregations forget just what a scandal the incarnation and the virgin birth really were, that behind the pretty nativity scene lies both a wonder and a scandal.

Invite people to think about their own experience—the ways in which they have failed to live up to the notion of the "perfect Christmas" and the ways that, despite that failure, they ended up finding themselves more graced and more faithful than they might have otherwise been.

AARON KLINK

RESPONSE

When have you failed to meet your own expectations of the "perfect Christmas"? Did that experience make you more faithful or prayerful?

PRAYER

Deliver me from my surface perfectionism, O God, and allow your grace to shine through. Amen.

✦ SATURDAY ✦

Matthew 1:18–25

REFLECTION

Joseph shows us a profound trust in today's Gospel. God does not appear to Joseph when he is wide awake and at prayer. There is no assurance of a burning bush or parting clouds on the mountaintop. There is only a dream. Can we trust dreams? Do we not quickly dismiss dreams if we can even recall them a few moments after we awake? The dream, however, was enough for Joseph. He had been asking many questions. "What should I do about Mary? What does the law demand? What does my heart tell me?" The dream answered these big questions.

DANIEL HARRIS

RESPONSE

When has God communicated with you through a dream? Did you trust that the dream came from God?

PRAYER

O God of dreams and visions, help me to remain open to your leading in whatever form you give it. Amen.

⊰ SUNDAY ⊱

Isaiah 7:10–16

REFLECTION

As in the great Advent hymn "O Come, O Come, Immanuel,"
the ancient biblical images of what God has promised stir us
beyond our clichés and our presumptions. The sign God gives,
despite our own refusals and our self-interests in deliverance,
goes beyond our ambivalences to God's eternal self-consistency.
God's covenant with the creation is to redeem it from the inside
out. The promise of a Messiah is grounded in God's intention to
restore us and to transform the world as we have come to make
it into our own image.

DON E. SALIERS

Psalm 80:1–7, 17–19

REFLECTION

The Fourth Sunday of Advent is a final step in a season of
expectation. The celebration of Christmas is just days away.
Families have been awaiting the arrival of loved ones. College
students, home for the holidays, have been catching up with
hometown friends. Children have been eyeing the pile of
presents with enthralled anticipation. Recent widows have been
looking to the coming of Christmas with questions, wondering
how to make it through the season that now seems so different.
Christmas Day is almost here . . . but it has not yet come. There
is still a time of waiting and hoping and wondering. So on
this Fourth Sunday of Advent, worshipers pause, offering to
God their hopes and then, with anticipation and expectation,
looking forward to the fulfillment of those dreams.

E. LANE ALDERMAN JR.

Romans 1:1–7

REFLECTION

It is always a strained day, this Fourth Sunday of Advent. The liturgically faithful cling tenaciously to the waning season of Advent and its songs and themes of waiting, patience, anticipation, and expectation. Meanwhile, those fully immersed in the flow (which includes just about all of us) of consumer culture are feeling strongly the urge to let loose a carol or two. Here we are with Paul's salutation to his Christian sisters and brothers in Rome. It is tempting to set this text aside and take up the Gospel lesson from Matthew 1, which commends itself to the Christmas-hungry crowd; or the Old Testament lesson from Isaiah 7, which plays well with those inclined to toe the Advent line. For those willing to venture beyond the obvious choices, I encourage you to spend some time with these opening verses from Romans 1.   DAVID J. WOOD

Matthew 1:18–25

REFLECTION

Our congregations on this Fourth Sunday of Advent will expect us to preach the good news that the savior is near. Even if they already know the answer that Immanuel is near, might we wonder if they are asking the right questions? Do contemporary believers still need a savior? What does a savior save us from? What does a savior save us for?   DANIEL HARRIS

RESPONSE

On this final Sunday of Advent, are you actively waiting for a Savior? If so, what do you need saving from?

PRAYER

As I await the birth of your Son, O Lord, may I realize anew that he was born to save me and all those I love. Amen.

❧ *Christmas Eve* ❦

*(These reflections are to be used between the
Fourth Sunday of Advent and Christmas Eve.)*

Isaiah 9:2–7

You have multiplied the nation,
  you have increased its joy;
they rejoice before you
  as with joy at the harvest,
  as people exult when dividing plunder. (v. 3)

Psalm 96

O sing to the LORD a new song;
  sing to the LORD, all the earth.
Sing to the LORD, bless his name;
  tell of his salvation from day to day. (vv. 1–2)

Titus 2:11–14

He it is who gave himself for us that he might
redeem us from all iniquity and purify for himself a people
of his own who are zealous for good deeds. (v. 14)

Luke 2:1–14 (15–20)

But the angel said to them, "Do not be afraid; for see—
I am bringing you good news of great joy for all the people:
to you is born this day in the city of David a Savior,
  who is the Messiah, the Lord." (vv. 10–11)

Isaiah 9:2–7

REFLECTION

On Christmas Day 1531, Martin Luther preached from the Christmas story at the morning service and from Isaiah 9:6 at the afternoon service. He began the afternoon sermon by quickly recalling that the congregation had heard the Christmas story earlier in the day. He told them that they would not hear it again; rather, they would learn how to make use of it. Luther then turned to the words of the prophet Isaiah, "For a child has been born for us, a son given to us."

As you reflect on this text for Christmas Eve, you may wish to begin with Luther's insight and explore what Isaiah's prophecy says about the significance of Christ's birth for us. Isaiah works with a rich mixture of metaphors and patches them together like a quilt of images: light shining in darkness, tramping boots and bloody garments, a child who is a father and a prince. Let Isaiah's images play in your mind. Perhaps think of them as swings that take you back and forth between the text and your context. PATRICK W. T. JOHNSON

Psalm 96

REFLECTION

It is Christmas Eve, and the pews are full of worshipers who have come to sing the comfortable old songs of their past. Into the quiet of this night has come a new song. It brings an invitation of grace. "The Lord is king! The world is firmly established" (v. 10). It brings a call to faithfulness as well. "He will judge the world with righteousness, and the peoples with his truth" (v. 13). E. LANE ALDERMAN JR.

Titus 2:11–14

REFLECTION

What a wonderful call to worship for Christmas Eve: "For the grace of God has appeared, bringing salvation to all!" (v. 11). It echoes the angelic announcements found in the reading from Luke. However, the text takes a turn we are not used to taking on Christmas Eve: "training us to renounce impiety and worldly passions, and in the present age to live lives that are self-controlled, upright, and godly" (v. 12). The reading from Titus reminds us that the salvation being announced has direct and immediate implications for our lives. The offer of a good life is intrinsic to the appearance of this grace.

DAVID J. WOOD

Luke 2:1–14 (15–20)

REFLECTION

For weeks television advertisements have told us how we ought to feel this night. We ought to feel warm and loving, especially if we have spent a small fortune on gifts for our family and friends. We hope that most in our congregations this night do feel great peace and joy, but let us take care not to presume. Some may come to church this night dealing with the death of a loved one, worrying about mounting financial debts, or struggling with tensions in their relationships. The good news from the Scriptures this night is more powerful than the pain that some may bring.

DANIEL HARRIS

RESPONSE

A child has been born for you. A Son has been given. How will you respond?

PRAYER

God of grace, I thank you on this Christmas Eve that there is always reason for praise. Your "world is fully established." Amen.

❧ *Christmas Day* ❦

Isaiah 52:7–10

Break forth together into singing,
    you ruins of Jerusalem;
for the Lord has comforted his people,
    he has redeemed Jerusalem. (v. 9)

Psalm 98

O sing to the Lord a new song,
    for he has done marvelous things.
His right hand and his holy arm
    have gotten him victory. (v. 1)

Hebrews 1:1–4 (5–12)

Of the angels he says,
    "He makes his angels winds,
        and his servants flames of fire."
But of the Son he says,
    "Your throne, O God, is forever and ever,
        and the righteous scepter is the scepter
        of your kingdom." (vv. 7–8)

John 1:1–14

In the beginning was the Word, and the Word was
with God, and the Word was God. He was in the beginning
with God. All things came into being through him, and
without him not one thing came into being. (vv. 1–3)

Isaiah 52:7–10

REFLECTION

The words of poet Robert Southwell, set to music by Benjamin Britten in his *Ceremony of Carols*, express this well: "This little babe, so few days old, has come to rifle Satan's fold."* Yes, this child "now weak in infancy, our confidence and joy shall be, the power of Satan breaking, our peace eternal making."** The humanity of God is found at Bethlehem. God became one of us that we (all, not just some) may become restored in God's likeness.

DON E. SALIERS

Psalm 98

REFLECTION

If it should seem on this Christmas Day that this presence is not available to us, that this victory is not yet won, or that the Christmas event is but a tale to make children happy and merchandisers rich, then the psalm is an invitation to sing anyway. It is a call to open our hearts, minds, and eyes to the world around us and to the possibility of a victory so wondrous as to be unthinkable, so unimaginable as to be hidden still from our comprehension. Singing this new song together can increase hope and build among us a new perception of divine presence. It can instill faith, because singing the song creates faith and imprints hope in our souls. This new song can reveal our already-given connections to the sea and all that is in it, to the earth and all its peoples, and to the floods that clap their hands in joy. The psalm reveals the presence of God in the events of the earth, of relationships among nations, of our own participation in this glorious, cosmic symphony of life over which rules the King of the universe. This is most assuredly one of the meanings of Christmas.

KATHLEEN M. O'CONNOR

---

*The stanza appears as "This Little Babe" in Britten's *Ceremony of Carols*. It is from a poem titled "New Heaven, New War," which was published in *The Poetical Works of the Rev. Robert Southwell*, ed. W. B. Turnbull (London: John Russell Smith, 1856), 100.

**Johann Rist, "Break Forth, O Beauteous Heavenly Light," trans. John Troutbeck.

Hebrews 1:1–4 (5–12)

REFLECTION

Reading these opening verses of Hebrews on Christmas Day helps us to see the full meaning of the incarnation. While this day may stand out on the calendar, both liturgical and cultural, it must never stand apart from the larger and long story of all that is disclosed to us in Christ—in birth, life, death, atonement, resurrection, and glorification.

DAVID J. WOOD

John 1:1–14

REFLECTION

This text reminds its readers that, amid life's chaos, the world belongs to God. The prologue asserts that Christ always was, as if to reveal that God's love and intention for humanity was not simply the result of human sin, but part of God's intention and love for the world from the start. That news and that person are here called "light." Even at Christmastime, which in much of the Northern Hemisphere is cold and dark, Christ's light shines. In the midst of the worries of the world, of illness, sickness, and doubt, Christ's light shines. How do we see and show that light to others? It may be as simple as welcoming the stranger who appears in church around the holidays; it may mean buying a cup of coffee for a homeless person on the street; it may mean protesting an injustice at a rally.

AARON KLINK

RESPONSE

Instead of merely wishing someone else a merry Christmas today, share the good news that Christ the Lord is born.

PRAYER

May I be a messenger of your good news, as the angels were to the shepherds. Christ is born today! Amen.

❧ *First Sunday after* ❦ *Christmas Day*

Isaiah 63:7–9

For he said, "Surely they are my people,
   children who will not deal falsely";
and he became their savior
   in all their distress.
It was no messenger or angel
   but his presence that saved them;
in his love and in his pity he redeemed them;
   he lifted them up and carried them all the days of old. (vv. 8–9)

Psalm 148

Praise him, sun and moon;
   praise him, all you shining stars! (v. 3)

Hebrews 2:10–18

Since, therefore, the children share flesh and blood,
he himself likewise shared the same things, so that through
death he might destroy the one who has the power of death,
that is, the devil, and free those who all their lives were
held in slavery by the fear of death. (vv. 14–15)

Matthew 2:13–23

Now after they had left, an angel of the Lord appeared to Joseph
in a dream and said, "Get up, take the child and his mother,
and flee to Egypt, and remain there until I tell you; for Herod is
about to search for the child, to destroy him." Then Joseph got up,
took the child and his mother by night, and went to Egypt, and
remained there until the death of Herod. (vv. 13–15a)

⊹ MONDAY ⊹

Isaiah 63:7–9

REFLECTION

Surely, if ever the church is to sing of God's saving grace, it is on the Sunday after the boxes are unwrapped and the tree has dropped its needles. So, often the church laments, "Where was God when we needed God the most?" Here in chapter 63, God laments the unfaithfulness and ingratitude of "my people." In verse 5, God grieves, "I looked, but there was no helper." The faithful covenant people of God were nowhere to be found, and so God grieves. Listening to all of chapter 63 on the First Sunday after Christmas will call the church to a long memory of God's faithfulness and the people's fickleness. Even more importantly—and unlike the human tendency to give up on those who disappoint and anger us—Isaiah calls the church to remember the one who maintains covenants, even when "my people" do not: "He became their savior in all their distress. It was no messenger or angel but his presence that saved them; in his love and in his pity, he redeemed them" (vv. 8–9).

GARY W. CHARLES

RESPONSE

When has God been faithful to you, even when you have not upheld your covenants?

PRAYER

Forgive me, Lord, that I have not always been faithful to you. Guide my spirit back to your true path. Amen.

✦ TUESDAY ✦

Isaiah 63:7–9

REFLECTION

While the First Sunday after Christmas may not seem the best
timing for any of today's readings, there may be no better day
to confront the truth that neither God's presence nor Christ's
birth rids the world of horror and death. Even the most
sheltered parishioner may have noticed a sharp dip in holiday
cheerfulness over the past week, as both neighbors and news
media buckle their seat belts for the new year. Any gospel that
seeks to avoid the realities of sea monsters, murderous political
leaders, dead children, wailing mothers—and yes, even the
chilling image of an angry God—is not a gospel big enough for
human life.

BARBARA BROWN TAYLOR

RESPONSE

Take a moment to list, either aloud or on paper, some of the
ways God has lifted and carried you.

PRAYER

God, you have saved me from distress in the past and I trust
in your ability to do so now and in the future. Thank you for
shepherding me through a world of pain. Amen.

✦ WEDNESDAY ✦

Psalm 148

REFLECTION

What is the purpose or nature of praise? In some instances, praising someone means little more than complimenting him or her. That is far more external to the identity of the one doing the complimenting than is entailed here. Instead, the praise here is an acknowledgment of *one's own* identity. To praise the Lord as universal sovereign is to proclaim one's own ultimate loyalty as the foundation of one's being. *That is what is being called for.*

L. SHANNON JUNG

RESPONSE

Look around you and know that mountains, trees, birds, and animals join you in praising their Creator!

PRAYER

God, I find my identity through praising you. Amen.

⇢ THURSDAY ⇠

Hebrews 2:10–18

REFLECTION

Redemption does not come without a cost. Dietrich Bonhoeffer, a theologian in Germany during Adolf Hitler's Third Reich, remarked in his classic book *The Cost of Discipleship* that salvation is costly because it cost a man his life. Bonhoeffer recognized that salvation is properly understood in the context of community, when individuals gather together to work out their faith with love and responsibility toward others. Often the only way this faithfulness and responsibility get exposed is when we find ourselves engaged in meaningful relationships with others. Service, which is central to the process of sanctification and at the heart of Jesus' ministry, involves a persistent commitment to advancing the well-being of those around us. This is extremely difficult in our contemporary culture, which is obsessed with self-gratification, indulgence, and personal autonomy. If we were dependent on our own capacities, it indeed would appear quite overwhelming. Here, in this Hebrews passage, the theme of God in Christ working to bring about the salvation of humanity is the assurance believers need to overcome the challenges, pitfalls, and burdens the new year may bring.

JOHNNY B. HILL

RESPONSE

What has been the cost of your redemption?

PRAYER

God, thank you for taking on the cost of discipleship in sending your Son, Jesus Christ. I will remember your sacrifice. Amen.

⚜ FRIDAY ⚜

Hebrews 2:10–18

REFLECTION

It is a cruel world, and when we are under great stress or harsh suffering, we are prone to feel abandoned by God. We cry out for help, and none seems to come. We are caught between the extravagant promises of God as found in the Bible and the reality of our own painful situation. Human suffering by innocent people is a baffling experience and tests the faith of the believer to the core. The fact of human suffering is used as a major argument against the existence of God. *"How can a loving God allow . . . ?"* has been thrown in the face of more than one pastor or teacher.

Although this lection does not give a complete answer to the question, it does give us some help in living with the issue. For whatever reason, suffering does exist in this cold, impersonal, fallen world. The believer is not exempt from it. Diseases attack our bodies, friends betray us, and in the face of temptation we find we cannot resist and succumb. Evil governments perpetrate holocausts, and institutions crush the many for the benefit of a few. The righteous do not always prevail, and evil persons triumph.

Trouble and difficulty will come, and all of us will have very serious bumps on the road. We are given guidance and help in this text for the times when trouble comes . . . and it will.

WILLIAM L. SELF

RESPONSE

Who do you know who is suffering right now, or who feels abandoned by God? Pray for that person.

PRAYER

God of the helpless and the suffering, comfort (*insert name here*) today with your Holy Spirit. Amen.

⇢ SATURDAY ⇠

Matthew 2:13–23

REFLECTION

The text alludes to God's protective care and power in uncertain times. As God protected the Messiah from the threat of death, so will God provide protection in our times of job loss, bad news, falling stock prices, and unprecedented social and economic uncertainty. Faithfulness and trust in God will yield protective care. God will protect us in uncertain times and hide us in secret places. The Messiah was looked after, provided for, and placed in an environment where he could be nurtured and grow, even in the midst of dangerous and violent circumstances. God will do the same for us.

FRANK A. THOMAS

RESPONSE

In today's text, God protected the Christ child from harm, but untold numbers of other children were slaughtered by Herod. Why would God allow this massacre of the innocents to take place?

PRAYER

God, I will never know the answer to every question about goodness and suffering, but help me to understand enough in faith that I can do your work in the world. Amen.

⇢ SUNDAY ⇠

Isaiah 63:7–9

REFLECTION

On this First Sunday after Christmas, after the birth of the Son of God, this passage from Isaiah reminds us about how we might imagine the parenthood of God, as parent to all God's children. Hebrew biblical scholar and theologian Walter Brueggemann asks the reader to consider God's attributes in Isaiah as both motherly and fatherly; that is, the fierce God of Isaiah 63:1–6 gives way to traditionally maternal imagery in verses 7–9. Here, in God's care and concern for Israel, the prophet tells us that God "lifted them up and carried them all the days of old" (v. 9). This imagery of bearing Israel has precedence in Isaiah 46:3–4, in which God reminds the remnant that they have "been borne by me from your birth, carried from the womb." God is with God's children like a mother who carries her children in her womb and then, once they have been delivered, lifts her children up to her hip to keep them out of harm's way. This God deals with them tenderly, in an "abundance of steadfast love" (v. 7c), looking on God's lost children with love and pity (v. 9b).   EMILY ASKEW

Psalm 148

REFLECTION

Psalm 148 celebrates the God who created and the God who has saved. Its exuberant praise is rooted in informed wonder at the intricacies of creation and in clear remembrance of an experience of God's saving power.   ROBERT J. OWENS

Hebrews 2:10–18

REFLECTION

In a final reminder of Jesus' solidarity with us, the preacher says, "Because [Jesus] himself was tested by what he suffered, he is able to help those who are being tested" (v. 18). We are in this together, Jesus and we. This is the paradox of Christmas. Because of the incarnation, this helpless infant in the cradle will carry us through our most severe times of testing.

PAUL WALASKAY

Matthew 2:13–23

REFLECTION

It is the custom in most homes and churches that set up manger scenes to take them down after Christmas and store them until the season returns the next year. Matthew's account of the Holy Family's trials suggests that this is wrong. Perhaps we should put away the shepherds (Luke) because they returned to their fields, and put away the magi because they returned to their distant home, but we should keep out Jesus, Mary, and Joseph. Just the three of them, all alone, facing the terrors of a brutal despot. No visitors. No sheltering barn. No cuddly looking sheep. No friendly oxen. Then we should move the Holy Family to another location in our church or our home. Perhaps to a window looking out on the larger world, the world where there is still violence and repression and terror, and where there are refugees fleeing, needing protection, human beings in whom the Christ is crying to us for protection.

THOMAS H. TROEGER

RESPONSE

If you have a crèche scene in your home or church, take the suggestion above and remove all of the "buffers" that protect the Holy Family, moving the three of them to an isolated place of danger.

PRAYER

God, let me rest in your protection as I face the menacing Herods of this world. Amen.

❧ *Second Sunday after* ❧ *Christmas Day*

Sirach 24:1–12

Wisdom praises herself,
    and tells of her glory in the midst of her people.
. . . .
Before the ages, in the beginning, he created me,
    and for all the ages I shall not cease to be. (vv. 1, 9)

Wisdom of Solomon 10:15–21

A holy people and blameless race
wisdom delivered from a nation of oppressors.
She entered the soul of a servant of the Lord,
and withstood dread kings with wonders and signs.
She gave to holy people the reward of their labors;
she guided them along a marvelous way,
and became a shelter to them by day,
and a starry flame through the night. (vv. 15–17)

Ephesians 1:3–14

With all wisdom and insight he has made known to us the
mystery of his will, according to his good pleasure that he set forth
in Christ, as a plan for the fullness of time, to gather up all things
in him, things in heaven and things on earth. (vv. 8b–10)

John 1:(1–9) 10–18

And the Word became flesh and lived among us,
and we have seen his glory, the glory as of a father's
only son, full of grace and truth. . . . From his fullness
we have all received, grace upon grace. (vv. 14, 16)

✦ MONDAY ✦

Sirach 24:1–12

REFLECTION

While Wisdom says nothing here about being God's first work of art (as she does in Proverbs 8:22–30), the contrast between her misty genesis and that of the mud creature Adam is striking. She does not even mention him, in fact. Perhaps this is because she was never earthbound the way human beings were. She shared God's perspective on things. When Wisdom looked at the world, she looked *down*; yet, for all the privilege of her position, something was missing. . . .

Wisdom is not bragging here, showing slides of her cosmic world tour. She logged all those miles because she was looking for something, she says. She was seeking a resting place on earth, a place to pitch her tent. As nice as it was to cover the earth like a mist, what Wisdom really wanted was a physical address.

So her Creator gave her not a suggestion but a command (v. 8)—that she make her dwelling in Jacob and receive her inheritance in Israel. Taking a moment to remember her genesis again (v. 9), Wisdom gave up the sky for the earth, accepting her God-given resting place in the beloved city of Jerusalem. She took root in a particular people, among whom she would grow tall as a cedar in Lebanon (v. 13).

BARBARA BROWN TAYLOR

RESPONSE

In this passage, Dame Wisdom is longing for a home—she craves place to claim as her own and a people with whom to forge an identity. What does home mean for you in this context?

PRAYER

O God of Jacob, grant me the wisdom to always seek to dwell where you are. Amen.

✦ TUESDAY ✦

Wisdom of Solomon 10:15–21

REFLECTION

We might wonder why the Wisdom of God was portrayed as
female. How do we respond to such a depiction of God? A
congregation that speaks comfortably of the Holy Spirit as "She"
probably considers itself very avant-garde. The discomfort
that church people can have about a feminine face to God is
echoed in a similar unease about women clergy. Recently a
consultant working with a pastor search committee spoke of the
next hypothetical pastor as a "she." Parishioners immediately
reacted, fearfully convinced that the bishop had already selected
the candidate. There would have been no such reaction to a
"he" reference.

A possible New Year's resolve: to listen with ears that are
less selective, hearing beyond easy confirmation of that with
which we are already comfortable. Perhaps the faithful can
ask of the God who makes all things new that our own firmly
grasped convictions might be refreshed by ancient feminine
wisdom, just as Jesus' own understanding was deepened by a
certain Syrophoenician woman (Matt. 15:21–28). Rather than
contenting ourselves with noble intentions about weight loss,
perhaps we could resolve to analyze the way we think.

MARTIN G. TOWNSEND

RESPONSE

Try speaking to Wisdom directly as the female personification
of God.

PRAYER

Holy Wisdom, thank you for your guidance and care through
generations. Help us to become a holy people and a blameless
race. Amen.

⇥ WEDNESDAY ⇤

Ephesians 1:3–14

REFLECTION

There is something exciting about the Second Sunday after Christmas—in part because it doesn't happen every year, in part because it seems so countercultural. The secular trappings of the "holiday season" have faded away, the Christmas trees of many are already lying by the side of the road, extended family members have returned to their homes, and many have returned to work and school. Liturgically, we are still in the Twelve Days of Christmas—coming to the end of the season, sure, but still very much in the thick of it. The years when we *do* get to celebrate a Second Sunday after Christmas, we are given an opportunity to delve more deeply into the mystery of the incarnation, to ponder and to relish the vastness of the gift that is ours in Christ.

In these opening verses of Ephesians we are taken far from the narrative of the nativity, and beyond the cosmic comfort of the "God with us" aspects of the incarnation. In these verses it is as if the camera lens is backing up and lifting up, until now we are high above the earth, high above the galaxy even, and now we can see that in Christ we have been given a part in God's eternal plan, and we are swept up in a hymn of praise to the glory and the wonder of it all.

LISA G. FISCHBECK

RESPONSE

Read Ephesians 1:3–14 aloud. What inheritance have you obtained in Christ?

PRAYER

God, thank you for richly blessing my life through your Son, Jesus Christ. I do not deserve this inheritance of grace. Amen.

✦ THURSDAY ✦

Ephesians 1:3–14

REFLECTION

The phrase "the mystery of his will" reminds us that much about the glory and the grace we have been given is beyond our understanding; it is part of God's mystery. It is a mystery how Christ's blood serves as means for our redemption. It is a mystery that Christ's sacrifice makes possible God's forgiveness once for all. It is a mystery that God "chose us in Christ before the foundation of the world" (v. 4). It is a mystery that we have been adopted by God in Christ, and now have been given an inheritance of redemption. We cannot understand it all.

LISA G. FISCHBECK

RESPONSE

What aspects of your faith are you certain of? What parts of your faith bring you uncertainty?

PRAYER

Holy God, I embrace the mystery of faith in the knowledge that your grace is beyond my understanding. Amen.

⇥ FRIDAY ⇤

John 1:(1–9) 10–18

REFLECTION

The first eighteen verses of the book of John form the prologue and contain the themes of the entire Gospel: the divine Savior has come into the world and has been rejected by many, but to all who believe he has given the power to become children of God and the gift of eternal life. If the prologue is the summary statement of the entire Gospel, then one verse culminates and sums up the entire prologue: "And the Word became flesh and lived among us, and we have seen his glory, the glory as of a father's only son, full of grace and truth" (v. 14). Eugene Peterson, in his contemporary rendering of the Bible, *The Message*, has given us an alternative version of the text:

> The Word was made flesh and blood and moved into the neighborhood. We saw the glory with our own eyes, the one-of-a-kind glory, like Father, like Son, generous inside and out, true from start to finish.*

I love this rendering of this text because of the choice of the word "neighborhood." The Word was made flesh and blood and moved into the neighborhood. Neighborhood reminds me of the place where I grew up and the people with whom I grew up.

FRANK A. THOMAS

RESPONSE

What aspects of your neighborhood are hospitable to Jesus? What would be unwelcoming about your neighborhood?

PRAYER

God, I invite you into my home, my neighborhood, my family. Dwell among us as flesh and blood, and as we serve each other may we actually be serving you. Amen.

*Eugene H. Peterson, *The Message: The Bible in Contemporary Language* (Colorado Springs, CO: NavPress, 2002), 1916.

✦ SATURDAY ✦

John 1:(1–9) 10–18

REFLECTION

Compared to the nativity stories, John's opening words, as magnificent as they are, have a more distant, reflective, intellectual ring to them. Instead of "a child wrapped in bands of cloth and lying in a manger" (Luke 2:12), John sets off echoes that go all the way back to creation: "In the beginning was the Word, and the Word was with God, and the Word was God" (John 1:1). If we had only the prologue to John and no nativity narratives, we would have no Christmas pageants, no Christmas carols, but what a loss it would be if we lacked John's splendid hymnlike poetry. What Matthew and Luke portray in homelier human terms, John gives us in grander theological declarations: "All things came into being through him, and without him not one thing came into being. . . . And the Word became flesh and lived among us, and we have seen his glory, the glory as of a father's only son, full of grace and truth" (John 1:3a and 14).

THOMAS H. TROEGER

RESPONSE

If we didn't have Matthew and Luke with their nativity stories, what would we know about Jesus just from the prologue of John? Would it be enough?

PRAYER

God, all things were made through Christ, and without Christ nothing was made. Thank you for revealing your glory through the human face of Jesus. Amen.

Sirach 24:1–12

REFLECTION

For Sirach, Wisdom is the transcendent majesty of God that becomes immanent in the world, and especially in Israel. For John, the Word is the transcendent majesty of God who becomes immanent in the world—and at first, at least, especially in Israel. To use traditional theological language, in Sirach, Wisdom is God's instrument both of creation and of redemption. In John, the Word is God's instrument of creation, and Jesus, the Word incarnate, is the instrument of redemption.

DAVID L. BARTLETT

Wisdom of Solomon 10:15–21

REFLECTION

This seems like a strange lection for Protestants and even stranger as a reading for the Second Sunday of Christmas. Protestants have trouble even locating the book called the Wisdom of Solomon. (It is between the Additions to the Book of Esther and Sirach. Does that help?)

The primary theological interest of this book is the centrality and role of Woman Wisdom. In chapter 10 she appears as a partner of both God and humankind. . . . In contrast to Sirach and Proverbs, this passage portrays her not as a past creation but as an eternal emanation from God. One might even understand Woman Wisdom as a dimension of YHWH.

L. SHANNON JUNG

Ephesians 1:3–14

REFLECTION

Nothing packs up and leaves town quicker than the Christmas spirit. On this Second Sunday after Christmas we begin to ask ourselves, Why? Why the tinsel and bells, why the presents and parties? There must be more. Yes, there is much more. God is beginning (or has begun) to make clear to us the divine purpose in the world, the plan of the ages and how we are a part of it. God has not left us alone to our own devices, nor are we left without meaning and direction for our lives. We are here for more than our own comfort and pleasure. We are a part of God's great enterprise of redemption, reconciliation, and the healing of God's broken world.

WILLIAM L. SELF

John 1:(1–9) 10–18

REFLECTION

It is worth pondering what it took to reveal God to humanity. It took creation—light and life. It took a human person—to the mystery of God Jesus gave a human face. It took the witness of another who could see Jesus' true identity. It took a sojourn of shared life—he "lived" among us—and the response of faith from those who perceived Jesus' true identity. It took a worshiping community to study Scripture, remember, and be led by the Spirit. It took the conferring of grace and truth. It resulted in a new status—a new relationship for those who could be called "children of God."

R. ALAN CULPEPPER

RESPONSE

The Gospel of John proclaims that in Christ, "the true light, which enlightens everyone," is coming into the world. How has Christ enlightened your understanding?

PRAYER

Logos of God, in your incarnation God's glory was made flesh. Thank you for choosing to dwell among us. Amen.

❧ *Epiphany of the Lord* ❧

*(These reflections are to be used when the Epiphany falls on a Sunday.
When it falls on a weekday, use these reflections for Epiphany day and
follow the reflections for the week of the Baptism of the Lord.)*

Isaiah 60:1–6

Lift up your eyes and look around;
> they all gather together, they come to you;
your sons shall come from far away,
> and your daughters shall be carried on their nurses' arms. (v. 4)

Psalm 72:1–7, 10–14

Give the king your justice, O God,
> and your righteousness to a king's son.
May he judge your people with righteousness,
> and your poor with justice.
May the mountains yield prosperity for the people,
> and the hills, in righteousness. (vv. 1–3)

Ephesians 3:1–12

Although I am the very least of all the saints, this grace was given
to me to bring to the Gentiles the news of the boundless riches of
Christ, and to make everyone see what is the plan of the mystery
hidden for ages in God who created all things. (vv. 8–9)

Matthew 2:1–12

On entering the house, they saw the child with Mary his mother;
and they knelt down and paid him homage. Then, opening their
treasure chests, they offered him gifts of gold, frankincense, and
myrrh. And having been warned in a dream not to return to
Herod, they left for their own country by another road. (vv. 11–12)

⁕ MONDAY ⁕

Isaiah 60:1–6

REFLECTION

Christians trained to read Isaiah as a prophet of Jesus may
assume that the "you" in today's passage is the child whom
the magi have come to adore. This child has been the focus
of attention for weeks now, after all. In him "the glory of the
Lord" has risen (v. 1). His light is the one to which all nations
shall come (v. 3a). Already, kings have been drawn to the
brightness of his dawn (v. 3b). Isaiah is clear that the "you" at
the heart of his good news is not Jesus but Zion (59:20). . . .

While Christians *do* celebrate the arrival of a human
Messiah, this Jewish reading of the text offers an angle for an
Epiphany sermon—one that does not rely on supercessionism
for its good news. For the prophet, God's glory is completed in
the glorification of God's people. Their radiance is essential to
any bright future of God's own imagining. If they hope to sit on
the sidelines while someone else shines instead of them, then
they have missed their central role in God's vision. They are
not God, but God's presence will be seen over them (v. 2
JPS). They are not kings, but kings shall walk by their shining
radiance (v. 3 JPS).

BARBARA BROWN TAYLOR

RESPONSE

Have you ever seen God's light shining in a human face? If so,
what about that person helped you think of God's love?

PRAYER

Let my light so shine before others, O God, that when they see
me they will have cause to praise you in heaven. Amen.

✦ TUESDAY ✦

Isaiah 60:1–6

REFLECTION

The term "darkness" has a rich background. It can communicate sin or suffering. It connotes estrangement from God and alludes to the situation in creation before God began to act (Gen. 1:1–3). The nations that now seem to Judah to be basking in the light of military and economic success will be covered by thick darkness. Military success is no evidence that the light of God's favor shines upon them! When nations and kings come to Jerusalem, it will not be in defeat or under compulsion, but in joy and expectation. The nations shall join Jerusalem in offering praise to the Lord.

CHARLES L. AARON

RESPONSE

Have you recently been in darkness, without hope, feeling abandoned by God? Read Isaiah 60:1–6 out loud to yourself as God's personal promise of hope to you.

PRAYER

God of hope, when I feel covered by thick darkness, shine forth with your light. Amen.

✢ WEDNESDAY ✢

Psalm 72:1–7, 10–14

REFLECTION

Psalm 72 has long been associated with Solomon. With its reference to the king's righteous judgment and to the international honor in which the king is held, this may have been composed for an anniversary celebration for King Solomon.* For the preacher the heart of this text could be verse 4:

> May he defend the cause of the poor of the people,
>   give deliverance to the needy,
>   and crush the oppressor.

In our own day politicians curry favor with the electorate by appealing to "the middle class," not to the poor and needy. Here a ruler is being praised for what he does for those from whom he can get little benefit. Administering justice and caring for the poor were the marks of a great king in ancient Israel.

MARTIN G. TOWNSEND

RESPONSE

Today, find a way to let people know how important you think it is that politicians support the needy, whether you link to a news story on Facebook, write a letter to your newspaper, or e-mail your congressional representative.

PRAYER

God, help our leaders to make righteous choices and defend those who are most vulnerable—and give me courage to support and vote for those who do, even when their decisions are unpopular. Amen.

*J. Barton and J. Muddiman, eds., *The Oxford Bible Commentary* (New York: Oxford University Press, 2001), 387.

✦ THURSDAY ✦

Ephesians 3:1–12

REFLECTION

How can the modern church separate and wall off sections
of the population when the goal of God in Christ is to unite
all God's children? The mystery of Christ is the union of
humankind through the union of all with Christ. Our churches
need to adopt this message, and our world needs to hear that
"In Christ there is no east or west, in him no south or north."
This revealed mystery, now open to all, is the proclamation by
Paul and for the modern church. This mystery was revealed so
that it could be proclaimed (v. 7). This is a ministry entrusted
to us today also. It was a gift of God's grace and God would give
power to proclaim it. It is God's mission and ours.

The mystery of the Epiphany is the inclusion of Gentiles
among God's people. Submission to God's gift of light carries
the obligation to accept and proclaim the inclusion of outsiders
within the mystery. This is symbolized by its link with the magi
following the light to the infant's manger; thus the Christ child
is for all people.

WILLIAM L. SELF

RESPONSE

In Ephesians, the author's concern is to let everyone know
the mysteries of Christ, and let the gospel illuminate the
whole world. In what ways might you be keeping the gospel
to yourself? How can you help those who are the "Gentiles"
outside your faith community to better know God?

PRAYER

O God, you have made flawed human beings into fellow heirs,
partners in the promise of Christ. Help me to live up to that
calling. Amen.

✦ FRIDAY ✦

Matthew 2:1–12

REFLECTION

Matthew . . . does not specify that there were three magi. The
number three is an inference from the gifts they offer him in
verse 11: "gold, frankincense, and myrrh." Because tradition
has concentrated on the three gifts given by three magi, it has
missed something in the passage that is much more central
to its interpretation: a word that occurs at the beginning,
in the middle, and at the end of the story (vv. 2, 8, 11). The
word, *proskyneō* in Greek, is translated by the NRSV as "pay
him homage." The phrase is a leitmotif in the story, far more
important than whether there were three magi bearing three
gifts. Paying homage to Christ gives the story its purpose, its
direction, and its culmination.

THOMAS H. TROEGER

RESPONSE

What gifts can you bring to Christ to pay him homage?

PRAYER

O God of lowly mangers and stables, I have no costly gifts to
offer you, but I give you my heart. Amen.

✦ SATURDAY ✦

Matthew 2:1–12

REFLECTION

Finally, what is particularly crucial in this regard is that
Matthew begins and ends this text with strangers, that is, with
Gentiles. This fact provides the widest expression and basis of
the theology of this passage. It means that Matthew's nascent
Christology affirms the fact that the Messiah's coming is an
arrival that has meaning for all people! The entry of the wise
men into the sacred texts, places, and actions of the Jewish faith
are for Matthew the sign that the Messiah has indeed arrived
in the person of the child. God, in the child, has breached
the boundaries of traditional faith, and the nations are now
entering to witness this Messiah, and doing so with joy!

SUSAN HEDAHL

RESPONSE

Imagine a birthday party to which the whole world is invited.
Such was Christ's birth. How should we celebrate?

PRAYER

God of the stranger and the friend, help me to receive everyone
I encounter as your beloved children, knowing your gospel is
for all nations. Amen.

⁂ SUNDAY ⁂

Isaiah 60:1–6

REFLECTION

God's transformative light appears in this passage in at least
three ways: First, we are reminded of the place of the prophetic
imagination in the work of hope, as the prophet's voice helps
prepare the human heart for God's transformations. Second, we
are reminded that power, to be truly of God, is attractive rather
than imposing; God's light shining through us will be a beacon
to all nations and will bring forward to good and sacred use the
gifts of the earth. Finally, we remember that the darkness shall
not last, neither as the dark days of winter nor as the dark days
of the soul, for the light rises now just over the horizon.

EMILY ASKEW

Psalm 72:1–7, 10–14

REFLECTION

All of the Epiphany texts point toward God's promised shalom
for the world; however, the psalm most emphatically instructs
us about our specific role as advocates in local, national, and
international affairs. Like God, we are to reach beyond our
church walls or geographic boundaries to show compassion to
any in need.

Of course, many church members believe that working for
justice is not a part of their calling and are quick to say that
"politics and religion" should not be mixed. Psalm 72 illustrates
that politics and religion are interwoven. The work of the king,
or the Congress, and the citizens is to defend the cause of the
poor.

DEAN MCDONALD

Ephesians 3:1–12

REFLECTION

The Epiphany of the Lord is made possible because of God's self-disclosure. God discloses or reveals God's self to human beings as an expression of God's inexhaustible love and mercy. The Epiphany speaks to an awakening, an enlightenment, and a revelation of the God revealed in the life of Jesus Christ. It is the kind of Epiphany that transforms lives and calls for new allegiances, goals, and directions.

JOHNNY B. HILL

Matthew 2:1–12

REFLECTION

When we follow the star to the Christ child and behold the Messiah, and after we have been overjoyed, have bowed down, have humbled our hearts and worshiped, and have given gifts to the child, we leave the season with an enflamed heart and an illumined memory. Our hearts are enflamed because of the divine revelations: we have been visited by the Messiah, and our memories are illumined because we cannot forget what we have seen.

FRANK A. THOMAS

RESPONSE

On this Epiphany Sunday, where has following the star led you? How has your life's path changed because you are a follower of Jesus?

PRAYER

God of love, help me to bring the light of your *shalom* to all people, knowing that wise people still seek the Christ child. Amen.

❧ *Baptism of the Lord* ❧

(First Sunday after the Epiphany)

Isaiah 42:1–9

Here is my servant, whom I uphold,
    my chosen, in whom my soul delights;
I have put my spirit upon him;
    he will bring forth justice to the nations. (v. 1)

Psalm 29

The voice of the LORD flashes forth flames of fire.
The voice of the LORD shakes the wilderness;
    the LORD shakes the wilderness of Kadesh.
The voice of the LORD causes the oaks to whirl,
    and strips the forest bare;
    and in his temple all say, "Glory!" (vv. 7–9)

Acts 10:34–43

"He commanded us to preach to the people and to testify that he
is the one ordained by God as judge of the living and the dead. All
the prophets testify about him that everyone who believes in him
receives forgiveness of sins through his name." (vv. 42–43)

Matthew 3:13–17

And when Jesus had been baptized, just as he
came up from the water, suddenly the heavens were
opened to him and he saw the Spirit of God descending
like a dove and alighting on him. And a voice from
heaven said, "This is my Son, the Beloved, with
whom I am well pleased." (vv. 16–17)

⤳ MONDAY ⤴

Isaiah 42:1–9

REFLECTION

> He has sent me to proclaim release to the captives
> and recovery of sight to the blind,
> to let the oppressed go free,
> to proclaim the year of the Lord's favor.
> (Luke 4:18–19)

Jesus received these words as powerfully as it is possible to
receive them and sought to mark every moment of his ministry
with the vision they expressed. His ministry did take care with
the bruised reed; he cupped his hands around the dimmest
wicks until they began to shine. The practices that the prophet
Isaiah called the people to cherish captured Jesus' imagination
and ought to capture ours as well.

The vision of this Servant Song is sweeping in its scope, but
specific in the practices it commends. It seems particularly
concerned with the suffering of prisoners, because it twice
repeats the call to release them: "to bring out the prisoners from
the dungeon, from the prison those who sit in darkness" (v. 7).

STEPHANIE A. PAULSELL

RESPONSE

Does it make you feel uncomfortable that Jesus spoke
of releasing captives? Do you think this is meant only
metaphorically, or as a literal release?

PRAYER

God of the helpless and forgotten, teach me how to pray for and
minister to those who are in prison. Amen.

⇥ TUESDAY ⇤

Isaiah 42:1–9

REFLECTION

In the first of Isaiah's Servant Songs (Isa. 42:1–9), it is God's voice we hear: "Here is my servant, whom I uphold, my chosen, in whom my soul delights" (Isa. 42:1). The first Servant Song celebrates the patient, nonviolent, merciful ministry of the Servant who "faithfully bring[s] forth justice" without breaking a "bruised reed" or quenching "a dimly burning wick" (Isa. 42:3).

STEPHANIE A. PAULSELL

RESPONSE

This passage from Isaiah presents the Suffering Servant as a paragon of nonviolence (vv. 1–2), but one who will not rest until he has established justice on earth (v. 4). Is it difficult for you to reconcile this text's model of silence and servitude with justice?

PRAYER

God, the former things have come to pass, and you are declaring "new things"—including a new model for establishing justice. Help me in humility to use your means, not my own, to contribute to the cause of justice. Amen.

⤳ WEDNESDAY ⤳

Psalm 29

REFLECTION

One of the very first images of the psalm is of water. "The voice of the LORD is over the waters; the God of glory thunders, the LORD, over mighty waters" (v. 3). This image is then recapitulated at the end: "The LORD sits enthroned over the flood" (v. 10).

Too often, powerful untamable water gets forgotten when it comes to baptism. Baptism can too easily become "the cute sacrament"—an adorable baby, a bowl of water, a sprinkling on the head. Too often our response to baptism is not "Glory!" in the temple but a heartwarming "Awww . . ." The God of Psalm 29 is not to be trifled with. Water is not just something in which to splash around. It gives life, but it also has the power to destroy. So when we are baptized in water, something life giving happens, and something is also put to death.

MARYANN MCKIBBEN DANA

RESPONSE

As you mark the Baptism of Our Lord this week, reflect on the power of water for cleansing and renewal.

PRAYER

God, you are Lord over the waters and over my life. Bless me with your peace. Amen.

✦ THURSDAY ✦

Acts 10:34–43

REFLECTION

This story of the radical transformation of Peter's perspective and action informs the way in which we can be enabled to transcend the limitations of our relationship with others. Our prejudices are deeply ingrained. Our perspective on what is right and proper in how we deal with others has permeated our whole understanding of who we are. We *can* be opened to new understandings and new perspectives as we confront again and again the ways of God in Jesus Christ. It is a difficult matter indeed for us to break through the limitations of how we see and deal with others. Our only hope is to be open to the Spirit and to seek ever new understanding of the God who "shows no partiality."

HARRY B. ADAMS

RESPONSE

It was only after a vision that Peter accepted the notion that God's message was intended for the Gentiles as well as the Jews. When has God challenged your perspective?

PRAYER

Open my mind and heart to receive new truths, O God, even if those truths take me out of my comfort zone. Amen.

✦ FRIDAY ✦

Acts 10:34–43

REFLECTION

At the center of Peter's confession is Jesus' death on a tree, his resurrection, and his appearance to the apostles. Jesus reveals the cruciform character of life in God. New life is given as it is spent and given up for others. Without overly specifying or speculating, we say that these fundamental theological convictions are the bedrock of faith.

TIMOTHY F. SEDGWICK

RESPONSE

One of the great ironies of the Christian faith is that only in losing our life will we gain it. What does this self-sacrifice mean for you?

PRAYER

O God, you spared nothing in rescuing humanity, not even your only begotten Son. Help me to understand how to pour out my life for others, and for you. Amen.

✦ SATURDAY ✦

Matthew 3:13–17

REFLECTION

The writer of Matthew employs the narrative structure found in the other Gospels: he places the baptism of Jesus at the very beginning of his ministry, a *preparation* for what will later follow. How do we understand baptism as preparatory to our lives in Christ? For what is God preparing each of the baptized? Further, for what is this communal act preparing the community? Theologian and ethicist Stanley Hauerwas writes that Christians are called to be a community "capable of forming people with virtues sufficient to witness to God's truth in the world."* How might your community be—or become— a community capable of forming people who will witness to God's truth? What does your tradition suggest those virtues might be? How are they previewed in the baptismal liturgy and/or baptismal vows your congregation witnesses? How might these virtues be understood from the succeeding chapters of the Gospel of Matthew, from which this witness to baptism is taken?

GREG GARRETT

RESPONSE

Why is baptism a necessary beginning to the Christian life?

PRAYER

God, help me to remember and practice the covenants of baptism: that I will love you, proclaim your word, serve your people, and resist evil. Amen.

---

*Stanley Hauerwas, *A Community of Character: Toward a Constructive Christian Social Ethic* (Notre Dame, IN: University of Notre Dame Press, 1982), 3.

✦ SUNDAY ✦

Isaiah 42:1–9

REFLECTION

This account of God's investment in creation, through the agency of a servant people, lies at the heart of the church's gift to the nations at Epiphany. Israel received from her prophet Isaiah what the church received from its Christ, and that is what the church testifies to the world—the revelation that the God who creates is a just God who restores sight to the blind, freedom to the captives, and grants strength to those who serve.

RICHARD F. WARD

Psalm 29

REFLECTION

The storm of Psalm 29 leaves an impressive mark on the Mediterranean landscape. The ground is strewn with snapped cedars and oaks. Amid the brokenness, the psalmist lifts his eyes to a God who reigns above the tumult and offers a prayer to a God whose strength is far greater than his own. With the company of the faithful, he sings: "Glory!"

ANDREW NAGY-BENSON

Acts 10:34–43

REFLECTION

As emphasized in this year's Gospel reading for this Sunday from Matthew (3:13–17) and in the readings from Acts for liturgical years B and C, baptism is not only an initiation into a new life but a matter of baptism in the Spirit (Matt. 3:16). In baptism by water we receive the gift and power of the Holy Spirit, just as Peter describes in Acts: "after the baptism that John announced . . . God anointed Jesus of Nazareth with the Holy Spirit and with power" (10:37–38). In baptism by water in the community of faith we experience the power of God at work. Here again, specifying and speculating about the work of the Holy Spirit leads in many directions. The more fundamental point is that entering this new life is a matter of dying to the old and birth into the new, a matter of cross and resurrection.

TIMOTHY F. SEDGWICK

Matthew 3:13–17

REFLECTION

The celebration of the baptism of the Lord is traditionally a time to contemplate both Jesus' baptism and our own. To make sense of both these mysteries, it is also necessary to contemplate the incarnation itself. For Christians of the first centuries of the church, and for contemporary readers who embrace that tradition, neither Jesus' baptism nor our own makes sense if not considered in the light of the incarnation. Reflecting on how we are restored in the waters of baptism requires reflection on how God created, entered into, and radically transformed those waters. Pondering the reasons for Jesus' own baptism requires pondering what it means for the Son of God to have become a human. In short, to understand baptism, we must understand the reality, the physicality, of being human, and what it means to say that God saved us by becoming just like us.

STEVEN D. DRIVER

RESPONSE

Today, in celebration of the baptism of the Lord, many churches will baptize new Christians. How will you receive them?

PRAYER

God, in the waters of baptism you have washed away my sin and brought new life. I promise to nurture those who are being baptized into a mature Christian faith. Amen.

❧ *Second Sunday after* ❦ *the Epiphany*

Isaiah 49:1–7

Listen to me, O coastlands,
  pay attention, you peoples from far away!
The LORD called me before I was born,
  while I was in my mother's womb he named me. (v. 1)

Psalm 40:1–11

I have not hidden your saving help within my heart,
  I have spoken of your faithfulness and your salvation;
I have not concealed your steadfast love and your faithfulness
  from the great congregation. (v. 10)

1 Corinthians 1:1–9

I give thanks to my God always for you because of the grace of
God that has been given you in Christ Jesus, for in every way you
have been enriched in him, in speech and knowledge of every
kind—just as the testimony of Christ has been strengthened
among you—so that you are not lacking in any spiritual gift as you
wait for the revealing of our Lord Jesus Christ. (vv. 4–7)

John 1:29–42

One of the two who heard John speak and followed him
was Andrew, Simon Peter's brother. He first found his brother
Simon and said to him, "We have found the Messiah" (which is
translated Anointed). He brought Simon to Jesus, who looked at
him and said, "You are Simon son of John. You are to be called
Cephas" (which is translated Peter). (vv. 40–42)

⤞ MONDAY ⤟

Isaiah 49:1–7

REFLECTION

All of life is your business, God sings to the Servant—every nation, every person, every life.

Surely this is the song God sings to each of us: that all of our work, no matter how local, must have the good of the whole world as its aim. In our globalized world, in which a seemingly innocuous action—a purchase, say—in one place can contribute to suffering in another, this is no easy vocation. Embedded in this call to be a light to the nations is a call to know the world in which we hope to shine. Through study and encounter, through travel and prayer, through seeking to understand the results of our choices of what to buy, what to wear, what to eat, we return, like the Servant, to God and receive a deeper vocation, one that encompasses strangers far off, as well as dear ones close at hand.

STEPHANIE A. PAULSELL

RESPONSE

For anything you purchase today, think very deliberately about who made it or grew it, and under what conditions.

PRAYER

God of the sparrow, help me to see and understand how the tiniest decisions about how I live my life can have great impact for justice. Amen.

✣ TUESDAY ✣

Isaiah 49:1–7

REFLECTION

American culture is fascinated with the notion of destiny and the idea that a person has the potential to go beyond one's station in life to reach the unattainable. The "American dream" of social mobility is alive and well, and it is manifest in the abundance of reality shows that promise instantaneous fame (or infamy) and a worldwide stage to exhibit one's talent. Such aspirations are further reflected in popular fiction stories of superheroes who suddenly overcome human physical limitations and discover supernatural powers. These cultural tendencies reflect a longing to be discovered, to be recognized as special, or to become something more. When we observe our current social patterns from a theological perspective, the deep-seated sense that humans are destined for greater things becomes apparent. In fact, this sense manifests itself in our society because we *are* destined for more than what we are. According to Scripture, we are called beyond our finitude, not only to a higher purpose as children of God, but to everlasting life through our Lord Jesus Christ.

Isaiah 49 illustrates this higher calling and the intimate care that God bestows upon the one whom God calls. Even before birth, God knew this unborn Servant, and God named, called, and equipped this one so that the tasks of restoration and salvation may be accomplished. JENNIFER POWELL MCNUTT

RESPONSE

Have you ever sensed that God had a purpose for you even before you were born? If so, what is that purpose?

PRAYER

Before you formed me in the womb you knew me, O God. Help prepare me for my service to you and your people. Amen.

✦ WEDNESDAY ✦

Psalm 40:1–11

REFLECTION

In the spring of 1985, U2's The Unforgettable Fire tour stopped in Hartford, Connecticut. . . .

The final encore that evening was "40," a lyrical adaptation of today's Psalm 40. As the band left the stage one by one, the enthusiastic crowd continued the song's refrain: "I will sing, sing a new song." Even as the crowd poured out of the stadium, huge bands of fans carried the tune onto the city streets: "I will sing, sing a new song." I thought little of it at the time, but that refrain springs forth from the psalmist's claim, "He put a new song in my mouth, a song of praise to our God" (v. 3).

The central claim of this psalm is well worth our singing and preaching: God hears our cries and delivers us from times of trouble, so we will respond with a joyful noise, a song of praise. Traces of this tune echo through the ages, from Israel's deliverance in Exodus to the praise songs Paul sings in prison. Time and again in Scripture God hears the lament of God's people, swings low, and gives us reason to hope. Time and again in the pulpit, preachers aim to tell "the glad news of deliverance in the great congregation" (v. 9).

ANDREW NAGY-BENSON

RESPONSE

If you have not heard the song "40" before, find one of U2's live performances of it on YouTube and listen to this "new song" to the Lord.

PRAYER

I praise you that you have lifted me from the pit and set my feet on the rock! Amen.

✦ THURSDAY ✦

1 Corinthians 1:1–9

REFLECTION

There is much to criticize in the Corinthian church, and Paul is about to roll up his sleeves and let them know it. First, though, he stops to tell the Corinthians the good news about themselves, the truth of who they are in the calling of God. They are the saints of God, made rich in Jesus Christ. All the criticism proceeds from this truth and no criticism undermines it. The Corinthians' identity as those "sanctified in Christ Jesus" does not depend on them or their efforts. Paul's rebuke to the church, however severe, does not threaten what God has done. This critique is merciful. It does not bind the Corinthians to their failures and divisions; it does not make their calling dependent on their reformation. It is not the sanctity but the failures that are untrue; they are false, not to an ideal that these Christians have yet to fulfill, but to a character with which they are already gifted. Godly, Christian critique is always an exhortation to receive what has already been given.

ALAN GREGORY

RESPONSE

Paul's approach of offering honey before vinegar helps the Corinthians realize their identity in Christ in spite of the flaws he points out to them. Is it easy or difficult for you to believe that your calling in Christ is not "dependent on [your] reformation"?

PRAYER

May your grace and holiness infuse my life, despite my failures. Amen.

⟿ FRIDAY ⟿

1 Corinthians 1:1–9

REFLECTION

Paul goes on to give thanks for the "grace of God that has been
given you in Christ Jesus" (v. 4). In spite of all the failures of
the people of Corinth, Paul can discern the gifts of God in
this community. Using the metaphor of wealth, Paul declares
that they have been "enriched" (v. 5). He asserts that they have
received the capacity for speech and that they have been given
knowledge. Furthermore, they are not lacking in any spiritual
gift (v. 7).

As we look at the church in our own time, the weaknesses
and failures are often all too evident. Paul can teach us to be
grateful for the gifts that God has given to the church even
with its frailties—gifts of understanding, gifts of caring, gifts of
words that help and heal, gifts of faithfulness to Jesus Christ,
gifts of shared community. The church is rich in blessings,
not because of the accomplishments of the people within the
fellowship, but because of the grace of God that has enriched
and sustained the people.

HARRY B. ADAMS

RESPONSE

What spiritual gifts are at work right now in your congregation?

PRAYER

May your peace inhabit my church, and may I be an instrument
of that peace. Where there is hatred, let me sow love. Amen.

⇥ SATURDAY ⇤

John 1:29–42

REFLECTION

> Christ has no body now on earth but yours,
>   no hands but yours,
>   no feet but yours,
> Yours are the eyes through which to look out
>   Christ's compassion to the world;
> Yours are the feet with which he is to go about doing good;
> Yours are the hands with which he is to bless men now.

This poem is attributed to Teresa of Avila, a sixteenth-century Spanish mystic, composed by her in a letter sent to her nuns toward the end of her life, although the actual documentation is obscure. Nevertheless, it has taken on a popular presence in Christian spirituality and reflects a common understanding of what some call an incarnational theology—the idea that we are to be Jesus Christ to the world. At its foundation, incarnational theology reminds us all that God became incarnate—became flesh—in Jesus Christ to embody fully God's love for the world. Teresa of Avila takes this incarnational theology one step further and calls on us to incarnate Christ in our own selves and to love the world as Jesus did, even to the point of "always carrying in the body the death of Jesus, so that the life of Jesus may also be made visible in our bodies" as the apostle Paul writes to the church at Corinth (2 Cor. 4:10).

RODGER Y. NISHIOKA

RESPONSE

What can you do to be the hands and feet of Jesus today?

PRAYER

Lamb of God, who takes away the sins of the world, abide in me today. Amen.

⤳ SUNDAY ⤳

Isaiah 49:1–7

REFLECTION

Verse 6 reveals that the Servant undertook the work of God in order that "salvation may reach to the end of the earth." Here Isaiah represents a shift from an exclusive to an inclusive restoration, in that the Servant comes to open the door of salvation for those to whom it has been closed. This illustrates that God has in store a greater destiny for humanity, more than could have ever been imagined, as the adopted children of God through the work of Jesus Christ. Let us, therefore, answer God's calling upon our lives with all our mind, heart, soul, and strength.

JENNIFER POWELL MCNUTT

Psalm 40:1–11

REFLECTION

The aspects of divine faithfulness and human witness and waiting intertwine the Psalms reading with the other Old Testament reading and the Gospel and Epistle readings for this Sunday. The Servant, as "a light to the nations" (Isa. 49:6), like the psalmist is an individual witnessing to the many, and John the Baptist serves as a witness to Jesus (John 1:29–36). Paul exhorts his addressees to wait for the revelation of the Christ (1 Cor. 1:7–8), just as the psalmist hopes and waits patiently for YHWH (v. 1). The character of God as "faithful" is emphasized by three of the readings (Ps. 40:11; Isa. 49:7; 1 Cor. 1:9).

LINDA DAY

1 Corinthians 1:1–9

REFLECTION

Because "God is faithful" (v. 9), Paul is confident that the Corinthians will no longer act like infants (3:1–5), but will grow to maturity. What God has done in the past by calling the Corinthians into the fellowship of the Son assures the community of God's faithfulness in the future. Despite the childish behavior of those who have received God's grace, God has not abandoned them, but will bring them to maturity in a unified church. To be in fellowship (*koinōnia*) with Christ, as Paul explains later (10:16–17; 12:13) is to be in fellowship with others in a corporate journey in a community that includes rich and poor, Jew and Greek (12:13).   JAMES W. THOMPSON

John 1:29–42

REFLECTION

This string of Sundays that we encounter in the lectionary as "after the Epiphany" serves to remind us that a baby in a manger is not enough to support our theological claims for the incarnation. We need more than Christmas, even if we wait patiently for the arrival of the magi. We need to see Jesus walk into the Jordan. We need to see the clouds part. We need to hear the booming voice name Jesus a beloved Son. We need to hear Jesus himself ask us, as he asks Peter and Andrew in this passage from John, "What are you looking for?" (John 1:38). We will be tempted to rush our reply, just as the children hurry the magi on their way to the manger. Before we answer, we need to be mindful that there are seven more Sundays "after the Epiphany," and six of them are devoted to the Sermon on the Mount. We would do well to wait to hear what Jesus has to say in the coming weeks before we answer his question and finish the celebration we started on Christmas.   DAVID TOOLE

RESPONSE

When and how has God been faithful to you?

PRAYER

God of faithfulness, help me to be faithful, an incarnation of Jesus. Amen.

❧ *Third Sunday after* ❧ *the Epiphany*

Isaiah 9:1–4

The people who walked in darkness
    have seen a great light;
those who lived in a land of deep darkness—
    on them light has shined. (v. 2)

Psalm 27:1, 4–9

One thing I asked of the LORD,
    that will I seek after:
to live in the house of the LORD
    all the days of my life,
to behold the beauty of the LORD,
    and to inquire in his temple. (v. 4)

1 Corinthians 1:10–18

Now I appeal to you, brothers and sisters, by the name of
our Lord Jesus Christ, that all of you be in agreement and that
there be no divisions among you, but that you be united in the
same mind and the same purpose. For it has been reported
to me by Chloe's people that there are quarrels among
you, my brothers and sisters. (vv. 10–11)

Matthew 4:12–23

As he walked by the Sea of Galilee, he saw two brothers,
Simon, who is called Peter, and Andrew his brother, casting a
net into the sea—for they were fishermen. And he said to them,
"Follow me, and I will make you fish for people." Immediately
they left their nets and followed him. (vv. 18–20)

⇥ MONDAY ⇤

Isaiah 9:1–4

REFLECTION

For Christians, the light of Isaiah's oracle breaks over us on the Third Sunday after the Epiphany, only a month after the shortest day of the year. Sunlight hours have begun to lengthen, the light remaining with us a little longer each day. The light Isaiah looks toward, however, is not light that grows gradually over time. The brightness of the light Isaiah proclaims shines on a people walking in darkness like a brilliant dawn suddenly breaking. This, surely, is the kind of light that illuminates every secret place, bringing a path obscured by shadows suddenly into view. It is the kind of light that gives direction and drives out fear.

Isaiah speaks his prophecy of light into a moment of tremendous fear for the people of Israel, a time of "distress and darkness, the gloom of anguish" (Isa. 8:22). Assyrian invaders have attacked the northern kingdom, shearing away portions of Israel to create Assyrian provinces. With its images of "the boots of the tramping warriors" and "garments rolled in blood" (Isa. 9:5), the oracle in Isaiah 9 reflects the oppressive military occupation under which Israel struggles to live. Isaiah speaks his word of light and hope into a time of desolation.

STEPHANIE A. PAULSELL

RESPONSE

When have you walked in darkness and difficult times, then seen a great light of hope?

PRAYER

Thank you for breaking the yoke of my burdens, O God of deliverance, and for increasing my joy. Amen.

⟶ TUESDAY ⟵

Psalm 27:1, 4–9

REFLECTION

In the midst of the confident assurances, the psalmist's confident language is hard won. The psalmist has experienced real hardship and trusts in God in spite of, or perhaps because of, those difficulties. Some psalms of praise border on the cheeriness of a pep rally—"God is in his heaven; all is right with the world." It is a message that has a place in our liturgical toolbox, but such messages can also feel false when used to paper over the difficulties of faith. Church people can tell when unabashed praise is sincere, and when the messenger is trying too hard. Psalm 27 strikes an authentic balance between God's goodness and the gritty reality of our lives.

. . . What might the fears of the psalmist have been? More to the point, with what fears do our congregations struggle? How do we understand God as our refuge, a place to hide? When is it healthy to hide, and when is it antithetical to the purposes of God and God's reign on earth?

MARYANN MCKIBBEN DANA

RESPONSE

The lectionary omits verses 2 and 3 of this psalm, which detail the violent fears of the psalmist, and skips ahead to the "happy" text of verse 4. Is it helpful or harmful to sanitize the passage in this way, hiding the most difficult parts of the psalmist's struggle out of sight? How often do we do this as Christians?

PRAYER

Lord, you have been present in my own "days of trouble" and will be again. I praise you that I can be honest about my struggles and doubts. Amen.

✣ WEDNESDAY ✣

Psalm 27:1, 4–9

REFLECTION

Years ago a beloved, longtime church member was wracked with worry about his son. Sunday after Sunday the man returned to the sanctuary. When the congregation sang its hymns, he stood without a hymnal. He listened to the familiar tunes, but he had lost his voice for singing. The congregation's alleluias felt far off.

One Sunday he rose during the time of congregational prayer. He offered a prayer of thanksgiving for the people in those pews. He thanked his fellow churchgoers for keeping the faith when he could not, for singing hymns when he could not, for seeing the goodness of God when his eyes were too cloudy to see it. To be sure, his concern for his son continued, but he had begun to recognize again the source of his strength. His words were his own, but they echoed an ancient faith: God *is* my light and my salvation. God *is* the stronghold of my life. I will sing to the Lord.

ANDREW NAGY-BENSON

RESPONSE

What do you fear most right now? Can you, like the psalmist, express confidence in God's care even amid your fears?

PRAYER

Lord, you are my light and my salvation; whom shall I fear? The Lord is the stronghold of my life; of whom shall I be afraid? Amen.

✦ THURSDAY ✦

1 Corinthians 1:10–18

REFLECTION

Although we cannot reconstruct the nature of the conflict with certainty, we can ascertain that the emphasis on individual freedom at the expense of the community (6:12; 9:1; 10:23) and the disregard of the rich for the poor (11:17–34) lie beneath the many issues that confront the Corinthian church. At the heart of the problems at Corinth is the fact that members are "puffed up" against each other (4:6). Paul's argument against human wisdom (1:20–23; 2:6–8; 3:18–23) and denial that he uses "persuasive words of wisdom" (2:4, my trans.) suggest that the Corinthian factions were created by those who claimed that the rhetorical power of their teachers was a demonstration of their wisdom.

JAMES W. THOMPSON

RESPONSE

Be honest with yourself: What in your life puffs you up with pride? How might that pride have created divisions in your church family?

PRAYER

Humility is a hard lesson, Lord. Teach me to keep my hope fixed on you, and not on earthly talents, wealth, or relationships. Amen.

✦ FRIDAY ✦

1 Corinthians 1:10–18

REFLECTION

Christian unity cannot be commanded; it must proceed from our "discerning the body" (1 Cor. 11:29), acknowledging that Jesus has bound us to himself. That body is recognizable to others insofar as Christians are "united in the same mind and . . . purpose" (v. 10). Doctrinal orthodoxy is not the issue here, still less a uniformity of speech and behavior. Later in his letter Paul will affirm, in spite of all the spiritual cliques in Corinth, the diversity of gifts and ministries. His concern here is more general and perhaps best expressed from the outsider's point of view: "so speak and act that no one will doubt you are brothers and sisters in Christ."

ALAN GREGORY

RESPONSE

When have you felt entirely united with your Christian brothers and sisters? How does that union differ from uniformity?

PRAYER

I know you are the God of *all* humanity, but my quarrels do not reflect that common heritage. Help me to listen to others and serve them in your name. Amen.

✢ SATURDAY ✢

Matthew 4:12–23

REFLECTION

Matthew's account, like Mark's, yields no preparatory details before the calling of Simon, Andrew, James, and John. This lack of detail, though, is not without its own significance. . . . Matthew's portrayal of the obedience of these would-be followers is radical for at least three reasons. First, they "immediately" (vv. 20, 22) follow him, seemingly with no qualifications or questions asked. Second, they leave their profession, a likely lucrative business of fishing, to walk after Jesus. There are no suggestions as to how they will be provided for, and there is no promise of "upward mobility." Finally, though not explicitly stated, their response is radical due to the fact that they also will leave their families. This call, put rather baldly by Matthew, is given unapologetically as being what Jesus demands.

Jesus' call to radical obedience has not changed over these many years; the demands have not been reduced. Jesus waits not for persons to apply to him in hopes of learning under him, as many young Jewish males would have done for their rabbinic education. Instead, rabbi Jesus is the one who seeks out followers, learners, apprentices who do not have to qualify for such a relationship, save the willingness to lay down everything else. What a call! What a mission! What a Savior!

TROY A. MILLER

RESPONSE

Could you, like these disciples, have dropped everything to follow Jesus?

PRAYER

The obedience and sacrifice you require feel intimidating, Lord. Help me to have the courage I need to follow you. Amen.

✧ SUNDAY ✧

Isaiah 9:1–4

REFLECTION

It is Epiphany, a season that gives the church time to reflect more carefully on the incarnation of the Word, the mystery that dawned at Christmas, and see it in action in the life of Jesus. The light from the candle at Christmas now fills the room, and Isaiah is one of its sources. The child of promise has now grown into adulthood and, according to Matthew, uses Isaiah as the text for the sermon that inaugurates his ministry. Gone are verses 5–7; included is verse 1, which gives him his focus— "those who were in anguish," who felt "in the former time" as if they were being held in contempt, not only by their oppressors but even by their God.

RICHARD F. WARD

Psalm 27:1, 4–9

REFLECTION

The vulnerability of the supplicant in Psalm 27 underscores the power of the metaphors employed for God. God as light, salvation, and stronghold in verse 1 make profound sense in relationship to the potential for harm described in verses 2, 3, and 12. The desire to remain in the secure presence of God is not unexpected from a beleaguered supplicant, nor is the joyful response that such protection would evoke.

CARMEN NANKO-FERNÁNDEZ

1 Corinthians 1:10–18

REFLECTION

Paul reminds the Corinthians that his vocation is proclamation, not baptism. This serves as a bridge to the following treatment of the "foolishness of the cross." He contrasts a polished, practiced, and refined rhetoric with preaching the cross. Paul is no mean rhetorician, of course. Even his critique of rhetoric has great rhetorical force. What he does, though, is provide a basic criterion for Christian preaching: do not obscure the cross. Words that strike because of their cleverness, sermons crafted first as entertainment, will hide the cross. A screen of distracting attractions will cover its fierce judgment and its urgent summons to life and love.

ALAN GREGORY

Matthew 4:12–23

REFLECTION

It is not a liturgical accident that today, "after" Epiphany (and Christmas) and before Lent and Easter, Jesus tells us to follow him, and that for the next six weeks we will be listening to him preach from the Mount. There is a sense in which we are being reminded in these weeks between Christmas and Easter that, for all their wonders, neither of these great celebrations is sufficient to sustain us in the hard work of following Jesus during the daily ordinariness of our lives.

DAVID TOOLE

RESPONSE

What does it mean today for you to do the "hard work of following Jesus" in your ordinary life, here in Ordinary Time?

PRAYER

I will follow you, my God, my refuge and my light. Amen.

🌿 *Fourth Sunday after* 🌿 *the Epiphany*

Micah 6:1–8

He has told you, O mortal, what is good;
 and what does the LORD require of you
but to do justice, and to love kindness,
 and to walk humbly with your God? (v. 8)

Psalm 15

O LORD, who may abide in your tent?
 Who may dwell on your holy hill?
Those who walk blamelessly, and do what is right,
 and speak the truth from their heart;
who do not slander with their tongue,
 and do no evil to their friends,
  nor take up a reproach against their neighbors. (vv. 1–3)

1 Corinthians 1:18–31

But God chose what is foolish in the world
to shame the wise; God chose what is weak in
the world to shame the strong. (v. 27)

Matthew 5:1–12

"Blessed are the poor in spirit,
 for theirs is the kingdom of heaven.
"Blessed are those who mourn,
 for they will be comforted." (vv. 3–4)

⤳ MONDAY ⤳

Micah 6:1–8

REFLECTION

One timeless question that many people have pondered and asked time and again is "What is God's will?" In the eighth century BCE, the prophet Micah asked a similar question, and the response given remains at the heart of right relationship with God, with humankind, and with all other communities of life on the planet. In eight verses, the poet describes the experience of a long-suffering God who remains faithful to an unfaithful people for whom the prophet makes intercession. The passage consists of a series of speeches that implore rather than accuse, despite initial sentiments of justified divine frustration directed toward a people chosen by God (Deut. 7:7)—a people entrusted with Torah who now are guilty of transgression (see Mic. 1–3).

CAROL J. DEMPSEY

RESPONSE

"What does the Lord require of you?" If you were asked this question, how would you respond?

PRAYER

Teach me to do justice, love kindness, and walk humbly with you every day, O God of Israel. Amen.

☙ TUESDAY ☚

Micah 6:1–8

REFLECTION

"What does God want?" the prophet asks. God wants us to do justice (v. 8)—to be a voice for oppressed persons, unprotected persons, widows, and foreigners, and to fight for the rights of handicapped persons, minorities, elderly persons, poor persons, and every person treated as less than God's child.

God wants us to love kindness. The Hebrew word *hesed* means God's loving-kindness. We respond to God's love by sharing it with others.

We are to walk humbly with God: listening for God's voice wherever God may be heard; listening to Jews, Muslims, and Buddhists; learning how other people make sense of their lives; thoughtfully examining what it means to live with faith.

BRETT YOUNGER

RESPONSE

Is showing compassion more important than believing correct doctrine?

PRAYER

God of *hesed*, loving-kindness, teach me to listen to your voice and love your people—*all* of your people. Amen.

✦ WEDNESDAY ✦

Psalm 15

REFLECTION

The norms established in verses 2–5a are challenging . . . .
"Those who walk blamelessly" (v. 2) is one point of entry. Who
among us does not carry some blame, some guilt that eats at
us? The struggle to be set free from that blame, to be forgiven, is
what brings us to worship. . . .

The people in God's presence "do not slander with their
tongue" (v. 3a), and this opens the door to a sermon on the sin
of gossip, which too often plagues churches. How easy it is to
slip from sharing news about a community to speculation and
titillation! The text reminds us that gossip, even when it seems
harmless, does evil to our friends. Far better to speak the truth
from our own hearts and let others do the same.

DREW BUNTING

RESPONSE

If you are tempted to gossip today, bite your tongue—literally.
And if someone around you starts to gossip, gently change the
subject.

PRAYER

May my words be gentle and loving, and help remind others of
Christ. Amen.

→ THURSDAY ←

1 Corinthians 1:18–31

REFLECTION

The first part of chapter 1 makes it clear that Paul was dealing with a church in Corinth that had divided itself into factions. These rival subcommunities had coalesced around favored teachers, resulting in arguments about which of the various "schools" possessed superior religious wisdom.

Remarkably, Paul refuses to take on the role of a referee in this situation. The apostle never considers the particular teachings that divide these groups from one another, nor is he interested in passing judgment on the differences in theology and practice that fuel the divisions. Instead, as we have seen, Paul proclaims his message about God's humbling of human religious pretension through the foolishness of the cross.

P. MARK ACHTEMEIER

RESPONSE

Paul single-mindedly focused on "nothing but Christ crucified," refusing to get involved in petty disputes in the church. What would it mean for you to follow this example?

PRAYER

God, you have chosen what is foolish in the world to shame the wise. Be my wisdom. Amen.

⇥ FRIDAY ⇤

Matthew 5:1–12

REFLECTION

Whenever we hear the Beatitudes, we are struck with their poetic beauty and, at the same time, overwhelmed by their perceived impracticality for the world in which we live. We admire the instruction, but we fear the implications of putting the words into actual practice. We live in a time when the blessings given are to those who succeed, often at the expense of others. To be poor in spirit, peaceful, merciful, and meek will get you nowhere in a culture grounded in competition and fear. Perhaps this is why most references to the Beatitudes imply that in giving this instruction, Jesus was literally turning the values of the world upside down. Who can survive in attempting to live into the spirit of the Beatitudes?

The answer resides not in their impracticality but in their *practicality*. We often approach them as an impossible challenge for ordinary living. Only the greatest of saints are up to the task. Therefore, we wait for the occasional figures like Martin Luther King, Dorothy Day, and Desmond Tutu to show us the way. In the meantime, the world does not get any better, and we remain unfulfilled in our pale expressions of Christian discipleship. The truth is that Jesus meant the Beatitudes to be for everyone. How can such a task be accomplished in our own time?

CHARLES JAMES COOK

RESPONSE

How would your life change if you interpreted the Beatitudes literally?

PRAYER

I am blessed, O Lord, when I am meek, pure, and humble, but these are not qualities that come naturally. Give me the strength to cultivate them. Amen.

✦ SATURDAY ✦

Matthew 5:1–12

REFLECTION

The narrative context of 5:1–12 is that it follows 4:18–22 (Jesus' calling of his disciples) and 4:23–25 (Jesus' proclaiming his message and healing crowds who follow him). Within this context, these opening verses provide a commissioning that undergirds the necessary instructions (the rest of the Sermon) for Jesus' chosen disciples and others in the crowd who desire to follow Jesus. As Jesus pronounces God's blessings, he frames the call to discipleship in terms of both who they are to be (their character) and its consequences for their lives in the present sociopolitical and religious context, as well as in God's future.

Finally, the theological heart of the Beatitudes is a call to be disciples who live out the virtues of the blessings in pursuit of righteousness grounded in God's righteousness (God's steadfast love, goodness, justice, and mercy). God's blessings are our command, because God first loved us, giving us the blessing of Jesus Christ, our salvation.

MARCIA Y. RIGGS

RESPONSE

In your own sociopolitical context, how would society change if people began really living the principles of the Sermon on the Mount?

PRAYER

Your call to discipleship is a blessing, O God. I will rejoice and be glad! Amen.

✦ SUNDAY ✦

Micah 6:1–8

REFLECTION

Justice, kindness, and the humble walk carry the reader beyond the confines of personal piety into life-giving, reciprocal relationships with God and with God's other beloved children.

W. SIBLEY TOWNER

Psalm 15

REFLECTION

In response to the Hebrew reading of this week's lectionary, Micah 6:1–8, the psalm corresponds with what to do beyond the ritual: doing justice and righteousness. "He has told you, O mortal, what is good; and what does the LORD require of you but to do justice, and to love kindness, and to walk humbly with your God?" (Mic. 6:8) Moral values are once again emphasized over the blind practices of hiding behind the edifice of institutional jargons. We are asked to live and dwell in God's house, not just be a captive of its building structure. To the question "Who may dwell?" we join the community of believers daring to answer, "We will live, doing God's justice for others!"

PAUL JUNGGAP HUH

1 Corinthians 1:18–31

REFLECTION

At first glance it may seem as if Paul did not get the liturgical memo that this is Epiphany season. More accurately, one may wonder why those who structured the Revised Common Lectionary are calling us away from these central themes of Epiphany to focus on a theology of the cross. The point is that it is all of a piece, as T. S. Eliot noted in "The Journey of the Magi,"

when he asked: "were we led all that way for birth or death?"*
The answer, of course, is yes. So, as Paul invites us on this
fourth Sunday of Epiphany to "survey the wondrous cross," the
preacher might see this, not as a call away from Epiphany, but
deeper into its great mystery: as an opportunity to discover (or
rediscover), as Isaac Watts did before us, a love that is so
amazing and so divine that it demands "our souls, our lives,
our all."

RICHARD M. SIMPSON

Matthew 5:1–12

REFLECTION

Living daily into the spirit of the Beatitudes involves looking at
them as a collection of the whole, rather than looking at each
one individually. Each is related to the others, and they build
on one another. Those who are meek, meaning humble, are
more likely to hunger and thirst for righteousness, because they
remain open to continued knowledge of God. If we approach
the Beatitudes this way, we see they invite us into a way of being
in the world that leads to particular practices. There are three
principles for living into the spirit of the Beatitudes: simplicity,
hopefulness, and compassion. These three principles allow us to
be in the world, while not being totally shaped by it. We offer an
alternative to what the world seems to be pursuing.

CHARLES JAMES COOK

RESPONSE

What will it mean for you to do justice and love kindness this
week in your family? At your workplace?

PRAYER

I know what you require, O God: that I will do justice, love
kindness, and walk humbly with you. Thank you for this call,
and guide my path as I try to live it out. Amen.

*T. S. Eliot, "The Journey of the Magi," in *Complete Poems and Plays, 1909–1950* (New York: Harcourt Brace & Co., 1952), 68.

THE WEEK LEADING UP TO THE

❧ *Fifth Sunday after* ❦ *the Epiphany*

Isaiah 58:1–9a (9b–12)

Is not this the fast that I choose:
    to loose the bonds of injustice,
    to undo the thongs of the yoke,
to let the oppressed go free,
    and to break every yoke? (v. 6)

Psalm 112:1–9 (10)

For the righteous will never be moved;
    they will be remembered forever.
They are not afraid of evil tidings;
    their hearts are firm, secure in the LORD. (vv. 6–7)

1 Corinthians 2:1–12 (13–16)

When I came to you, brothers and sisters, I did not come
proclaiming the mystery of God to you in lofty words or wisdom.
For I decided to know nothing among you except Jesus Christ,
and him crucified. And I came to you in weakness and in
fear and in much trembling. (vv. 1–3)

Matthew 5:13–20

"You are the light of the world. A city built on a hill cannot be hid.
No one after lighting a lamp puts it under the bushel basket, but
on the lampstand, and it gives light to all in the house. In the same
way, let your light shine before others, so that they may see your
good works and give glory to your Father in heaven." (vv. 14–16)

⤙ MONDAY ⤚

Isaiah 58:1–9a (9b–12)

REFLECTION

One year during Holy Week, a few Christians from well-endowed congregations in a major metropolitan area spent a night with homeless friends on the street. They were looking for the suffering Christ in the lives of those who spend their days and nights suffering from hunger, disease, and rejection. It was a chilly night, and rain rolled in close to midnight. Looking for shelter, the handful of travelers felt fortunate to come upon a church holding an all-night prayer vigil. The leader of the group was a pastor of one of the most respected churches in the city. As she stepped through the outer doors of the church, a security guard stopped her. . . . The security guard was friendly, but explained in brutal honesty, "I was hired to keep homeless people like you out." As the dejected group made their way back into the misery of the night, they knew they had found their suffering Christ, locked out of the church.

Isaiah would not have been surprised. Just like the city church, his people had every intention of excelling in their worship of God. Their intentions may have been as pure as the intentions of those who held vigil all through the night in the name of their God. Even so, their worship was a fraud. True fasting—and, by extension, true worship—leads not simply to a reordering of the liturgy, but a reordering of the life of the community.

ANDREW FOSTER CONNORS

RESPONSE

What is the "true fasting" that God requires of you?

PRAYER

Lord, I will loose the bonds of injustice and share my bread with the hungry, for in this you are honored. Amen.

✦ TUESDAY ✦

Isaiah 58:1–9a (9b–12)

REFLECTION

Isaiah's people appear to be very religious. They not only go to worship daily; they also fast frequently. The people complain that they have observed the fasts, but God has not answered their prayers. Isaiah has to point out that the wealthy are fasting on the holy days, but their employees still have to work (v. 3). God requires both worship and merciful attention to others.

Those who attend worship services usually do not appreciate having their insincerity pointed out, but Isaiah tells them that religious people can be the most quarrelsome (v. 4). The prophet sounds sarcastic (v. 5) when he calls them to the kind of worship that does more than anesthetize the conscience.

BRETT YOUNGER

RESPONSE

Isaiah points out the hypocrisy of his audience's outward religiosity and inward selfishness. If you are totally honest, how might some of his criticisms in verses 2–4 apply to you personally?

PRAYER

Keep me from self-centered hypocrisy, O Lord, and place me on a path of generosity. Amen.

*Rowen Williams, *Christian Trial* (Grand Rapids: Eerdmans, 2000), 6, 52, 69.

⇥ WEDNESDAY ⇤

Psalm 112:1–9 (10)

REFLECTION

Tremble as we do, we are always, always offered the amazing grace of both the promise of God's unconditional love and the humbling chance to have a purpose, to make a difference, to be a part of something bigger than ourselves. That is the obeying-God's-commands part of the deal. It turns out to be better than it sounds. Obedience, a word our culture hates, turns out to mean having a chance to make a difference, to make the world a better place. I have met very few people so jaded that they did not want to jump on that bandwagon.

Psalm 112 is a poem celebrating the happiness of obeying God's commands or, in a language that even contemporary culture can hear, the happiness of those who get to make a difference under God.

BARBARA S. BLAISDELL

RESPONSE

Is it difficult for you to obey God's commandments? Which ones in particular are the hardest for you to keep?

PRAYER

I will keep your commandments, O God of righteousness and justice, especially the one that Jesus said is most important—that we love one another. Amen.

✦ THURSDAY ✦

1 Corinthians 2:1–12 (13–16)

REFLECTION

In 1 Corinthians, Paul was dismayed that this same state of affairs existed in his church, because it was meant to be a radical alternative to the stratifications of imperial Rome. When Paul wrote, "When I came to you . . . I decided to know nothing among you except Jesus Christ, and him crucified" (vv. 1, 2), he was referring to an alternative way of residing in the world. He was contending that the disciples of the crucified one ought to stand with the oppressed and work for justice, reconciliation, and restoration. For Paul, this was the Christian way of residing in the world. Rowan Williams puts it this way: Jesus did not come to be "a competitor for space in the world." Rather, in his life, death, and resurrection "the human map is being redrawn, the world turned upside down," and "the whole world of rivalry and defense" is put into question.*

ROGER J. GENCH

RESPONSE

What would it mean in your life to "know nothing . . . except Jesus Christ, and him crucified"?

PRAYER

I praise you, God, that your foolishness has confounded the allegedly wise, and the resurrection of your Son has reordered the world. Amen.

---

*Rowan Williams, *Christ on Trial* (Grand Rapids: Eerdmans, 2000), 6, 52, 69.

✦ FRIDAY ✦

Matthew 5:13–20

REFLECTION

Human righteousness is about being the salt of the earth and the light of the world. As the salt of the earth, we are disciples of Jesus when we allow our characters to be formed by God's blessings. As the light of the world, we are followers of Jesus when accept the covenantal blessings as a call into relationships with despised groups because of what we believe—even if it means that we may be persecuted. As disciples of the Jesus who came not to abolish but to fulfill the law and the prophets, we seek to live righteously in ways consistent with the new interpretation of the law that Jesus provides.

MARCIA Y. RIGGS

RESPONSE

What does it mean in your community for you to be salt and light?

PRAYER

Let my light so shine that others may see my good works and glorify you in heaven. Amen.

✥ SATURDAY ✥

Matthew 5:13–20

REFLECTION

Jesus encourages his followers to bring light to a dark and broken world. The light is the light of the gospel, and it draws all people to its warmth and radiance. This mission has been primary, from the very beginning, throughout every age. Archbishop William Temple is often quoted as saying, "The church is the only organization on earth that exists for those who are not its members." In order for the light to be seen, we must be willing to go where the darkness exists, to engage and walk through it, so that, in time, the light can overcome it. Annie Dillard writes, "You do not have to sit outside in the dark. If, however, you want to look at the stars, you will find that darkness is necessary."* We must go into those dark places, bearing the light of Christ. The light is not given for our own personal enjoyment.

CHARLES JAMES COOK

RESPONSE

How can you be a light to others today in dark places?

PRAYER

Help me to bear your light into the world, O God, and heal its brokenness. Amen.

---

*Annie Dillard, *Teaching a Stone to Talk: Expeditions and Encounters* (New York: Harper Perennial, 1992), 43.

✣ SUNDAY ✣

Isaiah 58:1–9a (9b–12)

REFLECTION

The community's responsiveness to one another has a direct
effect on how God will respond to the community. Isaiah
instructs his listeners that when they live out a life of love in
accordance with Torah, God will answer them when they call
(v. 9). Theologically, Isaiah's proclamation heralds a vision of
worship that must exceed faithfulness to external practices
and rituals. Isaiah redefines worship as a lived experience of
being in "right relationship" with one another and with God,
made manifest through ethical practice rooted in and flowing
from divine love (see Deut. 6:1–8), which demands justice,
righteousness, and compassion.

CAROL J. DEMPSEY

Psalm 112:1–9 (10)

REFLECTION

The light of Epiphany and Christmas is behind us in this
Ordinary Time of the church year. We may even have forgotten
the excitements of the liturgy that led us through the feast time
of the holy days. Now, before we enter the time of fasting during
Lent (today's texts are not read in those years when the date
of Easter is very early), let us not forget that God Immanuel is
with us, even after the big star is no longer there to guide us.
However, the light of the flame continues to shine upon us. The
ritual required during the Ordinary Time is to reflect on one's
behavior and heart, to examine their congruency with each
other.

Are we truly walking the talk? Is the instruction truly
accompanied by right actions and desires?

PAUL JUNGGAP HUH

1 Corinthians 2:1–12 (13–16)

REFLECTION

Though Paul does not dispute that there are many mysteries, here he calls upon the Corinthians to relish the great mystery revealed among them—greater than any other thing, unseen and unheard, prepared by God from eternity. The source of 1 Corinthians 2:9 is debated, but the verse appears to derive from Isaiah 64:3–4 (though it varies from both the Hebrew and the Septuagint version by its reference to those who "love God"; cf. Sir. 1:10, rather than to those who "await his mercy"). Paul does, however, retain the general theme of being astonished by God, and may well have in mind the entire chapter (Isa. 64), which begins with an invocation of God to "tear open the heavens" and appear. This has indeed happened, exclaims Paul, in Christ Jesus!

EDITH M. HUMPHREY

Matthew 5:13–20

REFLECTION

When we are salt and light for others, we are more likely to fulfill the law as Jesus suggested: To love the Lord our God with all our heart, mind, and soul, and our neighbor as ourselves.

CHARLES JAMES COOK

RESPONSE

This week, think of two things you can do to help others. One good work is salt and the other light. Then go and do those things.

PRAYER

You do not desire outward sacrifice, but instead the sacrifice of my time, heart, and talents for your people. Teach me to give of myself unselfishly. Amen.

❧ Sixth Sunday after ❧ the Epiphany

Deuteronomy 30:15–20

If you obey the commandments of the LORD your God
that I am commanding you today, by loving the LORD your
God, walking in his ways, and observing his commandments,
decrees, and ordinances, then you shall live and become
numerous, and the LORD your God will bless you in the
land that you are entering to possess. (v. 16)

Psalm 119:1–8

You have commanded your precepts
    to be kept diligently.
O that my ways may be steadfast
    in keeping your statutes!
Then I shall not be put to shame,
    having my eyes fixed on all your commandments. (vv. 4–6)

1 Corinthians 3:1–9

For as long as there is jealousy and quarreling among you, are you
not of the flesh, and behaving according to human inclinations?
For when one says, "I belong to Paul," and another, "I belong to
Apollos," are you not merely human? (vv. 3–4)

Matthew 5:21–37

"So when you are offering your gift at the altar, if you remember
that your brother or sister has something against you, leave your
gift there before the altar and go; first be reconciled to your
brother or sister, and then come and offer your gift." (vv. 23–24)

✦ MONDAY ✦

Deuteronomy 30:15–20

REFLECTION

Walk around the block. Turn off the television. Get together with your friends. Invite a stranger to lunch or dinner. Clean out a drawer. Read a book of poetry. Quit doing what is not worth your time. Do something so someone else will not have to. Give money to a cause you care about. Stop arguing. Apologize to someone, even if it was mostly his fault. Forgive someone, even if she does not deserve it. Have patience. . . .

Worship with all your heart. Pray genuinely. Love your church. Believe that God loves you. Remember the stories of Jesus. See Christ in the people around you. Share God's love with someone who has forgotten it. Delight in God's good gifts. See that all of life is holy. Open your heart to the Spirit. Search for something deeper and better than your own comfort. Live in the joy beneath it all. Let God make your life wonderful.

Moses preached that we choose life in an amazing variety of ways. This text provides a wonderful chance for preachers to say to their congregations, "Today I set before you life and death, blessings and curses. Choose life."

BRETT YOUNGER

RESPONSE

The reflection above provides many different ways to "choose life," as Moses put it in this passage from Deuteronomy. Which will you implement? How will you choose life today?

PRAYER

God, you sent Jesus that we might have life more abundantly. Help me to find the paradox that when I live more simply, I live more abundantly. Amen.

✦ TUESDAY ✦

Deuteronomy 30:15–20

REFLECTION

We are a nation of choosers: paper or plastic? Small, medium, large, or super? Fries or chips? Organic or conventional? Having a choice has become a staple of the American dream. Political agendas of all flavors are sold on a platform of choice— everything from private school vouchers to health-care reform. More choice is always the preferred value. The choice offered in Deuteronomy does not sit well with a people inundated by choices. Actually "offered" is too generous—Deuteronomy does not *offer* a choice so much as *require* that a particular choice be made: "If you obey the commandments of the LORD your God . . . then you shall live. . . . But if your heart turns away . . . you shall perish" (vv. 16–18). . . .

However, the choice and its consequences are clear: Choose covenant, receive life; reject covenant, choose death. Choose covenant, gain land; reject covenant, lose land. Choose covenant, receive blessing; reject covenant, receive curse. Schooled in a society that shops around for a "wider selection," we resist any effort to have our choices curtailed. We resist having our choices cut, because it threatens the illusion of our autonomy—perhaps *the* central value of our culture.

ANDREW FOSTER CONNORS

RESPONSE

What choices have you had to make today? How might they culminate over time in choosing life or choosing death?

PRAYER

God who gave us the gift of free will, I need to choose this day, and every day, whom I will serve. Thank you for the promise of life. Amen.

→ WEDNESDAY ←

Psalm 119:1–8

REFLECTION

Psalm 119 is an extended meditation on the law. Along with
Psalm 1 and Psalm 19, it belongs to a genre known as Torah
Psalms because of their focus on the law. The first verse of
Psalm 119 summarizes the entire poem: "Happy are those
whose way is blameless, who walk in the law [Heb. *torah*] of the
LORD." In contrast to Christian traditions that view the law as
a burden on the ancient Israelites (see Acts 15:10), Psalm 119
expresses the Israelites' joy at having the perfect guidance the
Torah provides. The fact that Psalm 119 is the longest psalm—
as well as the longest chapter in the entire Bible—testifies to the
Israelites' conviction that the Torah was the greatest gift any
nation had ever received (Deut. 4:5–8).

KEVIN A. WILSON

RESPONSE

Do you view the law as a gift or a burden?

PRAYER

God of Torah and teaching, may my ways be steadfast in
keeping your statutes. I will praise you with an upright heart.
Amen.

✢ THURSDAY ✢

1 Corinthians 3:1–9

REFLECTION

Jean Vanier, the founder of L'Arche community, suggests that we all carry a deep wound of loneliness that is not easily overcome, and that this wound is so much a part of our human condition that we cannot escape it, try as we might. We want to belong in the worst way, so we join communities, but they always tend to disappoint us. . . .

These wounds were much in evidence in the church Paul founded in Corinth. The people of the church of Corinth, it seems, wanted desperately to belong. They must have had mainline Christian leanings, because they divided up into groups with buttons announcing, "I belong to Paul" or "I belong to Apollos" or some other charismatic leader. In Paul's view this rivalry betrayed a misunderstanding of the gospel. Paul came preaching Christ and him crucified, one who identified most deeply with our human woundedness, reconciling us to God—a God who alone can give a sense of who we are and whose we are as beloved people of God.

ROGER J. GENCH

RESPONSE

When have you been disappointed by your church community? What would it take to heal those divisions with the love of Christ crucified?

PRAYER

You have created us to need each other and to be in relationship, but sometimes we wound each other deeply. Help us to join in unity, not undermine each other with factionalism. Amen.

✤ FRIDAY ✤

1 Corinthians 3:1–9

REFLECTION

It is especially the lack of unity, and the cleaving to a particular human being as a "mascot" rather than to the Lord, that demonstrates how fallen humanity is still riddling the church ("I belong to Paul, . . . to Apollos," v. 4). Paul is following the logic of the prophet Isaiah, who reminded the Judahites that idol worshipers become like "their gods." Similarly, those who set themselves to follow a human being will never attain the glory promised by the Spirit of God, which Paul has celebrated in 2:7. It is, after all, the Spirit of glory who brings the church to maturity, so that its members also show forth the glory of Christ. In this knowledge, sober Christians will assess brothers and sisters (*adelphoi*, 3:1) who are in ministry (v. 5, *diakonoi*), such as Paul and Apollos, according to their real place in the household of faith. They are planters and waterers of a crop that belongs to God. Since seed, water, and growth come from God, it is a moot question whether the planter or the waterer is higher in significance.

EDITH M. HUMPHREY

RESPONSE

Where do you see Christians making idols of their leaders? What are the dangers of that idolatry?

PRAYER

Break down my golden calves, O God, and teach me to worship you alone. Amen.

✢ SATURDAY ✦

Matthew 5:21–37

REFLECTION

Torah forbids murder (Exod. 20:13; Deut. 5:17), but Jesus says
that not just murder, but anger, makes one liable to judgment.
It is interesting to see the commentators debate whether
such judgment against anger is absolute or not. Supporting
an absolute reading of Jesus' words, other Scripture passages
are equally strong in their condemnation of anger (Eph. 4:31;
Col. 3:8; cf. 1 Tim. 2:8; Jas. 1:20, but also Ps. 37:8; Prov. 14:29;
Eccl. 7:9). Against it, some commentators point out that the
Bible nonetheless records God's and Jesus' anger (Matt. 23:17;
Mark 3:5); others even refer to the biological basis of anger
that makes it inevitable (of course, if biological urges were the
measure of ethics, the next passage of Jesus' sermon makes even
less sense!). The concern of Jesus' saying, however, seems to be
less the *having* of anger than what one *does* with it: does anger
shape our relationships, or preclude reconciliation?

EDWIN CHR. VAN DRIEL

RESPONSE

In this passage, do you feel that Jesus was telling his followers
not to become angry at all, or to be careful of the ways they
dealt with their anger?

PRAYER

Cool my temper with your Holy Spirit, and teach me to utter
words of gentleness. Amen.

↦ SUNDAY ↤

Deuteronomy 30:15–20

REFLECTION

The flip side of these ominous warnings is that God desires for the community to be blessed. God desires life, not death. God hopes that Israel will make the right choice, for faithfulness. The right choice means blessings for the entire community, not just for some. The right choice means a home not just for God's people but for resident aliens as well. The right choice means economic policies that leave enough for everyone. The right choice means an equitable distribution of resources. The right choice means life—this is what God desires for us.

ANDREW FOSTER CONNORS

Psalm 119:1–8

REFLECTION

In verses 6–8, the psalmist turns to the results of obeying the Torah. Having kept God's commandments, he will not be put to shame. In a society like ancient Israel, where honor was of utmost importance, to be put to shame was to lose social standing (cf. Ps. 25:1–3). The psalmist states here that only through following the law will honor be kept intact. In verse 7 he states that after he has learned the law, he will be able to worship God with an upright heart. As the processional hymn in Psalm 24 makes clear, only those who have "clean hands and pure hearts" may ascend to the temple mount (Ps. 24:3–4). The connection between ethical behavior and the worship of God is strong. Only with a heart that is obedient to the law can God be worshiped in a worthy manner.   KEVIN A. WILSON

1 Corinthians 3:1–9

REFLECTION

Martin Luther suggested that Christians should begin each day by remembering our baptism, for in baptism one participates in the dying and rising of Christ. The water used in baptism reminds us of the story of creation, the story of the flood, and the story of the exodus. So it is a symbol of both that which threatens and that which gives life. It also reminds us of dying and rising with Christ and sets us on a path of walking with our woundedness in order to find life therein.

ROGER J. GENCH

Matthew 5:21–37

REFLECTION

Dorothy Day, the founder of the Catholic Worker movement, used to say to her fellow workers, particularly in difficult and stressful times: "If each of us could just remember that we are *all* created in the image of God, then we would naturally want to love more."* At the holy altar, standing shoulder to shoulder, hand in hand, we remember once again that in God's realm there are no outsiders. Every gift is accepted, each offering received.

CHARLES JAMES COOK

RESPONSE

To one degree or another, each of the readings for this week encourages us to reconcile with those who may have harmed us so we can worship God with a clear conscience. Is there anyone with whom you need to reconcile, or to whom you should offer forgiveness?

PRAYER

God, your forgiveness has taught me how to forgive others in turn. Give me the wisdom and the strength to reconcile with them. Amen.

*Paul Elie, *The Life You Save May Be Your Own* (New York: Farrar, Straus & Giroux, 2003), 275.

❧ *Seventh Sunday after* ❧ *the Epiphany*

Leviticus 19:1–2, 9–18

When you reap the harvest of your land,
you shall not reap to the very edges of your field,
or gather the gleanings of your harvest. You shall not
strip your vineyard bare, or gather the fallen grapes
of your vineyard; you shall leave them for the poor
and the alien: I am the LORD your God. (vv. 9–10)

Psalm 119:33–40

Turn my heart to your decrees,
    and not to selfish gain.
Turn my eyes from looking at vanities;
    give me life in your ways. (vv. 36–37)

1 Corinthians 3:10–11, 16–23

Do you not know that you are God's temple
and that God's Spirit dwells in you? If anyone destroys
God's temple, God will destroy that person. For God's
temple is holy, and you are that temple. (vv. 16–17)

Matthew 5:38–48

"You have heard that it was said, 'An eye for an eye and a tooth
for a tooth.' But I say to you, Do not resist an evildoer. But if
anyone strikes you on the right cheek, turn the other also; and if
anyone wants to sue you and take your coat, give your cloak as
well; and if anyone forces you to go one mile, go also the second
mile. Give to everyone who begs from you, and do not refuse
anyone who wants to borrow from you." (vv. 38–42)

⤜ MONDAY ⤛

Leviticus 19:1–2, 9–18

REFLECTION

When it came to money, in my family you were not supposed
tell the truth. I remember my parents fighting late into the
night, always about money—in particular, my mother's
spending. . . .

To avoid such scenes, I was taught never to tell my father
what anything cost. . . .

I remember as a little girl delighting in my brand-new
blue coat, but being afraid to wear it out the door past my
father. From an early age, material things elicited in me both
inordinate delight and misplaced shame, perhaps because we
did not tell the truth.

It is interesting that this passage from so many thousands
of years ago, and from such a different culture, still makes
the connection between generosity and truth telling. The
passage on sharing a portion of what you have with the poor
and the alien is followed by a call to honesty. "You shall not
steal; you shall not deal falsely; and you shall not lie to one
another" (v. 11).

The reading today has a word for me, and families like mine.
It has a word for the church. It is a call to tell the truth and to
take money out of the shadows.

LILLIAN DANIEL

RESPONSE

Read verses 9–14 aloud. How do these teachings on money
square with your own family's financial practices?

PRAYER

God, help me to put my money where my mouth is, using my
resources wisely as an instrument of your kingdom. Amen.

✦ TUESDAY ✦

Leviticus 19:1–2, 9–18

REFLECTION

Leviticus appears just this once in the entire Revised Common Lectionary cycle—and in most years, Lent begins before seven Sundays after Epiphany elapse. The omission is more than unfortunate; it eviscerates the heart of Israel's theology from the Christian preaching cycle. Leviticus records more words from the mouth of God than any other book of the Bible. The question of Christianity's relation to Israel's law cannot be avoided when we open Leviticus. Christians have often met the difficult question by avoiding it, appealing with great relief to the apostolic decree of Acts 15 lifting the burden of adherence to the ceremonial law for Gentile Christians. Might it be that, in shrugging off the burden, we also lose sight of the blessing that Leviticus intends to lavish on God's people?

SHELDON W. SORGE

RESPONSE

The commentator above points out that the lectionary cycle almost entirely avoids the book of Leviticus. Today, spend a few minutes perusing Leviticus. Which laws are still very much applicable for today? Which are not?

PRAYER

Teach me the best ways to honor you, O God, through right actions and a loving heart. Amen.

⁂ WEDNESDAY ⁂

Psalm 119:33–40

REFLECTION

For me at least, the word "righteousness" conjures up associations that are not particularly hopeful, helpful, or healthy. On first blush, "righteousness" evokes images of self-importance, self-righteousness, arrogance, rigidity, and on and on and on. I suspect I am not alone in that.

Jesus once told a story "to some who trusted in themselves that they were righteous and regarded others with contempt" (Luke 18:9).While it is commonly referred to as the parable of the Pharisee and the Publican, or the Pharisee and the Tax Collector, it is really a parable about false righteousness born of self-interest and true righteousness born of humility that gives way to God. "God, I thank you that I am not like other people: thieves, rogues, adulterers, or even like this tax collector. I fast twice a week; I give a tenth of all my income" (Luke 18:11–12). That prayer of the Pharisee is more an admiration of himself than adoration of God. That, I suspect, is one of the associations that are sometimes conjured up when we hear the word "righteousness."

MICHAEL B. CURRY

RESPONSE

What does the word "righteous" mean to you? What is the difference between righteousness and self-righteousness?

PRAYER

From the puffed-up vanities of self-righteousness, good Lord, deliver me. Take me to the rock that is higher, and equip me to serve your people. Amen.

✢ THURSDAY ✦

Psalm 119:33–40

REFLECTION

The quest for wisdom must have been foremost in the author's mind as these verses were composed. The writer twice implores the Deity, "Give me life" (vv. 37, 40). The Christian understanding of the Holy Spirit as "the breath of life" lets us consider this as a plea for divine presence and for the ability to live continuously within it. If one function of the law is to mediate the presence that caused Moses's face to shine after his descent from the mountain, then there is ample cause for wishing to observe that law with one's "whole heart" (v. 34).

"Life abundant" results not from rigid attendance to regulations, but from the constant, lifelong movement along the path of the commandments for which the psalmist expresses such ardent yearning. Seeking to understand the self-revelation of God within the Law—and the Prophets and the Writings and the gospel—brings us closer to the Holy One whose breath gives us life.

ELLEN J. BLUE

RESPONSE

Which aspects of your life right now provide you with "life abundant"? Which do not?

PRAYER

Give me life, O God! Breathe on me the inspiration of your Holy Spirit. Amen.

⤙ FRIDAY ⤚

1 Corinthians 3:10–11, 16–23

REFLECTION

Contemporary mainline North American churches face seemingly intractable divisions over ordination standards and the role of denominational governance. . . .

Paul has something different to say: a timeless reminder to the church to place God at the center of everything they do together. To make his point, Paul uses the metaphor of a skilled master builder: "Each builder must choose with care how to build on it" (v. 10). Other translations use the phrasing "But each one should be careful how he builds" (NIV), indicating words of caution about how the church is constructed.* Paul is urging that each person involved in creating, running, or sustaining a congregation be intentional with the process of being church. In the process of constructing a building, once a solid foundation is poured, each person adds her own expertise. Carpenters frame out the house, an electrician adds the wiring, plumbers add the plumbing, and so on, until the building is completed. If even one person contributes poor work, the building will not function well when it is complete.

KATE FOSTER CONNORS

RESPONSE

Drawing on Paul's metaphor of the church as a building in progress, what are you contributing to its construction? What are your special talents, and how are they used to build up the church?

PRAYER

May I be part of the building of your kingdom and your church, giving of myself and my talents. Amen.

---

*Richard B. Hays, *First Corinthians*, Interpretation series (Louisville, KY: John Knox Press, 1997), 54.

✣ SATURDAY ✣

Matthew 5:38–48

REFLECTION

The phrases of the Sermon on the Mount are so familiar and beautiful we can almost forget how demanding they are. "Turn the other cheek." "Go the second mile." "Love your enemies." "Be perfect, as your heavenly Father is perfect." How lovely, how close to home, how . . . impossible. Love your *enemies*? Respond to the fist by opening yourself up to more fists? Pray for your *persecutors*? As if that's not enough, *be perfect*. The final command is given as an afterthought:" "Oh yes, and besides all that, be flawless." Right. . . .

One thing this text expressly is *not* is an admonition doomed to failure—a word of judgment meant to drive us into the arms of grace. It will seem that way if it is taken as isolated moral admonition for straining heroes to accomplish through their lonely determination, like marathon runners. If, however, this is a blueprint for the life of the church, a constitution for a new society, then we have a chance.

JASON BYASSEE

RESPONSE

"Be ye perfect." Think about how this admonition of Jesus makes you feel: guilty or hopeful? Inadequate or empowered?

PRAYER

I cannot love my enemies, pray for my persecutors, turn the other cheek, or go the second mile without your grace, O God. Teach me to draw from your strength. Amen.

⤙ SUNDAY ⤚

Leviticus 19:1–2, 9–18

REFLECTION

The whole subject of holiness can make us uncomfortable. It is fine for God to be holy. Everyone knows that God is holy, but we have a pretty good sense that most of us are not holy—or holy enough. We are never holy enough. In fact, our discomfort on the matter has become a commonly understood expression of disdain, "holier than thou." Except for those in Holiness church traditions, most of us think true holiness is reserved for a few exceptional people of faith, like Mother Teresa or the pope or the Dalai Lama. Holy people live far removed from us and do with their lives things we cannot, or likely will not, do with ours. As appropriately modest as this may be, it is also a way of letting ourselves off the holiness hook. That is not biblical.

When we preach on Leviticus (as when we preach on Matthew), we remember that we are all on the hook for being holy. God says to Moses, "Speak to *all the congregation of the people of Israel* and say to them: You shall be holy, for I the LORD your God am holy" (19:2). Everyone, the whole congregation, is called to be holy. Being holy is what any person created in God's image is called to be . . . or, better put, to *do*.

KIMBERLY L. CLAYTON

Psalm 119:33–40

REFLECTION

Torah for the psalmist is the ongoing revelation of God's life-giving promise. The last line of the psalm, translated in the NRSV as "in your righteousness give me life" (v. 40), captures only part the original Hebrew *hayah*, which carries the meaning of giving and sustaining life, as well as revival and restoration, captured well by the KJV translation, "quicken me in thy

righteousness." For the psalmist, God's law has the power to
initiate and restore life.

APRIL BERENDS

1 Corinthians 3:10–11, 16–23

REFLECTION

Here we see that Paul was right. The only possible common
ground is Christ crucified. When we gather at the cross, we
have the opportunity to see it and to see Jesus from a variety of
perspectives. Respecting those perspectives of our neighbors
might help us to realize what Paul was preaching, that it is not
Paul or Apollos or Cephas or any of us who try to speak a good
word for Jesus Christ, it is not the world or life or death or the
present or the future—all of these belong to all of us, and we
belong to Christ, and Christ belongs to God.

JOSEPH R. JETER

Matthew 5:38–48

REFLECTION

In his Sermon on the Mount, Jesus lets us eavesdrop on his
instructions to the disciples. We too are encouraged to live
as sisters and brothers in God's realm. "Be perfect" is not an
indictment; it is a promise that carries the possibility that
we may love the world as God has loved us—fully, richly,
abundantly, and completely.

BARBARA J. ESSEX

RESPONSE

This week's readings all explore the concepts of holiness and
perfection. Where have you made progress toward holiness and
perfection this week? Where have you fallen short?

PRAYER

Guide me along the rocky path toward holiness, Lord, and
forgive me when I stumble. Amen.

❧ *Eighth Sunday after* ❦ *the Epiphany*

Isaiah 49:8–16a

But Zion said, "The LORD has forsaken me,
   my Lord has forgotten me."
Can a woman forget her nursing child,
   or show no compassion for the child of her womb?
Even these may forget,
   yet I will not forget you.
See, I have inscribed you on the palms of my hands.
                                    (vv. 14–16)

Psalm 131

But I have calmed and quieted my soul,
   like a weaned child with its mother;
   my soul is like the weaned child that is with me.
                                    (v. 2)

1 Corinthians 4:1–5

Therefore do not pronounce judgment
before the time, before the Lord comes, who will
bring to light the things now hidden in darkness and
will disclose the purposes of the heart. Then each
one will receive commendation from God. (v. 5)

Matthew 6:24–34

"So do not worry about tomorrow, for
tomorrow will bring worries of its own.
Today's trouble is enough for today." (v. 34)

✣ MONDAY ✤

Isaiah 49:8–16a

REFLECTION

The lamenters have their own reason for despair. They recall
the past history of abandonment that seems to suggest divine
forgetfulness. The paralyzing terror of history deprives them
of a capacity to hope. The prophet halts his triumphant song
to minister to them. This concern for flanking doubters is
significant. Second Isaiah, known for the lofty drumbeats of
marching to Jerusalem, turns to care for those who are bound
by the disabling past. God's salvation is also for those whose
vision of hope was impaired by the disappointments of the past
and present.

JIN HEE HAN

RESPONSE

What about your own past has you crippled with secret
fear, unable to allow yourself to hope for God's promise of
redemption and new life?

PRAYER

Do not forget me, O Lord! Remember me like a nursing mother
remembers and forever loves her suckling child. Amen.

Isaiah 49:8–16a

REFLECTION

When I was visiting a prisoner at the local jail, upon entering I realized that nobody knew where I was. As I walked down the long hall to the visitor's booth and was locked in myself, I realized that I was at the mercy of the guards. They had spoken crossly to me and had chastised me for forgetting to leave my bag behind. When they barked at me through the speaker in the tinted glass, I was frightened. I did not want them to be angry with me. I waited for a long time for the person I was visiting to arrive. Without a bag, I had nothing to do. There was nothing to read, no calendar to check—just me, locked up and waiting, with no time line. Suddenly I realized the obvious. I was getting the smallest possible taste of prison life. I felt trapped in darkness, hidden away where no one could see me. The seventy-two-year-old woman I was visiting told me that that was what she felt every minute of every day: invisible, bored, trapped, and out of the sight of the world. . . .

This passage reflects that note of despair: "But Zion said, 'The LORD has forsaken me, my Lord has forgotten me'" (v. 14). That is how prisoners feel. It is how sick people feel, and grieving people feel, and anxiety-ridden people feel. We all have had that moment when, in the midst of our suffering, we worry that we have been forgotten . . .—but God does not forget us.

LILLIAN DANIEL

RESPONSE

When have you felt forgotten or abandoned?

PRAYER

God who brings to light all things that are hidden, bring to my attention a forgotten person who needs my help today. Amen.

Psalm 131

REFLECTION

The psalmist's comparison of her soul to a deeply cared-for child in the presence of a loving parent brings to mind an occasion when my own daughter was visiting the room where she would soon begin prekindergarten. Despite the teacher's urgings to explore the surroundings, my daughter found my lap the best spot from which to view the classroom. After a bit, though, she slipped down and moved away to study an aquarium, while I continued to converse with the teacher. Then she returned to my lap, where I welcomed her. In time, she ventured out again to see what the shelves on another side of the room might hold. This pattern continued until she had seen every corner of the classroom.

God offers, the psalm assures us, the same kind of refuge, and thus provides the freedom to leave its confines and accomplish the work that is necessary for intellectual and spiritual growth. My use of the term "leave its confines" is not to imply that one can truly leave God's presence, but rather to emphasize that growth is the primary task of a child (and an adult) and that spiritual growth always involves risk taking of one sort or another.

ELLEN J. BLUE

RESPONSE

When has God been a mother to you?

PRAYER

Lord, you are my refuge and my strength. I will hope in you from this time on and forevermore. Amen.

→ THURSDAY ←

1 Corinthians 4:1–5

REFLECTION

This is not a passage that would make it onto a banner, or a cornerstone, or even a bulletin cover. No one wants to hear about judgment. No one wants to walk into church and see a banner (or hear a preacher) shaking a finger at them for being judgmental. No one wants to hear about judgment, because judgment is uncomfortable, whether it is a judgment about us or a judgment about others. Judgment implies a pronouncement of opinion about a person or persons. Whether the judgment comes from our own mouths or is pronounced by another, it often is hurtful. "Judgment" is the kind of word that conjures up childhood memories of a parent's admonishing words: "If you cannot say anything nice, do not say anything at all." This text certainly would not make it onto any Bible passage popularity list.

Nevertheless, Paul's words on judgment are words that demand a hearing.

KATE FOSTER CONNORS

RESPONSE

When have you felt unfairly judged? When have you unfairly judged others?

PRAYER

You alone are my judge, O God of justice and mercy. Help me to be merciful to others and refrain from judging them. Amen.

→ FRIDAY ←

Matthew 6:24–34

REFLECTION

This is a command from Jesus: "Do not worry about your life." The bucolic images of the birds and the flowers and the grass stand in contrast to the breathtaking nature of the command given. Fear nothing. It is said that this is the most oft-repeated command in the Bible. When angels appear to announce the incarnation, they tell Mary, Joseph, and the shepherds, "Fear not." When the disciples behold the level of Jesus' grandeur, he has to follow up very quickly with an admonition against fear. When Jesus is taken from them, whether in his death or his ascension, he comforts the little flock against fear. The order not to fear is perhaps not only the most reiterated in Scripture, but also the least obeyed. "Do not worry," our text says, "that's what Gentiles do" (v. 32).

JASON BYASSEE

RESPONSE

When you "consider the lilies of the field," do such exhortations not to worry about material things ring true for you? What makes it so difficult to release anxiety about money and the future?

PRAYER

Today's trouble is enough for today, O God. Give me peace from anxieties about the future. Amen.

✣ SATURDAY ✣

Matthew 6:24–34

REFLECTION

This passage will be especially challenging for listeners struggling to make sense of experiences virtually impossible to interpret in terms of divine providential care. Experiences of personal violation (sexual assault, for example), an untimely death of a loved one, chronic or recurring suffering, widespread hunger and malnutrition, the deterioration of the environment—such events can seem to be devastating rebukes to the portrait Jesus paints here of a God who lovingly attends to all basic, bodily needs.

Indeed, it is a great and difficult tension within Christianity that Jesus can both preach lyrical passages like this one and also cry from the cross, "My God, my God, why have you forsaken me?" (Matt. 27:46). There can be no easy answers here, and clearly naming such tensions can be a sensitive and credible homiletic strategy. Even the apparent contradiction just mentioned may point to an important liturgical resource in Christian life: traditions of lamentation (see, e.g., Ps. 22:1). Indeed, we might say that lament is the way Christians faithfully wrestle with apparent God-forsakenness.

MATTHEW MYER BOULTON

RESPONSE

Name some circumstances in your life that make it difficult to trust that God is in control. How do you respond when it feels like God is *not* taking care of your needs?

PRAYER

Teach me to be faithful, even as you are faithful, O God, and to trust in your eternal perspective when I do not understand the purpose of my suffering. Amen.

✦ SUNDAY ✦

Isaiah 49:8–16a

REFLECTION

We are not forgotten. We are inscribed on the palms of God's hands. Every day in Washington, D.C., people visit the Vietnam Memorial, searching for a name etched into the wall bearing so many names. They trace their fingers over the letters, touching something deeper than name alone. Not forgotten. Remembered. Inscribed. Still, not all names are there, for even our best memorials are limited. Not so the palms of God: every name is written, everyone is included. What joy to find your own name and names of those you love on God's outstretched palm!

KIMBERLY L. CLAYTON

Psalm 131

REFLECTION

The relationship that the speaker shares with God is elemental, aware of its source. The speaker understands that God's ways are "too great and too marvelous" to comprehend. So the psalm reiterates the theme of humility and trust found in other readings for the Eighth Sunday after the Epiphany, including 1 Corinthians 4:5, where Paul speaks of God "who will bring to light the things now hidden in darkness and will disclose the purposes of the heart," and the Gospel text from the Sermon on the Mount where Jesus bids his listeners to "consider the lilies" (Matt. 6:28).

APRIL BERENDS

1 Corinthians 4:1–5

REFLECTION

Describing himself using servant language, Paul aligns himself with God and reminds the Corinthian church that God is the one who does the judging. The church can learn from both messages: we can be God's servant, and in so doing, we can give up the need to judge, because that is God's job. Conversely, when we find ourselves the object of judgment, we can remember that human judgment does not hold authority.

KATE FOSTER CONNORS

Matthew 6:24–34

REFLECTION

Few of us are exempt from worry and anxiety. Most live with chronic anxiety, and we are scared of everything—losing our homes, losing our jobs, not having enough for retirement; caring for our children until they reach adulthood; avoiding danger and terror attacks. . . .

Jesus understands this; his call to worry-free living is not based on unrealistic views of the world. His words are for those who understand that God will not leave us without resources or support. We can face life with all its uncertainties and contingencies with the assurance that we are not alone—that God hears, sees, and cares about us and our situations. "Don't worry, be happy," because God is in control.

BARBARA J. ESSEX

RESPONSE

One theme in this week's passages deals with trusting God, whether it is to take care of our needs or to be the sole judge of our lives. What has helped you learn to trust God?

PRAYER

I cannot see the entire road ahead, my Lord, but give me enough light to see the next few steps on the path. Amen.

❧ *Ninth Sunday after* ❧ *the Epiphany*

Deuteronomy 11:18–21, 26–28

You shall put these words of mine in your heart and soul,
and you shall bind them as a sign on your hand, and fix them
as an emblem on your forehead. Teach them to your children,
talking about them when you are at home and when you are
away, when you lie down and when you rise. (vv. 18–19)

Psalm 31:1–5, 19–24

Blessed be the LORD,
>   for he has wondrously shown his steadfast love to me
>   when I was beset as a city under siege.
I had said in my alarm,
>   "I am driven far from your sight."
But you heard my supplications
>   when I cried out to you for help. (vv. 21–22)

Romans 1:16–17; 3:22b–28 (29–31)

For I am not ashamed of the gospel; it is the power
of God for salvation to everyone who has faith, to the Jew
first and also to the Greek. For in it the righteousness of
God is revealed through faith for faith; as it is written,
"The one who is righteous will live by faith." (1:16–17)

Matthew 7:21–29

"Everyone then who hears these words of mine and acts on them
will be like a wise man who built his house on rock. The rain fell,
the floods came, and the winds blew and beat on that house, but it
did not fall, because it had been founded on rock." (vv. 24–25)

✦ MONDAY ✦

Deuteronomy 11:18–21, 26–28

REFLECTION

In this Old Testament passage, we are told that these stories matter. Not only should we rehearse them over and over again; we should take them into our bodies: "You shall put these words of mine in your heart and soul, and you shall bind them as a sign on your hand, and fix them as an emblem on your forehead" (v. 18).

Furthermore, it is not enough that we understand them ourselves. We need to pass the wisdom down, one generation to the next. "Teach them to your children, talking about them when you are at home and when you are away, when you lie down and when you rise" (v. 19).

This text allows the preacher to remind the congregation of their crucial role as transmitters of the faith. This is a powerful word for church members who teach Sunday school, a reminder that their ministry is critical and desired by God. We do not all have children, but we can all be teachers of children. Sometimes the parent has the least likely shot at getting the message through, and it is another adult whom God can best use to shape a young mind.

LILLIAN DANIEL

RESPONSE

Think of an adult who took the time to nurture you in faith when you were younger. How can you pass that nurturing on to a young person today?

PRAYER

Inscribe your words in my heart and soul, and help me to teach them to the next generation. Amen.

☙ TUESDAY ☙

Deuteronomy 11:18–21, 26–28

REFLECTION

Squirreled away into the remotest corner of the lectionary,
this text comes around only when Easter is as late as possible,
Christmas falls on a Monday, and the congregation chooses
not to celebrate the feast of the Transfiguration. Yet the text is a
central biblical guidepost for daily discipleship.

Just as Isaiah assures us of God's persevering love by saying
that our names are engraved on God's hand (Isa. 49:16), so this
text urges us to bind God's law on our hands. Our hands are the
parts of our body most frequently and fully visible to us. When
we write the claims of this law on our hands, we constantly
remind ourselves: We belong to God.

SHELDON W. SORGE

RESPONSE

This passage from Deuteronomy demands that we display the
words of the Bible on our foreheads, publicly proclaiming our
loyalty to God. Do you feel comfortable being this public about
your faith? Why or why not?

PRAYER

Grant me the courage to put your words on full display in my
life, a profession of faith for all to see. Amen.

⤖ WEDNESDAY ⤚

Psalm 31:1–5, 19–24

REFLECTION

In the well-worn verses of Psalm 31 appointed for the Ninth Sunday after the Epiphany, the psalmist pleads with God, asking God to be a "rock of refuge." At the same time, the psalmist praises God's steadfast love. The psalm addresses one of the primary predicaments of people of faith: living in hope amid despair. It is at the same time a psalm of lamentation and a psalm of praise.

The rocky places portrayed in Scripture are often the places where God breaks in. The history of God's dealings with the people of Israel is punctuated by close encounters with God that take place on mountaintops (Gen. 22; Exod. 24, 34; 1 Kgs. 19). This phenomenon continues in the New Testament (Matt. 17:1–8//Mark 9:2–8//Luke 9:28–36). The psalmist's choice of metaphors makes good sense, given God's history of making fearsome appearances in the mountainous border regions between heaven and earth.

APRIL BERENDS

RESPONSE

When has God been a "rock of refuge" for you?

PRAYER

How abundant is your goodness, O God! Hide me in the shelter of your presence. Amen.

✦ THURSDAY ✦

Romans 1:16–17; 3:22b–28 (29–31)

REFLECTION

Theologically speaking, Paul raises an overwhelming number of issues in this passage; any one of which would be worthy of consideration in the church, but none of which he fully explains. Reading this passage, it would be legitimate for the contemporary church to ask questions like these: What precisely does Paul mean by such terms as gospel, salvation, faith, grace, redemption, sacrifice of atonement, and justified by faith? Can we define these terms in such a way that the person in the pew can understand them and use them in conversations and reflections about her faith and not have the terms become merely "talking points" of the faith? What is salvation? From what are we saved, and for what are we saved? Who can be saved? How are they saved? Is there a formula to obtain salvation that all people must follow precisely? What is the nature of human beings that makes us need salvation? Is salvation to be understood as a past event, a present activity, or a future promise, or some combination of all three time frames?

W. MICHAEL CHITTUM

RESPONSE

What do you think is the most important statement Paul makes in this passage?

PRAYER

All have sinned and fallen short of your glory, O God, and I am no exception. I praise you that I am justified by your grace as a gift, and not as the result of my own works. Amen.

✣ FRIDAY ✣

Matthew 7:21–29

REFLECTION

Matthew takes a bit more time to describe the storm that washes over the wise and foolish persons' houses than does his fellow evangelist Luke (see Luke 6:47–49).* "The rain fell, and the floods came, and the winds blew and beat against that house" (v. 27). Discipleship is no easy road, as anyone trying to live by the words of the Sermon can attest. It is certainly no way to decrease one's anxiety, blood pressure, or lack of self-esteem. Those who claim to love enemies will gain more of them. Those who refuse to be as anxious as the market demands will be a scandal to others. A storm is coming for all, those who live Jesus' words and those who do not—best to build on a solid foundation.

JASON BYASSEE

RESPONSE

In terms of being a disciple of Jesus, what would it mean for you to build your house "upon the rock"?

PRAYER

I will build my life on your sure foundation, Lord, for you are my rock and my fortress. Amen.

---

*I owe this observation to Daniel Harrington, *The Gospel according to Matthew*, vol. 1 of *Sacra Pagina* (Collegeville, MN: Liturgical Press, 1991), 109.

✢ SATURDAY ✢

Matthew 7:21–29

REFLECTION

The foundation must be solid. If the foundation is deep and on solid ground, the house will stand whatever comes. If the foundation is shallow or built on shifting ground, there is no way for the house to remain standing. New houses look pretty. Home inspections may uncover minor issues that are easily fixed, but the test of a house's strength comes only during bad weather. Although the roof looks fine, there is no way of knowing how sound it is until the rains come. Although the basement is cozy and spacious, there is no way of knowing how sealed it is until the floods flow. Although the windows look great, there is no way of knowing how strong they are until the winds blow. The strength of the house does not appear until the storms come.

Such is the life of the true disciple and of the community of faith. It is easy to learn the right words and to engage in rituals and rites, but the strength and character of the disciple is truly tested when the storms come. Those who build their faith on regular prayer, are community minded, and care about the environment are the disciples whose foundation is solid. Jesus calls us to a life of being and doing; words and deeds are interwoven. The life of the disciple—trust and service—springs from understanding that life is a gift from God and that God sustains that life.

BARBARA J. ESSEX

RESPONSE

How has your faith held up in hard times?

PRAYER

Help me to withstand life's storms, and to grow in love as your disciple. Amen.

✢ SUNDAY ✣

Deuteronomy 11:18–21, 26–28

REFLECTION

The primary claim that Jewish people were and are to keep in their hearts, talk about with their children, recite at home or away, when lying down at night and getting up in the morning, is the Shema: "Hear, O Israel: The LORD is our God, the LORD alone. You shall love the LORD your God with all your heart, and with all your soul, and with all your might" (Deut. 6:4–5).

If this were our first, our last, our every thought, imagine what could happen to the conversations in our homes and community, to the anxieties and responsibilities that disrupt our rest, to the mundane topics that take over our relationship with those we live with and love. If everything said and done among us began in this fact—that the Lord is our God, the Lord alone, whom we love first and fully—it would change the scope of our concern, the field of our vision, the quality of our relationships.

KIMBERLY L. CLAYTON

Psalm 31:1–5, 19–24

REFLECTION

The issues of evangelism and mission raised by Psalm 31 apply to congregations as well as to individuals. . . . Are our doors open? Do people know how to find us? Do we communicate a safe, nonthreatening presence? Do we offer guidance and counsel, while at the same time providing time and space for those who need to spend time waiting for the Lord? Do we take the opportunity to affirm God's steadfast love even in times of trial? Do we encourage one another to offer praise?

APRIL BERENDS

Romans 1:16–17; 3:22b–28 (29–31)

REFLECTION

The power of this passage lies in Paul's assurance that God so desires to be in relationship with us, that there is nothing we can do to escape the grasp of God's love. . . . For a broken people (and we all have brokenness), Paul's assurance of God's faithfulness to us is like a letter from an old friend that we can pull out when we need to be reminded that we are loved.

KATE FOSTER CONNORS

Matthew 7:21–29

REFLECTION

Exactly which "particular way" are we to live? Jesus does not specify or summarize this way of life here, and I take the omission to be advised. . . .

Indeed, we may go so far as to say that there is no "particular way" definable apart from Jesus, who is himself, Christians confess, the Way. In any given situation or circumstance, then, Christian discipleship is not a matter of attending to a specific ethical formula, but rather of attending to a specific, living person, Jesus Christ.

MATTHEW MYER BOULTON

RESPONSE

Recite the Shema, as listed above in the Deuteronomy reflection, three times.

PRAYER

I praise you for being the one God, you and you alone. I will love you with all my heart, all my mind, and all my strength. Amen.

❦ *Last Sunday after* ❦ *the Epiphany*

(Transfiguration Sunday)

Exodus 24:12–18

Now the appearance of the glory of the LORD was like a devouring
fire on the top of the mountain in the sight of the people of Israel.
Moses entered the cloud, and went up on the mountain. Moses was
on the mountain for forty days and forty nights. (vv. 17–18)

Psalm 2

Now therefore, O kings, be wise;
    be warned, O rulers of the earth.
Serve the LORD with fear,
    with trembling kiss his feet,
or he will be angry, and you will perish in the way;
    for his wrath is quickly kindled. (vv. 10–12)

2 Peter 1:16–21

For he received honor and glory from God the Father when
that voice was conveyed to him by the Majestic Glory, saying,
"This is my Son, my Beloved, with whom I am well pleased."
We ourselves heard this voice come from heaven, while we
were with him on the holy mountain. (vv. 17–18)

Matthew 17:1–9

Six days later, Jesus took with him Peter and James and his
brother John and led them up a high mountain, by themselves.
And he was transfigured before them, and his face shone like the
sun, and his clothes became dazzling white. (vv. 1–2)

✦ MONDAY ✦

Exodus 24:12–18

REFLECTION

The transfiguration falls on the Last Sunday after Epiphany, just before Ash Wednesday. Exodus and Matthew are very useful transitional texts as the people of God embark into the unknown with a God they barely know. Moses's meeting with God on Mount Sinai is essential to the people of Israel as they face a forty-year journey though the wilderness to the promised land. Likewise, the transfiguration in Matthew is essential to the disciples as they head into the terrifying time of the passion. Both texts are critical to us as we face into our own forty-day observance of Lent. Like Jesus, we set out into a spiritual wilderness to face temptations, to overcome our worst fears, to die to ourselves in order to gain faith that God is, indeed, present, loving, and wonderfully protective of our welfare.

ERICA BROWN WOOD

RESPONSE

As you head into the forty days of Lent, what challenges and temptations lie ahead? Can God's words on Mount Sinai strengthen you for the journey?

PRAYER

I will come up with you to the mountain, and receive the tablets of stone. I will heed your law and your commandments. I praise you for your appearance in glory! Amen.

→ TUESDAY ←

Psalm 2

REFLECTION

The Gospels tell us that Jesus rebukes the devil. Jesus has come to reveal a different kingdom, one defined not by power and might, but by humility and servanthood. Likewise, in the Gospel story of the transfiguration, Jesus signals that his mission is not about earthly glory. He does not stay long on that blessed mountaintop, basking in radiance. Instead, he leads the disciples back down the mountain, because he knows that his throne is not of this world, and that his true glory will be revealed on the cross.

Jesus does indeed become a king on a holy hill (Ps. 2:6), but it is the hill of Golgotha, not Zion. That day, he is clothed in shame, not in splendor. That day, we hear not God, laughing in derision (v. 4), but rather the crowds, mocking Jesus. That day, all messianic expectations are overturned, as the anointed one is crucified.

JOHN D. ROHRS

RESPONSE

Psalm 2 looks to a Messiah who would come clothed in earthly power and overturn the kings of the nations. Jesus, however, was a different kind of Messiah, renouncing power and ruling with love rather than fear. Do you think the people of Jesus' day were disappointed that he did not come to solve their political problems?

PRAYER

I confess I am drawn to the glittering idols of power, wealth, and prestige. Help me to see that Jesus' way of self-sacrifice and meekness—and not those idols—leads to eternal life. Amen.

✦ WEDNESDAY ✦

Psalm 2

REFLECTION

Like the ancient kings of Jerusalem, we are accountable for how we use the power we are given. In response to the behavior of the earthly kings and rulers who set themselves against the Lord, verse 5 says, "Then he will speak to them in his wrath, and terrify them in his fury." Abuses of power are abuses not only against those without power, but also against our God, who desires justice and mercy.

How are we called to use and understand our power? The psalm offers instruction for this: "Now therefore, O kings, be wise; be warned, O rulers of the earth. Serve the Lord with fear, with trembling" (vv. 10–11). Leading or holding power of any kind must be understood as serving God. Too often, people profess a humble faith and attend church on Sunday, while failing to live out that faith in their use of power Monday through Friday. Our faith must determine how we use our power; the two are inseparable. In fact, is this not the case for all aspects of our lives? The journey of discipleship asks that we devote all that we do to serving God.

ANDREA WIGODSKY

RESPONSE

In what ways are you required to exercise power? What temptations arise for you in the use of that power?

PRAYER

I want to be a steward of the gifts, money, and responsibilities you have given me. Show me how to live your kingdom values of love and mercy. Amen.

2 Peter 1:16–21

REFLECTION

Many churches today are woefully unable to provide a community of accountability for believers in their walk of faith. That being said, the epistle writer seems to be calling his readers back to the apostolic doctrine of the second coming mostly so as to scare them into being good. In some ways I am reminded of Jorge, the old monk in Umberto Eco's *The Name of the Rose*, who was driven to acts of murder in his desire to conceal a lost manuscript by Aristotle. He thought the book would cause people to lose their fear of God, and thus fall into disobedience, for, he said, "Law is imposed by fear, whose true name is fear of God."* The epistle writer's somewhat strident desire to reestablish in his readers a fear of God's judgment (see chap. 2) begs the question of whether such scare tactics actually result in lives that are formed in the shape of God's lavish grace. Certainly, we are not meant to use our freedom in Christ as a pretext for evil (1 Pet. 2:16); at the same time, lives of grateful and gracious service do not proceed easily from fear. They proceed most naturally and fruitfully from hearts overflowing with gratitude for God's steadfast love.

CHRISTOPHER GRUNDY

RESPONSE

The letter of 2 Peter seems to want to scare people into heaven. How do such scare tactics about judgment make you feel?

PRAYER

You are a God of love and mercy as well as justice. I am so grateful that the establishment of your kingdom is a cause for rejoicing, not dread. Amen.

*Umberto Eco, *The Name of the Rose* (New York: Harcourt Brace Jovanovich, 1983), 475.

✦ FRIDAY ✦

Matthew 17:1–9

REFLECTION

Peter, James, and John accompany Jesus up the mountain after hearing the news of Jerusalem and Jesus' imminent death. It is only human that in their minds they play out the next few days and weeks. They begin to look for alternatives, desperate for a second opinion, a way to stop time. They want to build a safe sanctuary away from the world, to be content in the moment, saving Jesus and themselves from the heartache to come. They cannot, nor can we.

We glimpse that moment in a hospital room as we sit with two people who have just heard the worst news of their lives and watch the patient reach out to assure the companion, the healthy one, that all will be well. . . . These are the moments when people begin to understand that where there is suffering, there is Holy Ground.* These are the moments when we realize God is present in suffering and sacrifice, just as God is present in the promise and potential of our lives.

This moment of transfiguration is just such a moment.

MARYETTA ANSCHUTZ

RESPONSE

It is natural for us to want to avoid suffering. How did the transfiguration help to prepare the disciples for Jesus' death? How might it help us?

PRAYER

Where there is suffering, your Holy Spirit is there, for you do not hide your face from our pain. Let me not hide my face from your own suffering as we approach your Passion. Amen.

---

*Robert Runcie, "Zeebrugge Ferry Disaster Sermon," in *Tongues of Angels, Tongues of Men* (New York: Doubleday, 1998), 740.

→ SATURDAY ←

Matthew 17:1–9

REFLECTION

The transfiguration does not intend to transport the faithful
into a transhistorical realm, where the Jesus known to
fishermen, tax collectors, and prostitutes suddenly appears in
ghostly mien, lit up from the inside, and having discourse with
famous figures long since dead! Rather, it intends to confess
that these untutored, down-to-earth men and women who
left everything and followed him, hardly knowing why—that
these same persons, later, knew that they had been drawn to
him because, for all his obvious humanity, something radiated
from him that spoke of ineffable and eternal truth. Some of
them remembered now, when he had left them, one incident in
particular when this radiance seemed to manifest itself almost
. . . visibly.

DOUGLAS JOHN HALL

RESPONSE

The transfiguration taught the disciples that Jesus was more
than just a teacher and prophet; he was the Son of God and the
Messiah. What does the transfiguration teach you today?

PRAYER

I thank you for the holy moment of transfiguration, when Jesus'
true identity was made plain. Show me anew the power of your
glory, O God of light. Amen.

✣ SUNDAY ✣

Exodus 24:12–18

REFLECTION

During the season of Epiphany the church probes more deeply the "good news of great joy" (Luke 2:10) that has come to all the world in the birth of Jesus. He is the light that "shines in the darkness" (John 1:5). To his light the nations are drawn, and in his light the people who dwell in "thick darkness" (Exod. 20:21) come and see the light of the grace and truth of the triune God.

ALLEN C. MCSWEEN JR.

Psalm 2

REFLECTION

The story of the transfiguration illustrates the message of Psalm 2. Whatever earthly power we may have ultimately is nothing compared to the power of God. Our human sense of being in control is an illusion, as the disciples learned that day on the mountain. This is not a loss. Rather, the knowledge that it is God—not we—who is in control comes as a huge relief. This relinquishing of power is the joy of the life of faith.

ANDREA WIGODSKY

2 Peter 1:16–21

REFLECTION

A rock concert? A sound and light show? Fourth of July fireworks? Those images come to mind when the Bible speaks about God appearing on Mount Sinai (Exod. 19:16–19) or the dazzling appearance of Jesus on the mountain of the transfiguration (Matt. 17:1–8). One always has to "come down" from such moments of religious ecstasy. The Israelites spend forty years in the wilderness, more complaining than in awe of the One who liberated them from slavery. The disciples will face the harshness of the passion that will expose their "little faith." To what extent can the memory of events in which the curtain of reality is pulled back to glimpse the glory of God inform our faith? That is the question which this final Sunday after the Epiphany, Transfiguration Sunday, poses.

PHEME PERKINS

Matthew 17:1–9

REFLECTION

God's glory and magnificence and power and majesty are unsurpassable, we say; but we must also declare that God's glory and magnificence and power and majesty are surpassed by God's willingness to shed them all in order that we might finally recognize God's love and gentleness. The measureless power that made the heavens and the earth concentrates in a hand reaching out to us.

Some would say that God is much too much to be contained within the walls of a church. Of course they are right. Some would remind us that God is so great that neither the earth below nor the heavens above can hold God. Certainly we must agree with them. God is certainly so great that God can never be contained in something as small as a crumb of bread or a sip of wine. We nod our heads, yes; but we must hasten to add: furthermore, God is so great, so majestic, so glorious, that God deigns come to us in a crumb of bread and a sip of wine, just as much of God as a hand can hold.

PATRICK J. WILLSON

RESPONSE

On this final Sunday before Lent, where has God appeared to you? What "transfigurations" are occurring in your life?

PRAYER

Holy God, we praise you for coming down into our unholy world. Thank you for revealing yourself in Jesus. Amen.

❧ *First Sunday in Lent* ☙

Genesis 2:15–17; 3:1–7

The LORD God took the man and put him in
the garden of Eden to till it and keep it. (2:15)

Psalm 32

You are a hiding place for me;
    you preserve me from trouble;
    you surround me with glad cries of deliverance. (v. 7)

Romans 5:12–19

Therefore, just as sin came into the world through one man,
and death came through sin, and so death spread to all because
all have sinned—sin was indeed in the world before the law, but
sin is not reckoned when there is no law. Yet death exercised
dominion from Adam to Moses, even over those whose sins
were not like the transgression of Adam, who is a type
of the one who was to come. (vv. 12–14)

Matthew 4:1–11

Then Jesus was led up by the Spirit into the wilderness
to be tempted by the devil. He fasted forty days and forty nights,
and afterwards he was famished. The tempter came and said to
him, "If you are the Son of God, command these stones to
become loaves of bread." But he answered, "It is written,

'One does not live by bread alone,
    but by every word that comes from the mouth of God.'"
                                                    (vv. 1–4)

⇥ MONDAY ↤

Genesis 2:15–17; 3:1–7

REFLECTION

The limits God sets to our freedom are not a matter of
enforcing conformity to arbitrary rules. The *torah* of God is
intended for the well-being of the "image bearing creature"
to whom God has entrusted the stewardship of creation. The
flourishing of human life in a good and bountiful, but limited,
creation requires both freedom and appropriate constraints on
the exercise of that freedom.

ALLEN C. MCSWEEN JR.

RESPONSE

As you move through this Lenten season, consider carrying a
small journal with you or using your phone or camera to record
words or visual images in your own response to the readings.
What are examples of where constraints are needed today?

PRAYER

Creator God, you entrust your creation to us all, even to me.
Help me be wise. Amen.

⤞ TUESDAY ⤝

Genesis 2:15–17; 3:1–7

REFLECTION

Care of the garden, God's earth, and all God's creation is more than a purpose. It is our mission. Living as servants of creation fulfills God's intention for us and lives up to the reasons why we were created in the first place. Caring for creation means doing God's work in the world. This is no pastime, nor is it a strategy for us to feel good about ourselves. God sends us into the garden because the garden needs service and preservation, and we are God's instrument for caring for creation.

JON L. BERQUIST

RESPONSE

Where are your hands needed for service and preservation of God's earth?

PRAYER

God, your creativity in our world reminds me of the many places where I can do your work.

❦ *Ash Wednesday* ❦

Isaiah 58:1–12

Is not this the fast that I choose:
 to loose the bonds of injustice,
 to undo the thongs of the yoke,
to let the oppressed go free,
 and to break every yoke?
Is it not to share your bread with the hungry,
 and bring the homeless poor into your house;
when you see the naked, to cover them,
 and not to hide yourself from your own kin? (vv. 6–7)

Psalm 51:1–17

Create in me a clean heart, O God,
 and put a new and right spirit within me.
Do not cast me away from your presence,
 and do not take your holy spirit from me. (vv. 10–11)

2 Corinthians 5:20b–6:10

We are treated as impostors, and yet are true;
as unknown, and yet are well known; as dying, and see—
we are alive; as punished, and yet not killed; as sorrowful, yet
always rejoicing; as poor, yet making many rich; as having
nothing, and yet possessing everything. (6:8–10)

Matthew 6:1–6, 16–21

"Do not store up for yourselves treasures on earth, where moth
and rust consume and where thieves break in and steal; but store
up for yourselves treasures in heaven, where neither moth nor rust
consumes and where thieves do not break in and steal. For where
your treasure is, there your heart will be also." (vv. 19–21)

Isaiah 58:1–12

REFLECTION

Authentic worship is not a matter of elegant ritual or
self-congratulating piety. It is a matter of both social justice and
costly personal concern for the bruised and battered of
the world.

ALLEN C. MCSWEEN JR.

Psalm 51:1–17

REFLECTION

As we begin the season of self-examination and repentance, we
follow the psalmist's example by focusing on how we are failing
to live as God calls us to live and how we are in need of the
salvation and redemption that comes from God alone.

ANDREA WIGODSKY

2 Corinthians 5:20b–6:10

REFLECTION

Being reconciled with God is the agenda of the Christian
life at all times, especially during Lent, as we undertake a
concentrated period of penance and renewal. As in Paul's
own case, reconciliation with God always causes us to have "a
ministry of reconciliation" (5:18) toward others.

CHRISTOPHER A. BEELEY

Matthew 6:1–6, 16–21

REFLECTION

Lent can be a dangerous time. People come to the church
looking for discipline and a new way to live; they come to be
challenged—prepared for the heartache and joy of the cross to
come. The problem with Lent, however, is a direct outgrowth

of this urgency: we contain the season to six weeks of doing good, rather than *building a Lent that becomes a life*. This, very simply, is what Jesus asks his disciples to do at this climax in the Sermon on the Mount. Do not be holy because it is what the world expects of you; rather, learn to live holy lives because a closer relationship to the God who sees in secret will be reward enough.

MARYETTA ANSCHUTZ

RESPONSE

Take out your journal today and reflect on other Lenten seasons and recall the practices in which you have engaged. Which of these have helped you "build a Lent that becomes a life"?

PRAYER

God of my life, may the ashes remind me this Lenten season of your renewing spirit in me. Amen.

→ THURSDAY ←

Romans 5:12–19

REFLECTION

If sin is original to our condition and therefore unavoidable,
it is also deeper and more insidious than we may think. By
turning against God, our neighbor, and ourselves, we bring
about the ruin of all that is good in the world: the consequence
of sin is death in the fullest sense of the word. Sin and death are
not mere annoyances or particular flaws of human life; they are
the central and ultimately destructive problem of our existence,
in which human society is catastrophically trapped.

CHRISTOPHER A. BEELEY

RESPONSE

As you move out and about today, what examples do you see of
the reality of sin in our world?

PRAYER

Help me, O God, to turn toward you, toward my neighbor, with
hands that bring good into your world. Amen.

⤖ FRIDAY ⤐

Matthew 4:1–11

REFLECTION

Temptation comes to us in moments when we look at others
and feel insecure about not having enough. Temptation comes
in judgments we make about strangers or friends who make
choices we do not understand. Temptation rules us, making
us able to look away from those in need and to live our lives
unaffected by poverty, hunger, and disease. Temptation rages in
moments when we allow our temper to define our lives or when
addiction to wealth, power, influence over others, vanity, or an
inordinate need for control defines who we are.

MARYETTA ANSCHUTZ

RESPONSE

As you journal today with words or images, what temptations
rule you?

PRAYER

In human condition, God of life, I often allow temptations to
take over. Help me. Amen.

✦ SATURDAY ✦

Matthew 4:1–11

REFLECTION

Temptation wins when we engage in the justification of little lies, small sins: a racist joke, a questionable business practice for the greater good, a criticism of a spouse or partner when he or she is not around. Temptation wins when we get so caught up in the trappings of life that we lose sight of life itself. These are the faceless moments of evil that, while mundane, lurk in the recesses of our lives and our souls.

MARYETTA ANSCHUTZ

RESPONSE

Recall a time when you experienced temptation winning.

PRAYER

Evil abounds, O God, in thoughtless words, in actions that harm another. Help me name this evil and be cleansed. Amen.

☀ SUNDAY ☀

Genesis 2:15–17; 3:1–7

REFLECTION

The garden is no small responsibility, and we are not to be lords of leisure over the garden, but to be its servants and slaves. We are responsible for the garden, now and into the future, so we must preserve and protect it.

JON L. BERQUIST

Psalm 32

REFLECTION

The psalmist embraces the joy of forgiveness but remains painfully aware of the power of sin, which had so recently infected his body and soul. This honest admission makes this a wonderful text to guide us as we embark on the journey of Lent, a journey of self-reflection, confession, and, ultimately, joyful redemption.

JOHN D. ROHRS

Romans 5:12–19

REFLECTION

Our sin is deep, unavoidable, and devastating, but the grace of Christ far exceeds the power of sin and death. God is on our side against sin and death, and nothing can separate us from his abundant grace and love in Christ Jesus (5:17, 20; 8:38–39).

CHRISTOPHER A. BEELEY

Matthew 4:1–11

REFLECTION

Lenten penitence engages the dark places in our lives that we
may come face to face with them, name them, understand
them, and seek forgiveness for them. It is not about guilt. It is
about freedom from the control that our fears and insecurities
have over us all, about the amendment of life and new
beginnings.

MARYETTA ANSCHUTZ

RESPONSE

What is your confession to God this first week of Lent?

PRAYER

On this Lenten journey I pray, sustaining God, that you will
help me see the places where my life needs amending. Amen.

❧ *Second Sunday in Lent* ❧

Genesis 12:1–4a

I will make of you a great nation, and
I will bless you, and make your name great,
so that you will be a blessing. (v. 2)

Psalm 121

The Lord will protect you from all evil;
God will protect your very life.
The Lord will protect you on your journeys—
whether going or coming—
from now until forever from now.
(vv. 7–8 CEB)

Romans 4:1–5, 13–17

For this reason it depends on faith, in order
that the promise may rest on grace and be guaranteed
to all his descendants, not only to the adherents of the law
but also to those who share the faith of Abraham (for he is the
father of all of us, as it is written, "I have made you the father
of many nations")—in the presence of the God in whom
he believed, who gives life to the dead and calls into
existence the things that do not exist. (vv. 16–17)

John 3:1–17

"The wind blows where it chooses, and you hear
the sound of it, but you do not know
where it comes from or where it goes. So it is
with everyone who is born of the Spirit." (v. 8)

❖ MONDAY ❖

Genesis 12:1–4a

REFLECTION

Abram is called by God to serve as a mirror. Instead of images, Abram will reflect blessings and curses on the land where he will sojourn. As the world blesses Abram, so will Abram reflect those blessings back to the world. As the world curses Abram, so will the world's curses be returned. That is not all. This mirror has two sides. The other side of Abram's task is to turn his mirror self so that the blessing that God shines on him shines on the nations as well.

JAMES MCTYRE

RESPONSE

With words or images, consider the ways you serve as God's mirror in this second week of Lent.

PRAYER

I am indeed blessed, O God. May the blessings I have received bless others this day. Amen.

✦ TUESDAY ✦

Psalm 121

REFLECTION

There is a big difference between having and keeping. For instance, I might *have* a favorite sweater. It is my possession. However, I *keep* my puppy dog. . . .

Likewise, God does not merely have us. God keeps us. We are God's beloved, and immeasurably dear to God. We are not merely possessions in the eyes of the Lord, because if we suffer, it hurts God too. Psalm 121 celebrates the fact that Lord is our keeper.

ROBERT W. FISHER

RESPONSE

What has been your experience of God protecting your life?

PRAYER

God, you keep me, love me, and protect me. I am grateful. Amen.

✦ WEDNESDAY ✦

Psalm 121

REFLECTION

God has already decided we are not throwaways. Someone has already assumed a certain amount of responsibility for us and stays vigilant even when we sleep and even when we slip. We can release ourselves into rejuvenating rest, partly because we know God's watchful eye and creative hand never cease.

DAVID M. BURNS

RESPONSE

As you move through this day, who are those whom God loves? Who are those whom God sees that we don't see?

PRAYER

Thank you, God, for always having a watchful eye over your creation. Amen.

✦ THURSDAY ✦

Romans 4:1–5, 13–17

REFLECTION

The God revealed in Jesus, bringing salvation to all who will accept it, is the same God revealed in Abraham, Moses, Isaiah, and Esther. The unique nature of Jesus will be seen as a unique revelation of the one God who is also revealed in many other places and ways. Salvation, then, is through the revelation and work of God (John 14 makes clear that Jesus and the Father are one) and can be known through other religions. How we understand the relationship between the God of Abraham and the God of Jesus has major implications regarding how we enter into religious dialogue with Jews, Muslims, and followers of other world religions.

WARD B. EWING

RESPONSE

Where do you wrestle with this text and this reflection?

PRAYER

My faith, O God, is indeed shared by many who love you and call you by name. Amen.

✢ FRIDAY ✦

John 3:1–17

REFLECTION

When Jesus tells Nicodemus that he needs to be born again by water and Spirit, he is asking Nicodemus to let God work in his life.

DEBORAH J. KAPP

What if Jesus was exercising a little rabbinical irony instead of divine judgment? It changes our place in the story; suddenly, there is room for *our* ignorance too! Nicodemus reminds us that even the best educated and most authoritative among us are still searching.

ANNA CARTER FLORENCE

RESPONSE

As you are out in the world today, where does the Spirit reveal God at work? Record what you notice with words or images.

PRAYER

Spirit of God, work in my life to help me do amazing things this day and forever. Amen.

✧ SATURDAY ✧

John 3:1–17

REFLECTION

So what does "being born" look like where you live? Why
would we want the chance to do it again? More accurately, since
we cannot birth ourselves, why would we need someone to
bear us again? Who bears us and bears with us today, and who
has borne us in the past? Is this clean work, or messy work?
How are our bodies and spirits involved? There are hundreds of
questions and images to hold up to the light, again and again, to
see how they grow in *your* neighborhood.

ANNA CARTER FLORENCE

RESPONSE

Reflect on your response to one of the questions asked in the
reflection.

PRAYER

God of my life, I give thanks for all my friends and family who
bear with me this day. Amen.

⊹ SUNDAY ⊹

Genesis 12:1–4a

REFLECTION

The faithful response of those who have gone before us has showered humankind with wealth, prosperity, freedom, creativity, and family beyond the imagination of Abraham the patriarch. God calls us to go; will our response offer blessings to those who follow us? If our history reads, "So she went, as God told her," blessings will flow for generations beyond our faithful response.

DONALD P. OLSEN

Psalm 121

REFLECTION

It is as hard to accept that the Lord is my keeper as it is to accept that the Lord loves me, but these two facts are intertwined. That is the key to understanding not merely what the Lord does for us, but why. God's love is the very foundation of God's trustworthiness. God loves us, and therefore God keeps us.

ROBERT W. FISHER

Romans 4:1–5, 13–17

REFLECTION

The wellspring of doxology is discovered when we realize we stand before God incapable of earning God's grace and are instead worthy of that grace simply by God's blessed choice.

LAIRD J. STUART

John 3:1–17

REFLECTION

Who among us has room to grow in our faith? The good news of this text is that God is prepared—even eager—to do the hard, messy, sweating labor that will bring us to maturity and new life.

DEBORAH J. KAPP

RESPONSE

Pause with these reflections as you consider your own response to these texts and their meaning for your life.

PRAYER

God, if you are willing to hang in with the hard work of my growth in faith, I am too. Amen.

❧ *Third Sunday in Lent* ❦

Exodus 17:1–7

He called the place Massah and Meribah,
because the Israelites quarreled and tested the LORD,
saying, "Is the LORD among us or not?" (v. 7)

Psalm 95

O come, let us worship and bow down,
let us kneel before the LORD, our Maker!
For he is our God,
and we are the people of his pasture,
and the sheep of his hand. (vv. 6–7)

Romans 5:1–11

Therefore, since we are justified by faith, we have peace
with God through our Lord Jesus Christ, through whom we have
obtained access to this grace in which we stand; and we boast in
our hope of sharing the glory of God. (vv. 1–2)

John 4:5–42

"God is spirit, and those who worship him
must worship in spirit and truth." (v. 24)

⇥ MONDAY ⇤

Exodus 17:1–7

REFLECTION

Like many other pieces of the long, complex narrative that tells of Israel's wilderness sojourn, this story of thirst and testing has at its center a critical question concerning God's presence. How can we know if God is with us, more literally, "in our midst"? What signs or evidence do we use for discerning the presence and providence of God?

FREDERICK NIEDNER

RESPONSE

As you begin this third week of Lent, note with words or images the places where you see God in your midst.

PRAYER

Sometimes I wonder if you are present, O God, and at other times I am so sure because the signs are so clear. Amen.

⤍ TUESDAY ⤎

Psalm 95

REFLECTION

This psalm delves into the awkward stance we suffer as people
of God who have had every reason to follow God's voice, yet
for some inexplicable reason have failed to do so. Why have we
gone against God's voice? We cannot say. It is an uncomfortable
place to have to stand.

ROBERT W. FISHER

RESPONSE

Consider times when you have gone against God's voice. How
did that place feel to you?

PRAYER

Shepherding God, help me to listen very hard to hear your
voice and to follow it. Amen.

Psalm 95

REFLECTION

If that is not enough to warrant our praise, then the psalmist reminds us that God also made us. Without God we would never have had the chance to get it right and get it wrong. We are alive because God allowed that it was a good thing to be. So come, give thanks and praise to the One who has made all these things possible.

DAVID M. BURNS

RESPONSE

What words of praise do you bring to God today?

PRAYER

With the psalmist, I offer my life in thanks to you. Amen.

✣ THURSDAY ✣

Romans 5:1–11

REFLECTION

So this passage sets us on the pilgrimage of hope. Hope comes from experiencing this progression as God feeds us and leads us through it. Hope also comes because before us is the cross, a sign both of the suffering of Christ and of the triumph over death that God made possible for him and for us. These two sources of hope are intertwined. It is the cross before us, like the north star, that calls us forward through this pilgrimage from suffering into endurance and character on our way to hope.

LAIRD J. STUART

RESPONSE

What signs of hope do you see in the world today? Note them with words or images in your journal.

PRAYER

Thank you for your peace in my life. Amen.

✦ FRIDAY ✦

John 4:5–42

REFLECTION

What rules is Jesus breaking to talk with *us*? What social conventions is he disregarding? What lines is he stepping across, in order to speak about what truly matters, and what may save our life? Human beings are, by definition, rooted in social contexts and ordered by those realities. Sometimes we let "the way it is" determine what we can or are willing to see. Jesus has a distinct fondness for overstepping boundaries. What traditions or customs or conventions might Jesus have to cross in order to speak to you?

ANNA CARTER FLORENCE

RESPONSE

What did Jesus see in the Samaritan woman that others did not see?

PRAYER

Help me to see, O God, beyond conventions, to all that is holy in another. Amen.

✣ SATURDAY ✣

John 4:5–42

REFLECTION

There is something beautifully simple in the staging of this scene as well as its premise: Jesus is thirsty at the well, and we are the ones with the bucket. The deeper metaphorical conversation that follows makes no sense until we really take this in. Can a little thing like a cup of cool water, offered in love, be the beginning of a salvation journey? Yes; and we will never know until we meet the stranger, and tend to the human need first.

ANNA CARTER FLORENCE

RESPONSE

This day, as you meet others, who needs a cup of cool water from you?

PRAYER

Help me pause, listen, and offer a cup to those I meet this day. Amen.

→ SUNDAY ←

Exodus 17:1–7

REFLECTION

A vision, coupled with the freedom to reach for it, is a powerful motivator. Freedom is also a taskmaster. It bears the yoke of choice—choosing whom you will follow, where, when, and why. Understanding the responsibility of that choice is the issue here, for these sojourners in the desert and for the sojourners in our pews and pulpits. Both suffer from misplaced authority. Both will murmur.

DONALD P. OLSEN

Psalm 95

REFLECTION

God wants us to remember God's graceful acts among us. God want us to trust God today and tomorrow without needing constant verification of God's goodness. How would life be different if we did? There is something life-saving about remembering that God is the one who knows what we need and that we do well not to assume God is here to grant our every want when we want it. God is in charge, not us.

DAVID M. BURNS

Romans 5:1–11

REFLECTION

Grace, not works, is what brings us life. One of the great insights contained in this understanding is the recognition that external conditions are of secondary importance. We may experience being loved and loving in the hospital, in unemployment, and even in emotional pain. This should not reduce the desire to end suffering in this world, especially

suffering caused by human action, but it does mean even in
hardship we can know the life of grace. That is good news.

WARD B. EWING

John 4:5–42

REFLECTION

This story narrates the dramatic transformation of the woman.
She begins the story as an outsider and becomes a witness; from
her status as a beginner in faith she becomes an apostle sent by
Jesus himself to testify on his behalf.* As such she is a model for
other women, for people who feel like nobodies, for newcomers
to the faith, and for people with a past. Jesus encounters and
welcomes many into the household of faith—even the least
likely and maybe, even, you and me.

DEBORAH J. KAPP

RESPONSE

Sit with these texts and these reflections. Look over your word
and picture images in your journal. What do you most need to
remember this third week of Lent?

PRAYER

Help me remember, God, you are in charge, not me. Amen.

---

*R. Alan Culpepper, *The Anatomy of the Fourth Gospel: A Study in Literary Design* (Philadelphia: Fortress Press, 1983), 137.

❧ *Fourth Sunday in Lent* ❦

1 Samuel 16:1–13

But the LORD said to Samuel, "Do not look on
his appearance or on the height of his stature, because
I have rejected him; for the LORD does not see as mortals
see; they look on the outward appearance, but
the LORD looks on the heart." (v. 7)

Psalm 23

You prepare a table before me
   in the presence of my enemies;
you anoint my head with oil;
   my cup overflows.
Surely goodness and mercy shall follow me
   all the days of my life,
and I shall dwell in the house of the LORD
   my whole life long. (vv. 5–6)

Ephesians 5:8–14

For once you were darkness, but now in the
Lord you are light. Live as children of light. (v. 8)

John 9:1–41

Jesus said, "I came into this world for
judgment so that those who do not see may see, and
those who do see may become blind." (v. 39)

↣ MONDAY ↤

1 Samuel 16:1–13

REFLECTION

Theologians, prophets, and Pharisees of all stripes would
do well to ponder the story of Samuel and David, in which,
ironically, an ancient, anonymous theologian who practiced his
art through narrative reminded readers, including peers and
colleagues of every age, that God does not see as mortals see.
God sees what human observers can never discern, including
the hidden depths of their own hearts (1 Sam. 16:7).

FREDERICK NIEDNER

RESPONSE

Consider your heart today. What do others see? What does
God see?

PRAYER

Thank you, God, for seeing me through your eyes of love.
Amen.

Psalm 23

REFLECTION

The shepherd walks with you in the midst of your trials. The darkness is not changed, but rather you are changed when you receive the gift of his presence.

ROBERT W. FISHER

In the middle part of this psalm the one who testifies suddenly addresses God directly. I wonder what would happen if a preacher suddenly got so carried away telling about the abundance of God's care, and the palpable presence of God, that the preacher slipped into direct praise of God. If you throw yourself into the structure and spirit of this psalm, it may take you there.

DAVID M. BURNS

RESPONSE

Consider the ways your life has been different because of being in the presence of the shepherd.

PRAYER

Let your prayer today be the reciting of this familiar psalm.

Psalm 23

REFLECTION

This gift of presence is especially meaningful for modern people who find authentic presence with one another an increasingly scarce commodity. More and more, it seems that our busy lives are pulling us away from family meals, from leisurely phone conversations, from long walks with very good friends. We find that human interactions of all sorts, from commerce to courting, are being increasingly facilitated by electronics. All the while, the ability to listen is being corroded, and the experience of being truly heard has become more significant than ever. If we learn from our walk with the shepherd just how healing it is to receive such presence, perhaps we will in turn offer it to others.

ROBERT W. FISHER

RESPONSE

How are you present to others today, really listening—in phone conversations, in texts, on Facebook, in FaceTime or Skype, and in face-to-face presence?

PRAYER

Help me be aware of how much I really listen, really give myself to the presence of others. Amen.

✦ THURSDAY ✦

Ephesians 5:8–14

REFLECTION

True worship results in transformed people who act out of genuine concern for others and for doing the will of God. From within the community that honors the dignity of every human being, we are free to listen carefully to the other, free to express our understanding, and free to find the new understanding that somehow bridges the division and moves toward truth.

WARD B. EWING

RESPONSE

Consider places of darkness and places of light today in your journaling with words and images.

PRAYER

Help me live as a child of light in your world. Amen.

⤳ FRIDAY ⤳

Ephesians 5:8–14

REFLECTION

What we most need, as bearers of Christ's light, are glimpses of our possibilities for exposing the works of that darkness.

DON WARDLAW

Now, those who were in darkness actually become like Christ. . . . *Now*, their lives—illumined by Christ—become living testimonies of the power of God.

GAY L. BYRON

RESPONSE

What darkness is God asking you to enter with Christ's light?

PRAYER

I am ever grateful, God of light, for your presence in this world. Help me to join with others in bringing light to the dark places in our community. Amen.

☩ SATURDAY ☩

John 9:1–41

REFLECTION

Providence is not a Christian explanation of history, nor is it a compelling rational answer to and explanation of the horrors of the twentieth century. Providence is a confession by those who are given the eyes of faith that in particular events God works in, around, through those things that oppose God, to accomplish God's purposes.

GEORGE W. STROUP

RESPONSE

What evidence of providence do you see?

PRAYER

God of my life, help me see the ways that I can join you in accomplishing your purposes in this world. Amen.

⊹ SUNDAY ⊹

1 Samuel 16:1–13

REFLECTION

What were God and Samuel thinking? Apparently, they first
thought it took a giant to slay giants. The larger story reveals
that it really took a faithful, dancing heart. Remember, it was
David who slew Goliath. Faithful, dancing hearts are what the
church needs too.

DONALD P. OLSEN

Psalm 23

REFLECTION

When we sit at the Lord's table and feel our foreheads anointed,
we get a holy kiss that heals our places of hurt. We see the
darkness around us lose its power in the midst of the Lord's
presence, and we are restored.

ROBERT W. FISHER

Ephesians 5:8–14

REFLECTION

For some of us, this Christ-driven boldness may find expression
in protesting the redlining practices of a local bank. For others,
this new Spirit-driven resolve may come to life in joining the
battle against the polluting chemical plant north of town.
Possibly this newly inspirited courage is voiced in the parish
leaders' demand that we as a congregation break out of our
insular mentality to address the poverty and crime in the
neighborhood.

DON WARDLAW

John 9:1–41

REFLECTION

The light of the world is in our midst, and we need not shut our eyes. In fact, the best thing to do is to open our eyes, wide. We will not be blinded by the light. We will be saved.

DEBORAH J. KAPP

RESPONSE

How has God's anointing presence at the table healed your hurt?

PRAYER

Open my eyes wide, O God, so I can be a light in your world. Amen.

❧ *Fifth Sunday in Lent* ❧

Ezekiel 37:1–14

"I will put my spirit within you, and you shall live, and
I will place you on your own soil; then you shall know that I,
the LORD, have spoken and will act, says the LORD." (v. 14)

Psalm 130

I wait for the LORD, my soul waits,
    and in his word I hope;
my soul waits for the Lord
    more than those who watch for the morning,
    more than those who watch for the morning.
                                    (vv. 5–6)

Romans 8:6–11

If the Spirit of him who raised Jesus from the
dead dwells in you, he who raised Christ from
the dead will give life to your mortal bodies also
through his Spirit that dwells in you. (v. 11)

John 11:1–45

Jesus said to her, "I am the resurrection and
the life. Those who believe in me, even though they die,
will live, and everyone who lives and believes in me
will never die. Do you believe this?" (vv. 25–26)

⇢ MONDAY ⇠

Ezekiel 37:1–14

REFLECTION

At the core of biblical narrative is the story of displacement—
of having wandered a long way from home, and longing to
return. This is the underlying plot of being cast out of Eden, of
being foreigners in Egypt, of the journey to the promised land,
of the longing of exiles in Babylon to return to the land of their
fathers.

KELTON COBB

RESPONSE

As you begin this fifth week of Lent, recall the places where you
have wandered in your life of faith.

PRAYER

Even when I have wandered far from home, O God, your Spirit
has been with me. For this I am grateful. Amen.

✢ TUESDAY ✢

Ezekiel 37:1–14

REFLECTION

What would an analysis of our spiritual bones indicate this
Lenten season? What would we find out about our spiritual
maturity if we examined our spiritual bones? Would we
show a deficiency of a substantial diet of study, reflection,
prayer, and a meaningful relationship with God? What would
this examination tell us about the richness of our spiritual
practices? How sincerely do we long and pray for the gifts
of the Spirit: love, joy, peace, patience, kindness, goodness,
faithfulness, gentleness, and self-control? What would be our
answer if the Lord spoke directly to us and questioned, "Can
these bones live?"

KATHERINE E. AMOS

RESPONSE

Pick one or more of the questions that are asked here and
journal in response.

PRAYER

When my spiritual bones are dry, refresh and renew them.
Amen.

✦ WEDNESDAY ✦

Psalm 130

REFLECTION

If the first human task in the depths is to cry out, the second is to wait. We are not to wait passively but to wait with hope. Hope is an intensive form of waiting, a statement that almost exactly describes the grammar of the Hebrew verb used here.

STEPHEN FARRIS

RESPONSE

For what are you waiting this day?

PRAYER

In my waiting and watching, I hope, and my hope is in your hands, God of my life. Amen.

→ THURSDAY ←

Romans 8:6–11

REFLECTION

Might we not see Lent in a different light if we conceived this season as a time of setting the mind on the Spirit in a disciplined fashion so that we might know peace—true peace, the peace that passes all understanding?

DOUGLAS TRAVIS

RESPONSE

Here you are at the end of Lent. How have you experienced it this time?

PRAYER

As this season is coming to an end, help me continue to set my mind on your Spirit of peace, O God. Amen.

⟶ FRIDAY ⟵

John 11:1–45

REFLECTION

Releasing persons and communities from the clutches of death also demands something of us, as did Lazarus's resurrection of his community. Though Jesus called Lazarus from the tomb, he urged those who were alive and well, "Unbind him, and let him go."

VERONICE MILES

RESPONSE

What persons in your community need to be unbound from the clutches of death?

PRAYER

I believe, O God, and I know I live because of you. Amen.

⇥ SATURDAY ⇤

John 11:1–45

REFLECTION

Resurrected women, men, and children today also require caring communities that are willing to nurture and strengthen them until they are able to walk alone; to remove the graveclothes of self-doubt, social isolation, marginalization, and oppression; to tear away the wrappings of fear, anxiety, loss, and grief, so that unbound women, men, and children might walk in dignity and become creative agents in the world.

VERONICE MILES

RESPONSE

What graveclothes is Jesus asking you and those in your community of faith to help tear away?

PRAYER

Sometimes I fail to see how others are bound in ways not visible to the eye. Open my eyes that I may see. Help me be one to support the unbinding. Amen.

Ezekiel 37:1–14

REFLECTION

The African American spiritual titled "Dese Bones Gwine Rise Again" has the refrain "I know it, deed I know it, dese bones gwine rise again."* This assurance can underlie all of our living. With the difficulty and joy of living, God continually challenges us to read the bones and then offer them up to God for the breath of restoration and resurrection.

KATHERINE E. AMOS

Psalm 130

REFLECTION

"Forgiveness with God" is not by itself very useful or helpful to anyone in the long night watches, in the pits, or left waiting. Implied instead is a movement of the believer, namely, the act of repenting. Repentance means saying good-bye to the old self and leaving an entrance for God to act, to bring morning to the soul.

MARTIN E. MARTY

Romans 8:6–11

REFLECTION

We live through Lent as those who know they are headed for glory, not because of our own spiritual accomplishments, but because the Spirit has bound us up with the glorified Christ, who is "the firstborn within a large family" (8:29).

AMY PLANTINGA PAUW

*Leonidas A. Johnson, *Go Down, Moses! Daily Devotions Inspired by Old Negro Spirituals* (Valley Forge, PA: Judson Press, 2000), xx.

John 11:1–45

REFLECTION

A few years ago, a friend gave me a poster with the slogan, "Consider the possibilities . . ."—ellipsis marks indicating that there is more to be said, this slogan provocatively reminds us to dream beyond the boundaries, to consider the possibility of resurrection, anticipating it so profoundly that we stand at the tomb of suffering and pain, listening for the voice of Jesus, ready to unbind those whom God delivers, even now.

VERONICE MILES

RESPONSE

Think on these reflections. What connections do you make with these texts and these reflections and your life of faith?

PRAYER

Open the eyes and ears of my heart, Lord, so I may see and hear you. Amen.

❧ *Palm/Passion Sunday* ❧

Psalm 118:1–2, 19–29

You are my God, and I will give thanks to you;
  you are my God, I will extol you.
O give thanks to the LORD, for he is good,
  for his steadfast love endures forever. (vv. 28–29)

Matthew 21:1–11

When he entered Jerusalem, the whole city
  was in turmoil, asking, "Who is this?"
The crowds were saying, "This is the prophet
Jesus from Nazareth in Galilee."(vv. 10–11)

Isaiah 50:4–9a

The Lord GOD has given me
>the tongue of a teacher,
that I may know how to sustain
>the weary with a word.
Morning by morning he wakens—
>wakens my ear
>>to listen as those who are taught. (v. 4)

Psalm 31:9–16

My times are in your hand;
>deliver me from the hand of my enemies
>>and persecutors.
Let your face shine upon your servant;
>save me in your steadfast love. (vv. 15–16)

Philippians 2:5–11

Let the same mind be in you that was in Christ Jesus,
>who, though he was in the form of God,
>>did not regard equality with God
>>as something to be exploited,
>but emptied himself,
>>taking the form of a slave,
>>being born in human likeness. (vv. 5–7)

Matthew 27:11–54

And about three o'clock Jesus cried with a
loud voice, "Eli, Eli, lema sabachthani?" that is,
"My God, my God, why have you forsaken me?" (v. 46)

✢ MONDAY ✦

Psalm 118:1–2, 19–29

REFLECTION

One is to give thanks, not because one has been victorious in battle, as this psalmist may have been, or for good things God gives. No, one gives thanks because God is good. God merits thanks intrinsically, in the nature of the case, because the chief feature in the experience of God and the witness to God is that "he is good; *his love endures forever*" (vv. 1, 29).

MARTIN E. MARTY

RESPONSE

In your journaling time this day, with words or images record your thanksgiving to God.

PRAYER

Thank you, O God, for your steadfast love that surrounds me. Amen.

☙ TUESDAY ❧

Matthew 21:1–11

REFLECTION

Our Holy Week liturgies are rooted in this strong Jewish sense
of the present faith community's being re-membered ritually
into God's ongoing, liberating action. So begins the church's
annual reentry onto the events of Holy Week by marking how
the empire of God, whose nearness Jesus came to proclaim
and embody, looks to welcome quite "a different kind of king"
indeed.

JOHN ROLLEFSON

RESPONSE

What kind of king did they expect? What kind of God do we
welcome this Palm Sunday?

PRAYER

God of my Lenten journey, help me remember the places where
your liberating work is needed this day. Amen.

✦ WEDNESDAY ✦

Isaiah 50:4–9a

REFLECTION

This powerful passage in Isaiah describes an intimate relationship between God and the writer. God personally whispers in the listener's ear what God needs for the listener to learn. This instruction is a revelation from God that provides not only divine wisdom but also the ability to use this wisdom to teach and care for the "weary." The instruction occurs not just once but continues "morning by morning." God "wakens [the] ear to listen" and teaches wisdom and compassion. We might ask ourselves, Have our ears ever been wakened by God? Are there occasions when God has felt this available and personal in our lives? Are we open to such experiences with God?

KATHERINE E. AMOS

RESPONSE

What is your response to the questions asked in this reflection?

PRAYER

Help me, O God, to have the words I need to sustain those who are weary. Amen.

✧ THURSDAY ✧

Psalm 31:9–16

REFLECTION

It is pointless to ask for grace from a graceless one, for the shining of a face from one who comes in scowling darkness, or for salvation from someone who is not loving "steadfastly," through thick or thin. This asking is most effective when it comes from someone who has long practiced what we might call "the conversation with God." We read and say and sing and chant psalms to further that conversation and the confidence that comes with hearing the Thou to whom these words are addressed.

MARTIN E. MARTY

RESPONSE

Who do you know who has had a long life of practicing "conversation with God"? What have you learned from her or him?

PRAYER

My times are indeed in your hand. Shine your face upon me this day. Amen.

⇢ FRIDAY ⇠

Philippians 2:5–11

REFLECTION

We should rejoice in processions that exhibit humility,
compassion, and a thirst for God's reign—participants in the
Montgomery bus boycott walking and carpooling to work,
South Africans moving in long, swaying lines to vote for the
first time. There we catch a glimpse of the creaturely glory God
has promised us in Christ Jesus.

AMY PLANTINGA PAUW

RESPONSE

In addition to the processions mentioned here, what other ones
can you recall where you caught a glimpse of the glory and
hope of God?

PRAYER

Help me join processions of humility, compassion, thirst, and
hope in this world. Amen.

✦ SATURDAY ✦

Matthew 27:11–54

REFLECTION

Matthew's narrative affirms that whatever lies ahead for
Jesus' followers has already happened to Jesus. Whatever they
might suffer, he has suffered already; the death they face is a
death he has already endured. The essential christological
claim in this Gospel is that Jesus—even at the most isolated
and isolating moment on the cross—is Immanuel, God with
us (1:23; cf. 28:20).

AUDREY WEST

RESPONSE

Pause and reflect on the meaning of Immanuel, God with us, as
it is revealed in Matthew's narrative.

PRAYER

My God, in your suffering, you draw to you all those who suffer
and are in pain. And in being Immanuel—God with us, you
offer us love and hope. Amen.

✦ PALM/PASSION SUNDAY ✦

Psalm 118:1–2, 19–29

REFLECTION

Anyone who in heart and mind accompanies Jesus through the week to come will find a world turned upside down. That person will see the hand of God in all that follows in the story and be enabled to say, "O give thanks to the Lord, for he is good, for his steadfast love endures forever" (v. 1, 29). In the end, the only appropriate response to reversal is praise.

STEPHEN FARRIS

Matthew 21:1–11

REFLECTION

The Liturgy of the Palms and the Liturgy of the Passion occupy the same stage, their dramas unfolding so close in proximity that we can scarcely make the emotional shift. Celebration and praise converge with loss and grief; strength and vulnerability share one liturgical moment, inviting us to shout "Hosanna!" while also bracing ourselves for the poignancy of the crucifixion and the mourning that follows. The Liturgy of the Palms punctuates the moment with a call to communal faith, courageous proclamation, and conspicuous action as we consider again our shared identity as the church and community of faith.   VERONICE MILES

Isaiah 50:4–9a

REFLECTION

As we listen for God and listen to God, we must remember that God does not just teach and ask for a response to the gift of new wisdom. God also promises to remain faithful and supportive as we act on this new wisdom by caring for the weary.

KATHERINE E. AMOS

Psalm 31:9–16

REFLECTION

"My times" includes all those negative references about the abandoned one who is praying this psalm. We are where we began: placing all confidence where it belongs, in the relation to a God who is worthy of trust and who acts on the basis of the divine character as the Trustworthy One.

MARTIN E. MARTY

Philippians 2:5–11

REFLECTION

So the heart of God is revealed. The divinity of our Lord is somehow inextricably linked with his willingness to empty himself, with his radical humility, with his ready willingness to identify with "the least of these" (cf. Matt. 25:40, 45).

DOUGLAS TRAVIS

Matthew 27:11–54

REFLECTION

For the crucifixion is not simply an event to be mourned or an entrée to the resurrection, but a reminder of the malevolence that ensues when faithful persons forget to remember that we stand with the One who has come in the name of the Lord.

VERONICE MILES

RESPONSE

How is the heart of God revealed to you in these texts this Palm/Passion Sunday?

PRAYER

As my Lenten journey ends, help me remember how the spiritual work I have done can become a way of life. Amen.

❦ *Holy Week* ❦

✦ MONDAY OF HOLY WEEK ✦

Psalm 36:5–11

How precious is your steadfast love, O God!
    All people may take refuge in the shadow of your wings.
They feast on the abundance of your house,
    and you give them drink from the river of your delights.
For with you is the fountain of life;
    in your light we see light. (vv. 7–9)

REFLECTION

God is refuge, which people find "in the shadow of your
wings." God is sustainer, through which people "feast on the
abundance of your house" and "drink from the river of your
delights." God is life and light in a world of death and darkness.
In each of these metaphors, the imagery indicates a notion of
the profound *nearness* of God: protection beneath God's wings,
feasting and drinking in the house of God, life being "with"
God and light being "in" God.

NICOLE L. JOHNSON

RESPONSE

This week pause and reflect on your experience of God as
refuge, sustainer, life, and light.

PRAYER

Shine your light, O God, on the places of darkness in your
world that need our care and response. Amen.

⊹ TUESDAY OF HOLY WEEK ⊹

Isaiah 49:1–7

Listen to me, O coastlands,
> pay attention, you peoples from far away!
The LORD called me before I was born,
> while I was in my mother's womb he named me. (v. 1)

REFLECTION

Disappointment in vocation is not a sign that God has not
called. It is just a sign that discernment is hard work and
engages the whole of a person's history—past, present, and
mysterious future. Things we could not know at the time
become gracefully clear as the years pass. God calls everyone
to something, and God can call us again and again, to different
things at different times. We respond to life, and within our
careful and prayerful response is the mysterious call of God.

BARBARA CAWTHORNE CRAFTON

RESPONSE

Today, reflect on your life and the different ministries God has
called you to over your lifetime.

PRAYER

For the many ways you have called me and will call me to be
your light in this world, I am grateful. Amen.

☙ WEDNESDAY OF HOLY WEEK ❧

Psalm 70

But I am poor and needy;
 hasten to me, O God!
You are my help and my deliverer;
 O LORD, do not delay! (v. 5)

REFLECTION

It is from the depths of our fear, anxiety, and even outright danger that humans are most able to recognize that they are "poor and needy" and are therefore in need of God's faithful love and deliverance. It is from such depths of suffering that we are able to shout with genuine praise along with the psalmist, "God is great!"

NICOLE L. JOHNSON

RESPONSE

In what ways are you poor and needy before God?

PRAYER

God, you are indeed great and good in my life, my help and my deliverer. Amen.

☀ MAUNDY THURSDAY ☀

John 13:1–17, 31b–35

"I give you a new commandment, that you love
one another. Just as I have loved you, you also should love
one another. By this everyone will know that you are my
disciples, if you have love for one another." (vv. 34–35)

REFLECTION

The witness of Jesus is as counterintuitive as the instinct to
power and privilege is subverted. This subversion, however,
is the way of love and the mark of a true disciple: "I give you
a new commandment, that you love one another. Just as I
have loved you, you should love one another. By this everyone
will know that you are my disciples, if you have love for one
another" (John 13:34–35).

This is the choice faced by all who have gathered to follow
Jesus in his hour.

TRYGVE DAVID JOHNSON

RESPONSE

What does loving another mean for you? Where is it hard?
Where is it easy?

PRAYER

I pray that I may be counted as one of your disciples. Amen.

⇥ GOOD FRIDAY ⇤

Isaiah 52:13–53:12

But he was wounded for our transgressions,
  crushed for our iniquities;
upon him was the punishment that made us whole,
  and by his bruises we are healed.
All we like sheep have gone astray;
  we have all turned to our own way,
and the LORD has laid on him
  the iniquity of us all. (53:5–6)

REFLECTION

Our reconciliation with God is the "medicine" we need. Its effects are to bring "healing" or "salvation," the fullness of life God intends us to have, with God and with others. The Sufferer brings fullness by making us new persons, healed from the wound of our sin by his own wounds. By his "bruises" we can be made whole.

DONALD K. MCKIM

RESPONSE

As you sit with the texts for Good Friday, consider the possibilities for the fullness of life God intends for humankind.

PRAYER

God who died for me, thank you for the fullness of life made possible by your sacrificial love. Amen.

→ HOLY SATURDAY ←

Psalm 31:1–4, 15–16

My times are in your hand;
>   deliver me from the hand of my enemies and persecutors.
Let your face shine upon your servant;
>   save me in your steadfast love. (vv. 15–16)

REFLECTION

On Holy Saturday, we make the decision to bind ourselves to
the history of Jesus and to the history of God. We experience
the brokenness of a more-than-good man who bound himself
to God. Christianity is not, on this day, glorious or triumphant.
The day itself is a time of quietly following enormous suffering,
when human compassion is one of the few gifts we can offer
and one of the few we can take.

NORA GALLAGHER

RESPONSE

In this last day before the alleluias, think about ways God has
been Immanuel in your life.

PRAYER

As I move out of the darkness of this day and wait for the light
of Easter, I am thankful, O God, that my time is in your hands.
Amen.

✣ THE RESURRECTION OF ✣
THE LORD
(EASTER DAY)

Jeremiah 31:1–6

I have loved you with an everlasting love;
   therefore I have continued my faithfulness to you. (v. 3b)

Psalm 118:1–2, 14–24

This is the LORD's doing;
   it is marvelous in our eyes.
This is the day that the LORD has made;
   let us rejoice and be glad in it. (vv. 23–24)

Colossians 3:1–4

So if you have been raised with Christ, seek the things
that are above, where Christ is, seated at the right hand of God.
Set your minds on things that are above, not on things that are
on earth, for you have died, and your life is hidden with Christ
in God. When Christ who is your life is revealed, then you
also will be revealed with him in glory.

John 20:1–18

Jesus said to her, "Mary!" She turned and said to him in Hebrew,
"Rabbouni!" (which means Teacher). Jesus said to her, "Do not
hold on to me, because I have not yet ascended to the Father. But
go to my brothers and say to them, 'I am ascending to my Father
and your Father, to my God and your God.'" Mary Magdalene went
and announced to the disciples, "I have seen the Lord"; and she
told them that he had said these things to her. (vv. 16–18)

Jeremiah 31:1–6

REFLECTION

We sing because we know that there is another way to run a world, a world where death is not the final word, where despair is not the winner, where human power and hierarchies are not thought to be inevitable and unchangeable.

JOHN C. HOLBERT

Psalm 118:1–2, 14–24

REFLECTION

God's graciousness toward us is not expressed in individualized, separate, and independent actions that have no relationship to each other. Individuals are saved and justified as part of a community.

THOMAS P. MCCREESH

Colossians 3:1–4

REFLECTION

If you have taken the step to be baptized with Christ, so you also must be serious about living the resurrected life with him. This means you are to organize your days with a certain conduct in mind, just as you are to fashion the decisions of your days around the moral identity of Christ Jesus. In essence, you are to orient your existence around the very things that matter to Christ.

PETER W. MARTY

John 20:1–18

REFLECTION

Realities about which we hold no doubt may not be large enough to reveal God to us. So we say without apology or hesitation: what we proclaim at Easter is too mighty to be encompassed by certainty, too wonderful to be found only within the borders of our imaginations.

MARTIN B. COPENHAVER

RESPONSE

What song of faith is on your heart this day? Sing it with joy and happiness.

PRAYER

Once you were dead and now you are alive! O God, be alive in my heart so I may live in the newness and light of Easter. Amen.

❧ *Second Sunday of Easter* ❧

Acts 2:14a, 22–32

"This Jesus God raised up, and of that
all of us are witnesses." (v. 32)

Psalm 16

Protect me, O God, for in you I take refuge. (v. 1)

1 Peter 1:3–9

Although you have not seen him, you love him;
and even though you do not see him now, you believe in
him and rejoice with an indescribable and glorious joy, for
you are receiving the outcome of your faith, the
salvation of your souls. (vv. 8–9)

John 20:19–31

Jesus said to him, "Have you believed because
you have seen me? Blessed are those who have not
seen and yet have come to believe."(v. 29)

⤻ MONDAY ⤸

Acts 2:14a, 22–32

REFLECTION

"When did Jesus become more than just a name to you?"
The name may be one you grew up hearing as part of your
daily life, or perhaps it was only mentioned in the midst of
all the secular festivities of Christmas and Easter. Whether by
gradual understanding or a lightning-bolt moment, somewhere
along the way your spirit awakened to the truth that Jesus is
more than the name of someone who lived a couple thousand
years ago.

KATHLEEN LONG BOSTROM

RESPONSE

When did Jesus become more than just a name to you? What
are your earliest memories of being told the stories of Jesus?

PRAYER

Jesus, I am a witness to your birth, your life, and your saving
death. Amen.

⇥ TUESDAY ⇤

Acts 2:14a, 22–32

REFLECTION

Let Jesus be more than just a name to you, Peter says. Let Christ
be your Savior. Hear with your heart as well as with your ears.
Then you can proclaim Jesus as Lord and know the joy of
Christ's amazing, saving grace.

KATHLEEN LONG BOSTROM

RESPONSE

As you live in response to the old yet ever new resurrection
story, be aware of the places you are being called to extend the
grace and joy of Jesus with another.

PRAYER

Savior of my life, let me join with others in living in response to
your promises. Amen.

✦ WEDNESDAY ✦

Psalm 16

REFLECTION

This ancient psalm understands the Lord's mercy and love so
well that it affirms faith in the Lord as the giver of life, even
against all odds. The Lord is the one who leads to life, and the
psalmist rests in the security of this belief.

THOMAS P. MCCREESH

RESPONSE

What affirmations of God's mercy and love can you make
this day?

PRAYER

Continue to show me the paths that lead to life. Amen.

✦ THURSDAY ✦

1 Peter 1:3–9

REFLECTION

Some Christians' convictions about the death penalty, about fair housing, about a living wage for the poor, about immigration reform, or about foreign policy make them opponents of popular social and political trends. Christians' varied experiences of the faith move some also to embrace movements for justice within the church that are decidedly unpopular with other groups of Christians.

E. ELIZABETH JOHNSON

RESPONSE

What is the outcome of your faith? Which of the issues mentioned in this reflection are important to you?

PRAYER

Gracious God, be present with all people of faith as we come together to address issues of public policy that affect how we live together in your world with peace. Amen.

✦ FRIDAY ✦

John 20:19–31

REFLECTION

Though we latter-day disciples may be blessed for believing
though not having actually seen those telltale signs ourselves,
we are disciples capable of greater faith and courage because
we trust that Thomas and the others saw them on our behalf.
Thereby we are assured that the risen one is indeed the crucified
one. Thus hope endures.

D. CAMERON MURCHISON

RESPONSE

As you consider this Easter story through postmodern eyes,
what is necessary for your belief?

PRAYER

I confess, O God, that sometimes, like Thomas, I need a sign.
And then other times, I rest in the mystery of believing without
proof. Amen.

⤳ SATURDAY ⤶

John 20:19–31

REFLECTION

If those in our congregations need something else, something
beyond the verbal, beyond the simple telling of the story,
something that looks and feels more like life, then that is OK
also, John seems to say. Jesus can still give them—each of us—
what we need. So, for instance, we are invited to come to the
Lord's Table, to open our empty hands, to touch and taste for
ourselves. On this Sunday—whether we experience it as Low
Sunday or approach it as the Second Sunday of Easter—Jesus
still has the power to give us what we need.

MARTIN B. COPENHAVER

RESPONSE

How would you tell the Easter story to someone who has never
heard it before?

PRAYER

Take my empty hands, Jesus, and help me receive the gift of
your risen power. Amen.

⇨ SUNDAY ⇦

Acts 2:14a, 22–32

REFLECTION

We need to use the tools of our day to announce the power and wonder of Jesus' resurrected life that has changed everything about us. In our world of death-dealing violence, of haves and have-nots, of those in and those out, the pretty people and the nobodies, we need to announce the fact that death holds no sway over us anymore. That means that hierarchies have no meaning, those who would dominate others have lost their power; in Jesus all things are truly made new.

JOHN C. HOLBERT

Psalm 16

REFLECTION

For all of the jubilation of Easter, Psalm 16 expresses a sort of quiet joy. This is the kind of joy that comes from having seen the worst and lived through it—joy that is tempered with the knowledge of what the world, and life, can do. It is a song of confidence and trust in the one who does not abandon God's people to death.

KIMBERLY BRACKEN LONG

1 Peter 1:3–9

REFLECTION

Remember, Jesus bequeathed two things to his disciples before departing: peace and joy. The first he breathed; the second he lived. "I have said these things to you so that my joy may be in you, and that your joy may be complete" (John 15:11).

PETER W. MARTY

John 20:19–31

REFLECTION

The One who has hardwired our brains to seek understanding also holds the key to the heart.

CLAYTON J. SCHMIT

RESPONSE

Pause and let your lungs fill with Jesus' breath of peace. Live Jesus' joy in all you do this day.

PRAYER

Help me breathe peace and live with joy in celebration of your life and love, Jesus, Savior of the world. Amen.

❧ *Third Sunday of Easter* ☙

Acts 2:14a, 36–41

"For the promise is for you, for your children,
and for all who are far away, everyone whom
the Lord our God calls to him." (v. 39)

Psalm 116:1–4, 12–19

What shall I return to the LORD
    for all his bounty to me?
I will lift up the cup of salvation
    and call on the name of the LORD. (vv. 12–13)

1 Peter 1:17–23

You have been born anew, not of
perishable but of imperishable seed, through the
living and enduring word of God. (v. 23)

Luke 24:13–35

Then they told what had happened on
the road, and how he had been made known to
them in the breaking of the bread. (v. 35)

✤ MONDAY ✤

Acts 2:14a, 36–41

REFLECTION

Descent into the waters portrays death to old ways, and rising
up signifies new birth in Christ, the actions embodying the call
for repentance, a changed mind (cf. Rom. 6:3–14).

We are not merely born to better ethical and moral behavior.
We are born to life in Christ, joined to Christ's body the church.
We need a transformed mind to begin to see through Christ's
eyes, and to guide our transformed lives participating in his
mission of reconciliation and justice. The intensity of this
call to discipleship presented in baptism is seen in the next
passage, where the new believers are led to radical changes of
lifestyle, including economic redistribution and new spiritual
disciplines.

GARY NEAL HANSEN

RESPONSE

As you continue your journey down an Emmaus road,
notice the places this week where the transforming work of
reconciliation and justice is needed. Name these places in your
time of meditation and prayer here and in prayers at church.

PRAYER

Help me see through your eyes, Jesus my Lord. Amen.

✧ TUESDAY ✧

Acts 2:14a, 36–41

REFLECTION

Just as God gave the Law to Moses and Israel on Mount Sinai to initiate the shaping of the identity of a people, so for Luke, the *Messiah* is responsible for the giving of the Spirit to shape the (new) identity of this new people. For these early Spirit-inspired followers of Jesus, the Messiah himself is a charismatic, Spirit-granting agent of God. So, what are the new ways in which God's Spirit inspires and shapes the identity of the Christian community today?

EMERSON B. POWERY

RESPONSE

What new things are you seeing and hearing, ways God's spirit is at work in communities of faith in your neighborhood?

PRAYER

Spirit-granting agent of God, Jesus Messiah, continue to inspire and shape our identity as your own. Amen.

Psalm 116:1–4, 12–19

REFLECTION

The psalmist responds with *public* thanksgiving to God and with *public* fulfillment of responsibilities to God offered within the gathered faith community. What a marvelous and *challenging* vision of the faithful life!

JEFF PASCHAL

RESPONSE

What thanks to God can you offer today? What commitments can you make with your faith community to live into God's vision?

PRAYER

With the psalmist, I ask, what shall I return to you for all your generosity in my life? Amen.

Psalm 116:1–4, 12–19

REFLECTION

All of this is in keeping with a profound understanding of God's gifts. The lives that we live and the breath we use to speak of that life are all gift, all the time. Prayer, in this account, is speech that knows (or means to know) what it is doing. . . .

. . . The energy we bring to our attempted obedience originates with the God we call the giver of all good things, the God whose purposes toward us, we are assured, do not end in entropy, corruption, or decay (Ps. 16:10). In the meantime, this redeeming power, the power signaled both in the biblical accounts and in our experience of the risen Christ, is to be realized primarily in the ebb and flow of our life together, our lives that partake of and participate within the body of Christ. Resurrection, in this sense, has nowhere to happen but here.

J. DAVID DARK

RESPONSE

Think on what you know and how you experience God's gifts of love and mercy. What is on your list?

PRAYER

Hear my requests for mercy, Lord of my life. Amen.

✛ FRIDAY ✛

1 Peter 1:17–23

REFLECTION

To love from the heart with no guarantees and no escape clause is a prophetic statement by any standard or life condition. To find meaning in ancient texts that have been broken open for review, providing palatable food for life, is a responsibility to take seriously. To bear the imperishable seeds (*the very "living and enduring word of God,"* v. 23) and shake them off for new birth in the next season is a step toward the church of the future.

JOY DOUGLAS STROME

RESPONSE

What new meanings in this text offer food for your thought and action?

PRAYER

God, plant new seeds of faith within me. Amen.

✤ SATURDAY ✤

Luke 24:13–35

REFLECTION

Broken bread nurses our broken faith and can nourish the
courage we need to leave our graveclothes behind and vacate
the vault of our defeated dreams. The weary travelers feel
alive; their hearts are renewed. The witness of the women at
the empty tomb is now their testimony too. In the breaking of
bread, the beams of resurrection's dawn have reached about
seven miles from Jerusalem. Their burning hearts illumine
their blind eyes and quicken their weary souls for a seven-mile
nighttime run in the moonlight of Easter. Their sacred city is
made holy again, and their pilgrimage of faith has just begun.

SHANNON MICHAEL PATER

RESPONSE

As you break bread with family, friends, neighbors, even
strangers at the coffee shop, give thanks for God's love.

PRAYER

As I walk down the road of faith, renew my heart, remind me of
your powerful presence, and help me recognize it in the face of
others. Amen.

✦ SUNDAY ✦

Acts 2:14a, 36–41

REFLECTION

In his Pentecost sermon Peter is inviting fellow sinners to start
again new. The Holy Spirit is guiding the people of God into
new life, and a sacred community called the church is being
born.

TIMOTHY B. HARE

Psalm 116:1–4, 12–19

REFLECTION

A character in one of Walker Percy's novels asks, "Suppose you
ask God for a miracle and God says yes, very well. How do you
live the rest of your life?"* The psalmist has made his answer
clear. How do you live, indeed?

JEFF PASCHAL

1 Peter 1:17–23

REFLECTION

There are perishable seeds and imperishable seeds. The
hothouse hybrids will not last through the winter. First Peter
would have us sow imperishable seeds and be prepared for all
the morning glory we can handle.

JOY DOUGLAS STROME

*Walker Percy, *Love in the Ruins: The Adventures of a Bad Catholic at a Time Near the End of
the World* (New York: Ivy Books, 1971), 320.

Luke 24:13–35

REFLECTION

Throughout the history of the church the story of the encounter of Jesus with bewildered and disconsolate pilgrims has illumined the theology of resurrection, the nature of faith sustained by the Holy Spirit, the promise of Eucharist through hospitality, and the necessity of communal practice.

MOLLY T. MARSHALL

RESPONSE

As one of God's faithful pilgrims, how do these texts and reflections speak to your own life of faith? Where are they a comfort? Where are they a challenge?

PRAYER

God of resurrections, help me to be prepared for all the morning glories you have arrayed before me. Amen.

❧ *Fourth Sunday of Easter* ❦

Acts 2:42–47

They devoted themselves to the apostles' teaching and fellowship, to the breaking of bread and the prayers. (v. 42)

Psalm 23

The LORD is my shepherd, I shall not want.
    He makes me lie down in green pastures;
he leads me beside still waters;
    he restores my soul.
He leads me in right paths
    for his name's sake.
Even though I walk through the darkest valley,
    I fear no evil;
for you are with me;
    your rod and your staff—
    they comfort me. (vv. 1–4)

1 Peter 2:19–25

For you were going astray like sheep, but now you have returned to the shepherd and guardian of your souls. (v. 25)

John 10:1–10

So again Jesus said to them, "Very truly, I tell you, I am the gate for the sheep." (v. 7)

❧ MONDAY ❧

Acts 2:42–47

REFLECTION

There are now many ways to pray, but to be "devoted" to it,
individuals and communities must pursue prayer intentionally
and with energy.

God's grace causes growth, but these are ways of nourishing
the plant.

GARY NEAL HANSEN

RESPONSE

Notice how you experience Christian community this week
when you pray and when you break bread with someone.

PRAYER

God of pauses, slow me down so that I may devote moments
of quiet wherever I am to being in prayer, speaking and waiting
for you. Amen.

⇴ TUESDAY ⇴

Psalm 23

REFLECTION

Every moment of life God is pursuing us, *hounding* us with goodness and kindness. What kind of God is this? The psalmist says this God is our shepherd, who grants our needs, causes us to rest and be restored, leads us in the right way of living, protects us from evil, honors and blesses us, and never stops pursuing us with goodness and kindness. What kind of creatures are we? Well, not exactly self-sufficient superstars— more like needy, dependent sheep.

JEFF PASCHAL

RESPONSE

How have you experienced God's pursuing you with goodness and kindness?

PRAYER

I am not a self-sufficient superstar, it's true, O God. I am your needy sheep. Thank you for your protection. Amen.

⊹ WEDNESDAY ⊹

Psalm 23

REFLECTION

Yes, our Lord is the shepherd; God is also our host. Throughout the entirety of our lives, we should never lose sight that we dwell in the house of the Lord. We rejoice in the constant presence and vigilance of a God who has cared for us, and will always care for us, both as individuals and as a community of the faithful.

JOHN E. WHITE

RESPONSE

How do you interpret the difference between knowing God as shepherd and knowing God as host?

PRAYER

Watching God, continue your shepherding care of all of the faithful. Amen.

✣ THURSDAY ✣

1 Peter 2:19–25

REFLECTION

Some Bible verses should never be read aloud in public. At least that is what the lectionary committee must have decided, because this reading leaves out the thesis sentence that begins this section of the letter: "Slaves, accept the authority of your masters with all deference, not only those who are kind and gentle but also those who are harsh" (1 Pet. 2:18). Awful as those words are, this verse gives preachers permission to talk about the need for biblical interpretation. What shall we do with texts that have been used to harm people? How will abused women hear words about enduring pain and beatings?

BARBARA K. LUNDBLAD

RESPONSE

Read all of this text from 1 Peter and think about how you would interpret this text today. How is it heard?

PRAYER

I pray this today for all those who have lived with unimaginable pain. Help me be aware of my role in supporting them and working to change abusive systems. Amen.

✢ FRIDAY ✢

John 10:1–10

REFLECTION

Is the church the gatekeeper and Jesus the gate to protect the morally weak and vulnerable within the fold or to privilege a community of the ethically pure? Is the church a hospital for sinners, as Augustine believed, or a society of the morally perfectible, as Pelagius thought? Does Christ as the gate keep the flock from corruption by the world, or did God so love the world that the gate swings open for the lost sheep in particular? Is Jesus alone the gate, so that, in the end, every disparate flock will be made one in him (John 17:20–21)?

CYNTHIA A. JARVIS

RESPONSE

Think about your answers to the questions raised in this reflection. If you were teaching this text in a setting with young adults, what would be your way into the discussion?

PRAYER

God, how wide is your gate of love? Help me see all those whom you welcome and whom I fail to see. Amen.

⤳ SATURDAY ⤲

John 10:1–10

REFLECTION

The image of the "gate" by which the sheep can go to "find pasture" is used to express Jesus' role of bringing God's saving love to the world (3:17)

DONALD SENIOR

As the blossoms of the Easter lilies fade, we are invited to continue to embrace the riddle of faith: by dying, the shepherd provided abundant life. Sometimes it is hard to see and understand; but the single hand still claps.

SHANNON MICHAEL PATER

RESPONSE

What pastures does your church provide, places where people can experience God's saving love?

PRAYER

Thank you for your saving love graciously offered to all. Amen.

☙ SUNDAY ☙

Acts 2:42–47

REFLECTION

The real question for the contemporary church may be to understand what momentum, what new spiritual and political movement, is at work today, refreshing our ensconced and institutional religious tradition.

SUSAN B. W. JOHNSON

Psalm 23

REFLECTION

Perhaps Mitchell Dahood's translation, "sitting still," is the most accurate, rendering the verse, "I will sit still in the house of God for the length of my days."

The themes of trust and a complete yielding to God are not named explicitly in this psalm but permeate both the imagery and the text.

ALICE W. HUNT

1 Peter 2:19–25

REFLECTION

The text ties to the other lections for the day as it closes in shepherd imagery. In the arms of the shepherd, our soul is being guarded. The shepherd knows our name and leads us through this age and the next. With our soul guarded by the good shepherd, the freedom to act alternatively in the world starts to look like a possibility.

JOY DOUGLAS STROME

John 10:1–10

REFLECTION

Recovering shepherding imagery could call the church to
simplicity, sacrifice, and solidarity—needed in a time when
many have lost their way.

MOLLY T. MARSHALL

RESPONSE

Consider the shepherd imagery in the texts and the reflections
for this week. What new ideas emerge from your experience
with these readings?

PRAYER

I will try to sit still in your presence, O God, so you may speak.
Amen.

❧ *Fifth Sunday of Easter* ❦

Acts 7:55–60

But filled with the Holy Spirit, [Stephen]
gazed into heaven and saw the glory of God and Jesus
standing at the right hand of God. (v. 55)

Psalm 31:1–5, 15–16

My times are in your hand;
    deliver me from the hand of my enemies
        and persecutors.
Let your face shine upon your servant;
    save me in your steadfast love. (vv. 15–16)

1 Peter 2:2–10

Once you were not a people,
    but now you are God's people;
once you had not received mercy,
    but now you have received mercy. (v. 10)

John 14:1–14

"Do not let your hearts be troubled. Believe in God,
believe also in me. In my Father's house there are many
dwelling places. If it were not so, would I have told you
that I go to prepare a place for you?" (vv. 1–2)

✦ MONDAY ✦

Acts 7:55–60

REFLECTION

What does Christian faith have to say about rampant consumerism and our complicity in it? What does Christianity have to say about our nationalistic impulses and the self-interest that guides the foreign policies of many nations? What does our faith have to say about environmental stewardship and our current patterns of living? Though many of us may never be asked to die for our faith, our faith still calls us to measure our priorities, to take a stand, and to express our beliefs through action. For those of us in this position, Stephen's story is still very much a relevant model of faithfulness and obedience.

TIMOTHY B. HARE

RESPONSE

Consider the priorities of your faith, the places where your beliefs are expressed in action. What is most important?

PRAYER

As I seek to connect my faith to my living, remind me of all those saints who have gone before me who have taken a stand. Today I remember them: Rosa Parks, Mother Teresa, Ruby Bridges, Sojourner Truth, Dorothy Day, Myrlie Evers, Queen Esther . . .

✦ TUESDAY ✦

Psalm 31:1–5, 15–16

REFLECTION

One clearly must be among the oppressed to fully understand
this psalm. The truth rings out, "We have all been oppressed."
Some have been oppressed in our want, others in our
abundance. Know that we are all in need of the redemption that
only our God can provide.

JOHN E. WHITE

RESPONSE

What redemption from oppression do you most need?

PRAYER

God of my life, my times are in your hands. Amen.

✦ WEDNESDAY ✦

1 Peter 2:2–10

REFLECTION

When we let ourselves be built into a spiritual house by the presence of the living Christ, the results may not be very impressive. Some of these living stones are very well educated, others have not finished high school. There is a woman who sits in the balcony because she does not think her clothes are good enough for the nave. . . . Seven teenagers are in the side section slightly hidden behind a pillar. You know they are texting their friends who are sitting at the end of the row. "At least they are here," you say to yourself. You would text them yourself from the chancel, if you knew how.

All these living stones are assured that they are now God's people. They have become a holy priesthood. . . .

Once we were not a people,
but now we are God's people;

. . . What does this promise look like where you are?

BARBARA K. LUNDBLAD

RESPONSE

"What does this promise look like where you are?"

PRAYER

I am indeed fortunate to be included in your spiritual house, to be one of your people, to receive your mercy, O God. Amen.

✦ THURSDAY ✦

1 Peter 2:2–10

REFLECTION

God's own people are empowered through Christ to sing,
protest, dance, pray, and march. No stereotype can define
us, because we have been claimed by God. No ridicule can
undo us, because we have been named by God. No shallow
expression of faith can represent us.

JOY DOUGLAS STROME

RESPONSE

How has God empowered you to protest? to dance? to pray? or
to march?

PRAYER

God, you claim me. God, you name me as your own. Thanks be
to you. Amen.

✢ FRIDAY ✢

John 14:1–14

REFLECTION

What has troubled the disciples' hearts is the very real sense that their time with Jesus has come to an end. We have the same relationship to time: its brevity robs us of those we love. Consider the *metanoia* that is God's grace to one who hangs her heart on the God who has all the time God needs for her and for those she loves. The place Jesus is preparing in God's own life is *eternal life*, which, as Robert Jenson often says, is simply another name for God. As in the beginning of this Gospel God has come to dwell with us in Jesus Christ, explore the content of the Christian hope contained in the promise that we will dwell through him in God.

CYNTHIA A. JARVIS

RESPONSE

Think about the hope you have in God's promise.

PRAYER

When my heart is troubled, God of my life, remind me of your indwelling Spirit that surrounds me. Amen.

✤ SATURDAY ✤

John 14:1–14

REFLECTION

Doorframes are liminal places: a space between rooms, a portal from the outside to the inside. Teens need a companion who can be both midwife and chaplain, someone who will help them navigate the loss of infancy and facilitate a safe crossing to the terrain of adulthood. For the adolescent disciples, that will soon be the Holy Spirit. The Comforter will come to cure their diseased hearts and help them stand firm in the coming transformation.

SHANNON MICHAEL PATER

RESPONSE

What youth or young adults do you know who need your presence in their life as they move in and out of doors and spaces and rooms?

PRAYER

I pray that your comforting presence will be known and experienced by all of your adolescent disciples. Amen.

✦ SUNDAY ✦

Acts 7:55–60

REFLECTION

God's love cannot be destroyed. It is poured out with
unhindered generosity, much the way God's gift of the church
in Acts will not be prevented. Bishop Jeremiah Park of the
United Methodist Church is fond of reminding confirmands,
"God loves you, and there is nothing you can do about it!"
There is great emotional power to such a simple confession,
because it acknowledges the truth of God's victory and at the
same time leads us to accept it for ourselves.

TIMOTHY B. HARE

Psalm 31:1–5, 15–16

REFLECTION

As we commit our spirits to the not-yet-seen ends of the never-
not-redeeming God, we strain and exult, complain and hope,
worry and celebrate through and within the prayers Jesus
learned and repeated, tension included. These are the dramas
of divine relation in which we discover ourselves, the context
of our life and worship. It is the space where redeeming love
functions. There is no other.

J. DAVID DARK

1 Peter 2:2–10

REFLECTION

We make our way into Ordinary Time with the most
*extra*ordinary claim: Christ is risen! Risen indeed. It is enough
to sustain us. It is enough to support us. It is enough to
empower us for the days ahead. Alleluia! Amen.

JOY DOUGLAS STROME

John 14:1–14

REFLECTION

What we know of God in Jesus Christ is that God has chosen not to be God without us. In this is love (1 John 4:10), the love that is God. This is a Word worth a Sunday morning.

Finally, and contrary to the covenant we make with one another ("until death do us part"), God's promise to love us, to make room for us, to know and be known by us, never ends (1 Cor. 13:8). Therefore our hearts need never be troubled.

CYNTHIA A. JARVIS

RESPONSE

What new thoughts about God emerge from your engagement with these texts and reflections? If you are teaching these texts with a group in the church, which of these reflections might be helpful in starting the discussion?

PRAYER

Thank you for your love that never ends. Amen.

❧ *Sixth Sunday of Easter* ❧

Acts 17:22–31

"From one ancestor he made all nations to inhabit
the whole earth, and he allotted the times of their existence
and the boundaries of the places where they would live, so that
they would search for God and perhaps grope for him and find
him—though indeed he is not far from each one of us. For 'In
him we live and move and have our being'; as even some of your
own poets have said, 'For we too are his offspring.'" (vv. 26–28)

Psalm 66:8–20

Come and hear, all you who fear God,
  and I will tell what he has done for me. (v. 16)

1 Peter 3:13–22

And baptism, which this prefigured, now
saves you—not as a removal of dirt from the body,
but as an appeal to God for a good conscience, through
the resurrection of Jesus Christ, who has gone into heaven
and is at the right hand of God, with angels, authorities,
and powers made subject to him. (vv. 21–22)

John 14:15–21

"If you love me, you will keep my commandments." (v. 15)

✣ MONDAY ✣

Acts 17:22–31

REFLECTION

The challenge is to say to those around us, "We see your spiritual hunger. Might we offer sustenance from our rich store of spiritual resource?" The challenge is to find the imagery and language that allow us to enter another's world in order to speak our truth honestly, respectfully, and effectively.

RANDLE R. (RICK) MIXON

RESPONSE

As you move through this week, listen to the languages you hear, the expressions people use. What imagery and language do you think we need to use in sharing what we know of God?

PRAYER

You are never far from me, O God. Thank you. Amen.

⇢ TUESDAY ⇠

Acts 17:22–31

REFLECTION

What does it mean to be so fully rooted and grounded in God,
so centered in our own experience of the Christian story, that
we cannot keep from sharing it? In the words of the old hymn,
when we feel our faith in our very bones, "how can we keep
from singing?"

RANDLE R. (RICK) MIXON

RESPONSE

What part of the Christian story centers you the most?

PRAYER

Creator God, you are the source of my breath, the reason for
my being. Amen.

→ WEDNESDAY ←

Psalm 66:8–20

REFLECTION

Testimony is the means by which we are reminded that God's
faithfulness to us is not limited to us. God's love is not limited
to those in the sanctuary. The object of God's redemptive love is
creation-wide.

THOMAS L. ARE JR.

RESPONSE

Continuing to think about what you hear and see this week,
listen for testimonies.

PRAYER

God, you have done amazing things in my life. This day, I thank
you for . . . . Amen.

✢ THURSDAY ✦

Psalm 66:8–20

REFLECTION

If our testimony does not demonstrate a holy love that is creation-wide in scope, it will not be a faithful testimony to the God who truly has listened.

THOMAS L. ARE JR.

RESPONSE

What is your testimony to how God has acted in your life?

PRAYER

Loving God, help me to love as you do, without caution, without judgment. Amen.

✦ FRIDAY ✦

1 Peter 3:13–22

REFLECTION

Many Christians question and refuse to submit to a neoliberal globalization that creates poverty throughout the third world so that a small group of Western industrialized nations (mainly Eurocentric and self-professing Christians) can use and abuse the vast majority of the world resources. This invites the hostility of the dominant culture, and attempting to radically change these structures to reflect the liberating message of the gospel is to ensure persecution.

MIGUEL A. DE LA TORRE

RESPONSE

What in this reflection causes you to pause to think? What is your response?

PRAYER

Guide my steps, O God, that I may learn to walk more carefully and thoughtfully in your world. Amen.

✦ SATURDAY ✦

John 14:15–21

REFLECTION

The love Jesus wants his hearers to embrace is not an abstract
philosophical concept but the lived reality revealed in the life,
relationships, and actions of a simple Nazarene who looks
and talks like them and lives simply among them. He feeds
the hungry, touches lepers, heals the sick, and speaks and acts
toward women with care and regard. Love is seen in his life
as service and compassion. It is also seen in his fierce protests
against those who abuse this vision of the value of each person
and the importance of an ethic of mutual regard and care.
Instead of power as domination, Jesus invites those who meet
him to imagine power that has as its goal the well-being of all
persons regardless of social status.

NANCY J. RAMSAY

RESPONSE

Which of the images of Jesus pictured here is most popular and
known in your congregation? Which of these images is less the
object of your focus and response?

PRAYER

Help me see those you are calling me to love. Amen.

✦ SUNDAY ✦

Acts 17:22–31

REFLECTION

Much of the art and creative productivity in this world, at its deepest level, is expressive of the *Spiritus Creator*, God's ever-creating Spirit present within all creative process. Rather than shunning this creative potential, Paul recognizes it all around him and celebrates it as something that could potentially open us to the God who wants to be known in Jesus Christ.

JOHN S. MCCLURE

Psalm 66:8–20

REFLECTION

This psalm is an enduring reminder that whatever our experience, God is the patient and listening Presence, the power to transport us from the wilderness to the promised land within.

ROBERT V. THOMPSON

1 Peter 3:13–22

REFLECTION

The author realizes that for the recipients of 1 Peter to obey Christ is to live apart from the empire of their time. Likewise, for us today, to obey and follow Christ is to live apart from the empire of our present era.

MIGUEL A. DE LA TORRE

John 14:15–21

REFLECTION

What if we were to recognize that Christ is truly present *among* us when we keep his commandments to love and serve one another? Look around you in your community—your church community as well as the greater community in which you live and serve—and see where you can discern that outline around the picture of Jesus on the move. See where, in the familiar life of this group of people, you can discern the presence of the Spirit of truth.

LINDA LEE CLADER

RESPONSE

In this last week of Easter, what in these texts and reflections is most essential for you to remember about the life you are called to live?

PRAYER

Help me be strong enough to live apart from the values of the world and to follow Jesus. Amen.

❧ *Ascension of the Lord* ❧

Acts 1:1–11

They said, "Men of Galilee, why do you stand
looking up toward heaven? This Jesus, who has been
taken up from you into heaven, will come in the same
way as you saw him go into heaven." (v. 11)

Psalm 93

The floods have lifted up, O Lord,
  the floods have lifted up their voice;
  the floods lift up their roaring. (v. 3)

Ephesians 1:15–23

I pray that the God of our Lord Jesus Christ,
the Father of glory, may give you a spirit of wisdom
and revelation as you come to know him, so that, with
the eyes of your heart enlightened, you may know what
is the hope to which he has called you, what are the
riches of his glorious inheritance among the saints,
and what is the immeasurable greatness of his
power for us who believe, according to the
working of his great power. (vv. 17–19)

Luke 24:44–53

While he was blessing them, he withdrew from
them and was carried up into heaven. And they worshiped
him, and returned to Jerusalem with great joy; and they were
continually in the temple blessing God. (vv. 51–53)

✦ MONDAY ✦

Acts 1:1–11

REFLECTION

When and where do we find ourselves standing, "looking up toward heaven," hoping that Jesus or someone will do it for us? How are we hamstrung by our inability to see beyond the conventional into the miraculous promises that are still given to us today as followers of the Way? What would it take for us, as individuals and as communities of faith, to travel this thoroughfare that leads from God to God?

RANDLE R. (RICK) MIXON

RESPONSE

Consider your response to one of the questions asked in this reflection.

PRAYER

Sometimes, like the followers of Jesus, I too stand and look up, wondering what I can do. Help me live into the promises with faith and commitment. Amen.

✣ TUESDAY ✣

Acts 1:1–11

REFLECTION

Luke, the physician, is showing us a picture of the humanity of Jesus taken into the heart of God, and in that picture we see all of humanity taken up into God's heart, perhaps more deeply than ever before. This is profound good news for us in the in-between times. As the world changes, we confront new forms of insecurity. We experience oppression and sometimes violence. We confront suffering and death. We long for healing and wholeness. We work for justice. *Through it all* we carry with us this vision of our real value to God, of the Human One, who made himself at *home* with our humanity, for a time taken up into God, sustained, valued, and held, before returning home to restore the world.

JOHN S. MCCLURE

RESPONSE

Use the camera on your phone or any kind of camera you have available to you. As you are out and about this day, take random pictures of the "humanity of Jesus taken into the heart of God."

PRAYER

I pray today for all your children I have seen with my eyes and my camera this day. All are valued and loved by you. Amen.

Psalm 93

REFLECTION

The flood waters are real, but they are not ultimate. Never have the powers of evil and chaos been able to drown out the praise of God's people who in humble yet bold defiance sing what is true yesterday, today, and in every tomorrow: the Lord is sovereign. The ascension of the Lord celebrates on *one* day that which is true *every* day.

THOMAS L. ARE JR.

RESPONSE

What have been the floods you have experienced in your life?

PRAYER

In the midst of chaos, flood waters that threaten to drown, and in the midst of the evil of violence in which we live, help me to continue to praise you and find ways to live as your disciple. Amen.

✤ THURSDAY ✤

Ephesians 1:15–23

REFLECTION

For many marginalized communities, the importance of the
cross is that it is the location where Christ chose solidarity with
the world's marginalized. Christ becomes one with the crucified
people of his time, as well as with all who are crucified today
on the crosses of racism, sexism, classism, and heterosexism.
These crosses are places of violence, littered with broken lives
and bodies. Jesus' solidarity with the world's failures and the
world's powerlessness points to the God of the oppressed. Here
is the importance of the cross. God is not the God of those who
crucify, only of those who are crucified. The paradox of the
cross is that, in spite of what it symbolizes, there is resurrection.

MIGUEL A. DE LA TORRE

RESPONSE

Today in your journeys, notice crosses that you see in your
community. How is the cross viewed in your congregation?

PRAYER

Help me see, O God, those who bear the scars of racism,
sexism, classism, and heterosexism. Help me be your hands of
healing. Amen.

⇥ FRIDAY ⇤

Luke 24:44–53

REFLECTION

It is important to realize that as Jesus ascends to God so that this urgent work of the church may begin, he blesses us. Jesus begins his final conversation with the disciples and those who are with them with words of peace. Blessing conveys to those who receive it the goodness and favor of God.

NANCY J. RAMSAY

RESPONSE

Name the ways God has blessed you. What blessing will you pass on to others this day?

PRAYER

Thank you for those who have blessed me this day. Amen.

→ SATURDAY ←

Luke 24:44–53

REFLECTION

To what extent are we to take this story of a commissioning,
two thousand years ago, and apply it to our own mission as
disciples and apostles of Christ? To what, exactly, have we
ourselves been witnesses? Upon what do we stand when we
undertake to proclaim a gospel of God's forgiveness and mercy?
How do we acknowledge and share the blessing we have
received?

LINDA LEE CLADER

RESPONSE

Consider your response to one of the questions asked in this
reflection on the Luke text.

PRAYER

Having been blessed by you, God of my life, and having been
blessed by so many in my life, I share my blessings with others.
Amen.

✦ SUNDAY ✦

Acts 1:1–11

REFLECTION

It still takes a community of faith, Spirit-filled, to spread the good news and bring in the reign of God. That is our challenge and our commission as the body of Christ, followers of the Way.

RANDLE R. (RICK) MIXON

Psalm 93

REFLECTION

Heaven is not a place where God is an individual satisfied within "himself," but a place where God communally acts and communally *is* with us—here and now. We must all become concerned about each other's "personal" journey to God—that God's whereabouts need not be privately remote.

MICHAEL BATTLE

Ephesians 1:15–23

REFLECTION

Christ is entirely present, fully present in the church. Christ is fully present in the world. The claim seems at best paradoxical and at worst self-contradictory, but it is a way of affirming two great claims that Ephesians makes. Christ gave his entire self for the church. Christ gave his entire self for the world. Put it another way: Christ fills both church and world, but both church and world contain him whole.

DAVID L. BARTLETT

Luke 24:44–53

REFLECTION

This God to whom we bear witness intends to offer salvation to all the nations, and that is no easier to swallow now than then. The Spirit that clothes us at Pentecost is necessary for the witness to which we are called.

NANCY J. RAMSAY

RESPONSE

Using words or images (photography, pictures, or drawings) illustrate the nature of the Spirit that clothes you.

PRAYER

Continue to reveal to me the places where the witness of my life and faith are needed. Amen.

❧ *Seventh Sunday of Easter* ❧

Acts 1:6–14

All these were constantly devoting themselves to prayer, together with certain women, including Mary the mother of Jesus, as well as his brothers. (v. 14)

Psalm 68:1–10, 32–35

Father of orphans and protector of widows
   is God in his holy habitation.
God gives the desolate a home to live in;
   he leads out the prisoners to prosperity,
   but the rebellious live in a parched land. (vv. 5–6)

1 Peter 4:12–14; 5:6–11

Humble yourselves therefore under the mighty hand of God, so that he may exalt you in due time. Cast all your anxiety on him, because he cares for you. (5:6–7)

John 17:1–11

"And now I am no longer in the world, but they are in the world, and I am coming to you. Holy Father, protect them in your name that you have given me, so that they may be one, as we are one." (v. 11)

✦ MONDAY ✦

Acts 1:6–14

REFLECTION

Though the times have changed radically, it is still real human beings, men and women with names, identities, histories, and hopes, who gather to wait for the coming of the Spirit. It is we who make up today's church as we gather to pray for the coming of the Spirit in our own lives and in the life of our congregations. Even now, we wait for Pentecostal power.

RANDLE R. (RICK) MIXON

RESPONSE

Name people you know who reflect God's spirit in their lives.

PRAYER

Today I lift up in prayer women and men, youth and children whose stories have shaped my life of faith. Surround them with your love and presence. Amen.

→ TUESDAY ←

Acts 1:6–14

REFLECTION

At least by implication, this passage recognizes the central place of community in the life of the church. It is not enough to go it alone. They met, traveled, and worked together. We too must meet, travel, and work together in Christ's name. We need each other's witness and support, challenge and care, in order to live into the possibilities and expectations of God's realm.

RANDLE R. (RICK) MIXON

RESPONSE

Who are the people in your community, your company of witness and support?

PRAYER

Thank you, God, for all those who love me, support me, challenge me, and care for me. I am a different person because of their presence in my life. Amen.

Psalm 68:1–10, 32–35

REFLECTION

Let God rise up. Ascribe power to God, the rider in the heavens. Blessed be God. This is the language of praise, uttered by those who know the powers that erode and seek to destroy life, and yet have come to know God as one who calls the walking dead to breathe. As James Mays says, "This song belongs to the lowly, who in the midst of the powers of this world remember and hope for the victory of God"*

THOMAS L. ARE JR.

RESPONSE

What in this psalm gives you hope? What in this psalm challenges you?

PRAYER

In your holy habitation, God, protect all those who have no one. Amen.

---

*James L. Mays, *Psalms*, Interpretation series (Louisville, KY: Westminster John Knox, 1994), 229.

✦ THURSDAY ✦

1 Peter 4:12–14; 5:6–11

REFLECTION

Whether referring to persecution or to the more common
distresses and frustrations we all feel every day, the point is
that as Christians we are not flying solo. In other words, the
Christian faith is not individualistic. It is not solely about my
personal relationship with Jesus Christ. This is important,
for sure, but at its core, Christianity invites people to become
part of one body of Christ, which is larger than the troubles,
successes, or frustrations of any one person. Too often,
Christianity is reduced to the singular. Too often, faith is
focused on one's personal relationship with Jesus and little else.
This text, and 5:9 in particular, reminds us that as Christians we
are a part of the whole.

GORDON MCCLELLAN

RESPONSE

Consider the neighbors God is calling you to love. Who are
they?

PRAYER

Take all that concerns me. Take all that I worry about. Humble
me, O God. Amen.

⤙ FRIDAY ⤚

John 17:1–11

REFLECTION

It is just possible that this *is* what Christian unity looks like—a body, as Paul said, with many parts, a dance with many dancers, a song with many voices. The challenge to us, in response to all this variety, is to say yes. Yes, those *other* people really are Christians too. Yes, there is pain in all this diversity, but there is also possibility. Yes, there is struggle, but there is also glory.

LINDA LEE CLADER

RESPONSE

What does Christian unity look like to you?

PRAYER

God, open my eyes and ears to the places where I need to say yes. Amen.

⁂ SATURDAY ⁂

John 17:1–11

REFLECTION

What if the answer to Jesus' prayer for unity was not about solidifying into a monolithic block but, rather, was about joyful interplay, glorious dancing? If we tried that idea on for awhile, could it affect how we view our own disagreements with our brothers and sisters? Perhaps the vision toward which we strive is not one of total agreement but of the ability to join, in our disparate ways, in the common dance of faith. . . .

. . . This Christian community of ours can be wild and frustrating and crazy, but we place our trust in that prayer of Jesus. The disciples Jesus loved, and the community he loves now, lived and still live—enveloped by that prayer.

LINDA LEE CLADER

RESPONSE

What examples of living in unity are evident in your church or with other congregations in your community?

PRAYER

God who is Creator, Redeemer, and Spirit, I place my trust in you and pray that we may be one in sharing your love in this world. Amen.

✢ SUNDAY ✣

Acts 1:6–14

REFLECTION

This text calls Christians to be both Great Commandment people—loving God with our whole being and our neighbors as ourselves; and Great Commission people—carrying the good news of God's love in Christ to ends of the earth.

RANDLE R. (RICK) MIXON

Psalm 68:1–10, 32–35

REFLECTION

The psalmist reminds us that God's reconciling grace is not just for the individual but for the community. God provides a home for those who have no home. It is not the mighty but the desolate, the prisoners, and the needy who have reservations in God's "holy habitation" (v. 5).

MICHAEL BATTLE

1 Peter 4:12–14; 5:6–11

REFLECTION

The ability to empathize, to achieve solidarity, and to find common ground ultimately stems from an understanding of one's self as part of a larger whole. The further removed we are from this understanding, the less able we are to engage the world in Christlike love, the very essence of which is to love our neighbor as we love ourselves.

GORDON MCCLELLAN

John 17:1–11

REFLECTION

To find God in the faces of all humankind surely is a goal of the eternal life into which Jesus invites us to live our commitments now. The God of Abraham intends that all the families of the earth be blessed.

NANCY J. RAMSAY

RESPONSE

What are the challenges and the promises of these texts and reflections?

PRAYER

O God, I really do want to see you in the face of each person I meet this day. Amen.

❧ *Pentecost* ❧

Numbers 11:24–30

So Moses went out and told the people the words of the Lord;
and he gathered seventy elders of the people, and placed them all
around the tent. Then the Lord came down in the cloud and spoke
to him, and took some of the spirit that was on him and put it on
the seventy elders; and when the spirit rested upon them, they
prophesied. But they did not do so again. (vv. 24–25)

Psalm 104:24–34, 35b

May the glory of the Lord endure forever;
  may the Lord rejoice in his works—
who looks on the earth and it trembles,
  who touches the mountains and they smoke.
I will sing to the Lord as long as I live;
  I will sing praise to my God while I have being. (vv. 31–33)

Acts 2:1–21

All of them were filled with the Holy Spirit and began to speak
in other languages, as the Spirit gave them ability. (v. 4)

John 7:37–39

On the last day of the festival, the great day, while
Jesus was standing there, he cried out, "Let anyone who
is thirsty come to me, and let the one who believes in me
drink. As the scripture has said, 'Out of the believer's heart
shall flow rivers of living water.'" Now he said this about
the Spirit, which believers in him were to receive; for as yet
there was no Spirit, because Jesus was not yet glorified.

⇥ MONDAY ⇤

Numbers 11:24–30

REFLECTION

If we try to respond to the crying needs of the world as individuals, we will soon find ourselves in despair. The Pentecost experience and the gift of the Holy Spirit mean that no one needs to carry any burden alone. For leaders, as well as all others, God's Spirit is always available to guide, always willing to lead, and always present in every circumstance.

CAROLE A. CRUMLEY

RESPONSE

Think about all the witnesses of faith who surround you in celebrating this Pentecost experience. Name them!

PRAYER

God of fire and wind, renew the face of the earth. Amen.

⇥ TUESDAY ⇤

Numbers 11:24–30

REFLECTION

What spiritual disciplines help you to practice turning to God? What ways of praying open you to God's guidance? Where do you find support for your spiritual journey? Who listens with you to the movement of the Spirit in your life and encourages your response to God's callings? Where is an honest, authentic spiritual community in which you can reveal your doubts and fears and deepen in your knowledge and love of God? What action in the world invites your God-given talents and engages your passion for living? Where do you find the courage to live out those invitations?

CAROLE A. CRUMLEY

RESPONSE

Pause and think about your response to one or more of the questions asked above.

PRAYER

Spirit who moves with both force and gentleness, surround me with hope and courage as I move faithfully into the world you have created. Amen.

✦ WEDNESDAY ✦

Psalm 104:24–34, 35b

REFLECTION

The ecological crisis may indeed lead us into a deeper
relationship with our God and help awaken us to the true
meaning of life, which is to love all that exists. The psalmist
pleads for the "glory of the LORD to endure forever" (v. 31) and
speaks of a God "who looks on the earth and it trembles, who
touches the mountains and they smoke" (v. 32). This time in
our history may be a moment of grace that will transform our
lifestyles from consumerism to a life in harmony with creation.

CONSTANCE M. KOCH, OP

RESPONSE

Where are you a consumer of the created world? Where are the
places you live in harmony with creation?

PRAYER

You invite me to always go deeper, God of wind and fire. As you
look on this earth, look also on me as I struggle to be a good
steward of your creation. Amen.

✥ THURSDAY ✥

Acts 2:1–21

REFLECTION

Freedom in the Spirit versus structure and order—this dynamic has never disappeared in the life of the church. With Spirit-led freedom came tremendous gains in shattering received religious and cultural patterns of all types, including crossing the Jew-Gentile barrier, making advances against sexism, and moving people toward radical economic sharing and away from selfishness.

DAVID P. GUSHEE

RESPONSE

What boundaries is God's Spirit inviting you to cross?

PRAYER

You shake my world, confront my prejudices, and hold my life in front of me, O God. Amen.

⇥ FRIDAY ⇤

Acts 2:1–21

REFLECTION

No matter how you look at it, Acts 2 shows a big God with a
big word at work expanding out into a big world. These are the
kind of God and the kind of story that inspire listeners and
create, not little people of the little word, but believers who are
madly expressive.

JANA CHILDERS

RESPONSE

Consider your life of faith. In what ways is it "madly
expressive"?

PRAYER

God, you are indeed so much bigger than I can imagine. Help
me to let you be that kind of God, not one that I would try to
put in a small box. Amen.

☽ SATURDAY ☾

John 7:37–39

REFLECTION

When thirsty people come to Jesus, he does not merely hand them a spiritual beverage, momentary relief for thirst; he gives them instead the indwelling of the Holy Spirit (this is why this text appears in the lectionary at Pentecost). Through the Spirit, believers participate in the unceasing life of God, and the water of abundant life flows and flows through them.

THOMAS G. LONG

RESPONSE

For what do you thirst? What needs quenching in your life?

PRAYER

Dwell deeply in my life, satisfying all hungers and quenching all thirsts. Amen.

→ SUNDAY ←

Numbers 11:24–30

REFLECTION

In the midst of whatever hardship we are in, we can open
ourselves to God's transforming Spirit and live from the
knowledge that we are not alone. We can turn to that indwelling
Spirit and let it guide us through all dimensions of the day and
night. We can trust in God's leadership. When we do this, our
lives and our leadership are truly Spirit-led.

CAROLE A. CRUMLEY

Psalm 104:24–34, 35b

REFLECTION

This psalm is not a naive, "all is wonderful" song, but rather a
song at a more basic level, a song about where each of us lives.
The psalmist affirms that at the very ground of all existence is
a powerful and generous and gracious God. At the heart of our
very hearts is the Spirit of God who knows our names. It is the
same Spirit who called out those men and women to proclaim
the mighty acts of God on Pentecost.

NIBS STROUPE

Acts 2:1–21

REFLECTION

Many Christians have become accustomed to thinking of
the Holy Spirit as more of a Hawaiian breeze than a Chicago
gale. However, this important passage may at least remind
contemporary congregations that the Spirit does not always
arrive as a still, small voice or a faint stirring in the heart. The
Holy Spirit's power is not always subtle, fragile, or polite. Even
today it can be electric, atomic, and volcanic.

JANA CHILDERS

John 7:37–39

REFLECTION

Pentecost cannot be declared a "dead horse." We cannot afford to dismount from the celebration of the gift of the Holy Spirit, because the options are unthinkable. There cannot be a world where there is no Spirit. There cannot be a world where humans are not touched by the Divine, even if they do not understand it and cannot explain it. There cannot be a world where God does not infuse the very mind and will of God within human life.

STEVEN P. EASON

RESPONSE

Continue with your response, There cannot be a world where . . .

PRAYER

Spirit of the living God, be an electric presence in my life, calling forth all the gifts you have given me. Amen.

❧ *Trinity Sunday* ❦

Genesis 1:1–2:4a

God saw everything that he had made,
and indeed, it was very good. And there was evening
and there was morning, the sixth day. (1:31)

Psalm 8

When I look at your heavens, the work of your fingers,
the moon and the stars that you have established;
what are human beings that you are mindful of them,
mortals that you care for them? (vv. 3–4)

2 Corinthians 13:11–13

Finally, brothers and sisters, farewell. Put things in
order, listen to my appeal, agree with one another, live in peace;
and the God of love and peace will be with you. (v. 11)

Matthew 28:16–20

And Jesus came and said to them,
"All authority in heaven and on earth has
been given to me. Go therefore and make disciples
of all nations, baptizing them in the name of the Father
and of the Son and of the Holy Spirit, and teaching
them to obey everything that I have commanded
you. And remember, I am with you always,
to the end of the age." (vv. 18–20)

⤳ MONDAY ⤶

Genesis 1:1–2:4a

REFLECTION

The Creator's first pronouncement is that the creation is good. The goodness here is not an aesthetic or ethical proclamation about the nature of light; rather, goodness concerns the use to which it can be put for God's intention. We do not learn what that purpose is in these verses, but God is pleased. The light is "good." God names it.

MELINDA A. QUIVIK

RESPONSE

Look around you as you move outside today. Join the Creator in naming all that you see that is good.

PRAYER

Creator God, thank you for caring for me. Amen.

⤑ TUESDAY ⬿

Genesis 1:1–2:4a

REFLECTION

Scripture is theocentric not christocentric. Scripture is about God and how God works through Christ and through the Holy Spirit. . . . The opening of Scripture clearly sets the tone for how we are to understand God. God is one. God is a universal God. God creates, sustains, orders, preserves, provides, and loves. The first creation account offers an important opportunity to speak about the centrality of God in Scripture: "In the beginning, God."

DAVE BLAND

RESPONSE

As you read these first words in the Bible, what do you learn about God?

PRAYER

Your care, O God, for all creation is so great. Thank you for being mindful of all living things. Amen.

⇥ WEDNESDAY ↤

Psalm 8

REFLECTION

Out of the billions of creatures in the universe, out of the billions of human beings on the earth, we are bold to claim that God knows our names. We make this bold claim that we are children of God, not because of who we are or what we have done, but because of who God is and what God has done as Creator, Redeemer, and Sustainer. This claim is both a wondrous discovery and, at times, a frightening awareness.

NIBS STROUPE

RESPONSE

Pause and consider the things that God has done and is doing in your life.

PRAYER

I am indeed your child, Holy Parent. Thank you for calling me by name and calling me out to live in response to your love. Amen.

✦ THURSDAY ✦

Psalm 8

REFLECTION

This text points us to the fullness of the divine mystery. . . .

. . . By affirming that God is one, that God is present with us in many ways, *and* that these ways are never susceptible to our complete intellectual encompassment, we see that diversity is at the very heart of God. Respect for diversities of many kinds is therefore part of our calling as responsible persons of faith.

DAVID G. TRICKETT

RESPONSE

Who will you see or meet today who needs your respect?

PRAYER

God of all, remind me today of the responsibilities I have as one who is loved by you. Amen.

⇢ FRIDAY ⇠

2 Corinthians 13:11–13

REFLECTION

The rediscovery of the Trinity has been deeply affected by the urgent need to reconceive the relationality of the human person in a profoundly brutal era. The *social Trinity* has surged to the forefront of theological reflection as a paradigm for what it means to be human and to relate humanely to our fellow Christians and all neighbors.

To say that God is triune is to mean that God is social in nature. It is also to say that those made in the image of God are likewise intrinsically social.

DAVID P. GUSHEE

RESPONSE

What new thoughts about the Trinity does this reflection evoke for you?

PRAYER

Of all the things that sustain my life of faith, O God, your grace, your love, and your abiding presence are ones for which I am indeed grateful. Amen.

✦ SATURDAY ✦

Matthew 28:16–20

REFLECTION

Disciples are students. They are like interns. Interns are watching, practicing under supervision, asking questions, making mistakes, and learning from them. Jesus said very clearly, "Go therefore and make disciples of all nations" (v. 19a). Go make students of Christ. Put people in internships, into a lifelong learning process. That is a major paradigm shift from making church members or whatever else we substitute for discipleship.

STEVEN P. EASON

RESPONSE

In what ways have you discipled another?

PRAYER

I confess that like the disciples, I am watching, practicing, asking questions, and making a mistake every now and then as I live into my faith. Guide my steps. Amen.

Genesis 1:1–2:4a

REFLECTION

Humans are given dominion, not domination; they are caregivers, not exploiters (cf. Ps. 72:8–14). We do unto creation as God has done unto us; we express love and care toward the world. Being image bearers of God is also at the heart of how we see other humans, which results in treating them with dignity, regardless of race, age, gender, social or economic status.

DAVE BLAND

Psalm 8

REFLECTION

When we do not love, we destroy God's image within us. When we hate, use violence, kill, disregard, and discard, we are destroying God's image. This psalm and this feast call us to a responsible awareness that it is God who is love who has made us in that image of God. So we must be people who love, who give of ourselves, always reaching out in praise and in love for one another and for all the earth.

CONSTANCE M. KOCH, OP

2 Corinthians 13:11–13

REFLECTION

Paul's final words give voice to the possibility of hope even in the despair of dark brokenness. He voices the assurance that people do not face this overwhelming challenge alone. As in all of Paul's undisputed letters, he acknowledges and claims the presence of the grace of God. As God has proven time and again, God can bring about resurrection, even when death is a certain reality. God can find reconciliation, even when that road seems forever closed.

DAVID M. BENDER

Matthew 28:16–20

REFLECTION
The very fact that the task is utterly impossible throws the disciples completely onto the mercy and strength of God. The work of the church cannot be taken up unless it is true that "all authority" does not belong to the church or its resources but comes from God's wild investment of God in Jesus the Son and the willingness of the Son to be present always to the church in the Spirit.

THOMAS G. LONG

RESPONSE
In what ways are you an image bearer of God?

PRAYER
Merciful God, I offer my life to you to be your student, your disciple in your world. Amen.

❧ *Proper 3* ☙

Isaiah 49:8–16a

But Zion said, "The LORD has forsaken me,
　my Lord has forgotten me."
Can a woman forget her nursing child,
　or show no compassion for the child of her womb?
Even these may forget,
　yet I will not forget you.
See, I have inscribed you on the palms of my hands;
　your walls are continually before me. (vv. 14–16)

Psalm 131

But I have calmed and quieted my soul,
　like a weaned child with its mother;
　my soul is like the weaned child that is with me. (v. 2)

1 Corinthians 4:1–5

Therefore do not pronounce judgment before the time,
before the Lord comes, who will bring to light the things now
hidden in darkness and will disclose the purposes of the heart.
Then each one will receive commendation from God. (v. 5)

Matthew 6:24–34

"But if God so clothes the grass of the field, which is
alive today and tomorrow is thrown into the oven, will he
not much more clothe you—you of little faith?" (v. 30)

→ MONDAY ←

Isaiah 49:8–16a

REFLECTION

Isaiah proclaims that the people themselves are inscribed into the palms of God's hands. See the image: when God raises a hand in gesture of blessing, we look into the divine palm as in a mirror. The gesture of blessing holds the people up to themselves as a sign of God's own compassion. One epiphany is laid upon another.

MELINDA A. QUIVIK

RESPONSE

Take a moment and look at your hands. What blessings have you received in these hands? What blessings have you given?

PRAYER

Loving God, knowing that my life is held in the palm of your hand is a blessing and a sign of hope in my life. Thank you. Amen.

✣ TUESDAY ✣

Isaiah 49:8–16a

REFLECTION

Today, many have felt exiled from faith, and are seeking a way home. For them it is a distant "land." Seekers are finding many ancient yet new pathways through various spiritual practices. These practices draw on the tried and true ways of meditation, centering prayer, *lectio divina*/sacred reading, and silence. Today's pilgrims also seek God in nature and in the world's concerns. They seek God in service and travel, in prayer groups and worshiping communities, in the eyes of friends and strangers, in the ordinary routine of daily life and in set-aside times of retreat. In these ways, they both find and are being found by God.

CAROLE A. CRUMLEY

RESPONSE

Which pathways have been helpful to you as you have been "found by God"?

PRAYER

If my pathway seems blocked, O God, help me learn from other pilgrims. Amen.

Psalm 131

REFLECTION

Our calling as children of God is to find space to allow God's Spirit to speak to us in our sadness and in our rage, to help us hear that there are possibilities of life—yes, even great possibilities of life—in this need and in this longing to be connected. Authentic communities are built upon it, and at its best the church builds this kind of community and thrives upon it, a community where we can celebrate our individuality and also acknowledge our need for God and for one another.

NIBS STROUPE

RESPONSE

What in your soul needs quieting this day so there is space to hear God's voice?

PRAYER

Spirit of God, remind me of the community of faithful people who surround my soul both in happiness and in sadness. Today I give thanks. Amen.

✦ THURSDAY ✦

1 Corinthians 4:1–5

REFLECTION

We face questions of how to choose Jesus in a world that offers to the nondestitute instant access and instant gratification. How do we choose Jesus in a world that is more than ever divided along economic and political lines? How do we choose Jesus in a postmodern world that emphasizes individuality and tends to question all authority? How do we choose Jesus in a world that offers so many other choices to worship—self, work, power, entertainment, consumerism, technology, divisiveness? Church members join their Corinthian spiritual ancestors in daily engagement with these questions.

DAVID M. BENDER

RESPONSE

What is the challenge for you in choosing Jesus?

PRAYER

With so many options available to me, help me as I wrestle with the questions. Amen.

✛ FRIDAY ✛

Matthew 6:24–34

REFLECTION

What do you gain by hanging onto the anxiety anyway? Jesus asked that question. What is so valuable about panicking? What do you have to lose if you let go of that anxiety and gain a deeper sense of composure based on trust in the providence of God? That is the tradeoff Jesus is asking us to consider. It is callous to just tell someone who is in a dire situation not to worry. There is plenty to worry about; we are human beings, and worry comes all too easily. However, if we the church are going to ask for a nonanxious life, we have to offer something in its place. Abandon your anxiety, for a life that is surrendered to the loving providence of God. If there is no such providence, if you are just engaged in wishful thinking, then you die a fool who trusted in God. Consider the alternatives.

STEVEN P. EASON

RESPONSE

What worries are on your mind this day?

PRAYER

God of my life, I confess that sometimes the things I worry about consume my time and energy, leaving little space for seeing beyond myself. Amen.

✦ SATURDAY ✦

Matthew 6:24–34

REFLECTION

If we look long enough and hard enough at the birds of the air and the lilies of the field, suddenly there will break into our imagination a slice of that alternative reality, a world not of tooth and claw but a world of providential care, a world in which the One who created it delights in tending the garden and nourishing the creature.

THOMAS G. LONG

RESPONSE

Notice the birds today. Look for flowers that are growing. What signs of God's care do you see?

PRAYER

God, you are indeed a gardener who cares for all living things, for all creation, and, yes, even for me. Amen.

✦ SUNDAY ✦

Isaiah 49:8–16a

REFLECTION

This text invites our amazement at the inability of human beings to fathom a power that is both judgment and grace. . . . . . . God's way with God's people is both a hard challenge and an enveloping cradle. One without the other is too shallow an understanding of God and of our relationship with God.

MELINDA A. QUIVIK

Psalm 131

REFLECTION

Along with the other fourteen pilgrimage songs, Psalm 131 then is a song about life "on the way." The psalmist is in liminal space between home and the eventual destination and is therefore vulnerable to dangers along the way. Each of these psalms, in its own way, grapples with the life of faith throughout the journey.

V. STEVEN PARRISH

1 Corinthians 4:1–5

REFLECTION

Even if some judging among believers is unavoidable, we may take a page from the apostle Paul's book. It may be far better for us, as for Paul, if we can arrange our lives so that judging operates as "a very small thing" (v. 3) and not as the be-all and end-all of our life together.

JANA CHILDERS

Matthew 6:24–34

REFLECTION

So Jesus invites us, through the birds and the lilies, to see truly the world of loving providence in which we live. Once we have seen that, really seen it, then we can turn back to the world of mortgages and tuitions, even a world of crosses and tyranny, and go out in faith and confidence that ultimately, as Julian said, all manner of things shall be well.

THOMAS G. LONG

RESPONSE

What new ways of seeing are evoked for you in these Sabbath reflections?

PRAYER

Help me to truly see the world through your eyes, Creator God. Amen.

❧ *Proper 4* ❧

Deuteronomy 11:18–21, 26–28

You shall put these words of mine in your heart
and soul, and you shall bind them as a sign on your hand,
and fix them as an emblem on your forehead. Teach them
to your children, talking about them when you are at home
and when you are away, when you lie down and when
you rise. Write them on the doorposts of your
house and on your gates. (vv. 18–20)

Psalm 31:1–5, 19–24

Love the LORD, all you his saints.
 The LORD preserves the faithful,
  but abundantly repays the one who acts haughtily.
Be strong, and let your heart take courage,
 all you who wait for the LORD. (vv. 23–24)

Romans 1:16–17; 3:22b–28 (29–31)

For I am not ashamed of the gospel; it is the power
of God for salvation to everyone who has faith, to the Jew
first and also to the Greek. For in it the righteousness of
God is revealed through faith for faith; as it is written,
"The one who is righteous will live by faith." (1:16–17)

Matthew 7:21–29

"Not everyone who says to me, 'Lord, Lord,' will
enter the kingdom of heaven, but only the one who
does the will of my Father in heaven." (v. 21)

❖ MONDAY ❖

Deuteronomy 11:18–21, 26–28

REFLECTION

Moses continues to elaborate on the ways God's word is to
be kept: Speak of it constantly, he urges, teaching it to your
children, pondering it yourselves: when you travel, when
you are at home; in the house, outside the house; working,
walking, resting; dawn to dusk, and then at dawn again—in
short, always. Write the words where you will see them, he
admonishes. These words are for keeping.

Moses stresses what is at stake. These words are for life: Your
life depends on remembering them, keeping them, loving them.

BARBARA GREEN

RESPONSE

What words of God will you write on your heart today? What
words will you carry with you as you meet this day?

PRAYER

God of all the prophets across time, write these same words
on my heart and in my soul that I may remember them, keep
them, and love them. Amen.

✦ TUESDAY ✦

Deuteronomy 11:18–21, 26–28

REFLECTION

Anytime people share in the gift of caring for those in need, we are all enriched. We might say that in caring for others we are all "blessed." The Deuteronomist clarifies this by putting into Moses's mouth the invitation to receive blessings from following the ways of God, and the warning that dishonoring God's ways leads to sadness, impairment, and affliction.

MARY ALICE MULLIGAN

RESPONSE

Recall a story of how you have been blessed in caring for another.

PRAYER

Thank you, God, for the blessings in my life, both the ones that come through my giving and the ones that are simply a gift I receive. Amen.

✢ WEDNESDAY ✢

Psalm 31:1–5, 19–24

REFLECTION

There are those prayer warriors who maintain a trust in Love even when they feel the greatest scorn. There are those disciples who can smile even when they are dying painfully. There are those believers who have managed to carry their heavy weight of doubt for years, and still have a strong back of faith. Then there are the "outsiders" or the "de-churched" or the "believers in exile" or the "seekers" who are yearning for a refuge in a safe community where they are accepted as they are, doubts and blisters and all, and are loved into thinking of their new church as *home*—rock, refuge, rescue, deliverance, fortress, abundant shelter.

STEVEN D. MILLER

RESPONSE

Who are the outsiders or seekers or nones (those who check none of the above in relation to religious affiliation) whom you have met this week?

PRAYER

God of refuge, use me to represent your love and care with those who long for a place where they can come, "doubts and blisters and all." Amen.

⇥ THURSDAY ⇤

Romans 1:16–17; 3:22b–28 (29–31)

REFLECTION

It is clear in the text that the faithfulness of Jesus is what makes
his life effective for our salvation. Faith then implies action.
Living by faith can mean acknowledging our unity in Christ,
and stressing our unity in diversity when we disagree, trusting
God to work through each of us to resolve our conflicts.

DIANE GIVENS MOFFETT

RESPONSE

If one of those seeking faith asked you, What does it mean to
live by faith? what would you say? What story would you tell?

PRAYER

Order my steps, O God, that how I live my life may reveal my
trust in you. Amen.

✣ FRIDAY ✣

Matthew 7:21–29

REFLECTION

The essential theological message of this passage for Christian believers today is to live reflectively, representing the will of God and the advice of Jesus as best they may, so that they do not merely know the Gospels, but live the good news.

STEPHEN BUTLER MURRAY

RESPONSE

What Gospel story is at the heart of your faith?

PRAYER

God of my life, as this day unfolds, remind me to pause, being open to reflection on the places where you are present. Amen.

✦ SATURDAY ✦

Matthew 7:21–29

REFLECTION

Being a Christian is more than calling yourself one, and a
church that is actively living out God's message will be more
attractive than one indifferent to Jesus' reign. For people
seeking increased relevance from the church, Jesus' declaration
that heaven is for those who *do* the will of God (as opposed to
those who simply talk about it) may be highly intriguing. While
Jesus' stern words may give pause to those who came into
worship feeling comfortable with their faith, the exhortation
may prove a helpful motivation to those same people who wish
to have their spiritual lives reinvigorated.

ALEXANDER WIMBERLY

RESPONSE

Think about people you know who are comfortable with their
faith and those who are not. What differences do you notice?

PRAYER

God, I sometimes wonder if others, who witness my life, would
call me Christian. Amen.

✦ SUNDAY ✦

Deuteronomy 11:18–21, 26–28

REFLECTION

For the knowledge of God to touch our hearts and shape our
souls, we must learn from others whom it has touched and
shaped, and then we must in turn impersonate the faith and
teach it to the next generation.

BARBARA G. WHEELER

Psalm 31:1–5, 19–24

REFLECTION

The psalm closes with the summons to the community to wait
for the Lord. . . . This waiting for God is made possible, then
and in any age, by actual experience of the divine presence, an
actual demonstration of God's goodness in one's life. Strangely,
this experience of God's goodness may be hidden from the eyes
of everyone except the worshiper.

WALTER J. HARRELSON

Romans 1:16–17; 3:22b–28 (29–31)

REFLECTION

In this set of verses, it is God who is righteous. It is God who
has graciously acted on our behalf through Jesus Christ to give
us an opening and access to God's own righteousness. It is God
who moves beyond distinctions between Jews and Gentiles, to
make plain that God is God of *all*. Our response is to have faith
in God through Jesus Christ. With this, the door to salvation is
graciously open.

DIANE TURNER-SHARAZZ

Matthew 7:21–29

REFLECTION

Both activity and inactivity can be detrimental. There is
a holistic presentation of what determines faithful living:
doing the will of God. Mere hearing or acting will not suffice;
Matthew stresses hearing and doing, inward adherence to the
Word and outward practice of the Word. One is not greater
than the other.

LUKE A. POWERY

RESPONSE

In what ways has your heart been touched or your soul been
shaped by someone this week?

PRAYER

Mother God, Today I lift up in prayer all those who have
touched and shaped me this week. I am grateful for their
presence in my life and for their witness of a faithful life. Amen.

❧ *Proper 5* ☙

Hosea 5:15–6:6

For I desire steadfast love and not sacrifice,
  the knowledge of God rather than burnt offerings. (6:6)

Psalm 50:7–15

"Offer to God a sacrifice of thanksgiving,
  and pay your vows to the Most High.
Call on me in the day of trouble;
  I will deliver you, and you shall glorify me." (vv. 14–15)

Romans 4:13–25

Therefore his faith "was reckoned to him as
righteousness." Now the words, "it was reckoned to
him," were written not for his sake alone, but for ours
also. It will be reckoned to us who believe in him who
raised Jesus our Lord from the dead, who was
handed over to death for our trespasses and was
raised for our justification. (vv. 22–25)

Matthew 9:9–13, 18–26

As Jesus was walking along, he saw a man called
Matthew sitting at the tax booth; and he said to him,
"Follow me." And he got up and followed him. (v. 9)

⊹ MONDAY ⊹

Hosea 5:15–6:6

REFLECTION

It is my experience that individuals, families, communities,
and congregations do experience God's restoration. It is my
hope that this restoration may be also experienced by nations
and by the earth itself. Individuals are likely to say that they
experience God's restoration as forgiveness from sin, peace in
the face of uncertainty, courage in the face of challenge, hope
in the face of despair, recovery in the face of addiction,
health in the face of illness. Families are likely to say that
they experience God's restoration as joy in being together, in
reconciliation after disagreement, as strength in the face of
shared loss, as the ability to remember in the face of relentless
change.

H. JAMES HOPKINS

RESPONSE

How have you experienced the activity of God's restoration in
your life?

PRAYER

God of my life, you surround me with the bounty of your love
and care. Restore those places in me that need healing, hope,
and reconciliation. Amen.

✦ TUESDAY ✦

Hosea 5:15–6:6

REFLECTION

Communities are likely to say that they experience God's restoration when they are able to replace injustice with justice, inequality with equality, division with unity, and discouragement with opportunity. Congregations are likely to say that they experience God's restoration when diversity replaces homogeneity, when vision replaces fear, when worship replaces worry, when ministry replaces murmuring.

H. JAMES HOPKINS

RESPONSE

What in your community of faith needs God's restoring hand?

PRAYER

God of justice, help me be aware of my murmuring and the places where acting on vision is needed in my church and in my community. Amen.

✣ WEDNESDAY ✣

Psalm 50:7–15

REFLECTION

Companionship with God, biblical writers clearly understand, pleases God, even as it blesses and enriches human life. The difference is, however, evident to see. Devotion to God includes devotion to God's ways. Sharing goods with God involves readiness to share life and goods with fellow human beings.

WALTER J. HARRELSON

RESPONSE

How is your companionship with God evidenced in your life?

PRAYER

God, what comfort it is to know that when I call on you, you are there. Thank you for your abiding presence in my life. Amen.

✢ THURSDAY ✣

Psalm 50:7–15

REFLECTION

Having blessings for which to be thankful is a result of God's grace. Being able to offer thanks to God verbally or physically is a result of grace. Having the ability to think through the many ways we have been blessed is a result of grace. . . . When we as believers take the time and exert the effort to thank God for God's many blessings, we are also building our faith. Recounting what God has done reinforces our belief in what God can do.

DEBRA J. MUMFORD

RESPONSE

Consider the blessings you have received in your life. What then do you learn about what God is able to do?

PRAYER

God of grace, thank you for the many ways you have been a blessing in my life. Amen.

→ FRIDAY ←

Matthew 9:9–13, 18–26

REFLECTION

One should not automatically assume that we are not tax collectors and sinners in some way and in need of mercy. However, one must also acknowledge the ways some believers exclude others because they are different. While Christians can be viewed as the "sick," the socially marginalized today are truly the prisoners, prostitutes, pimps, AIDS victims, dope dealers, and the like. These are the ones whom many drive by, rather than sit by, like Jesus.

LUKE A. POWERY

RESPONSE

Who are the marginalized in your community whom no one wants to see or sit by?

PRAYER

God of all, remind me whom you call me to sit by, whom you call me to see, whom you call me to listen to this day, this week. Amen.

✦ SATURDAY ✦

Matthew 9:9–13, 18–26

REFLECTION

Those engaged in social ministry toward those mentioned may
be affirmed in their ministry, whereas others may feel convicted
by the mercy ministry of Jesus. This will depend on the
congregational context. One thing is for sure: Jesus reaches out
to the margins, calling us to follow him in this mercy mission.
To whom do we minister? If we follow him, we will not only sit
with outcasts, but touch them.

LUKE A. POWERY

RESPONSE

How have you received God's mercy? To whom are you being
asked to extend God's mercy?

PRAYER

I confess, O God, that sometimes I draw the margins of your
mercy too narrowly. Help me to see the wideness of your love
and the healing touch present in my hands. Amen.

✦ SUNDAY ✦

Hosea 5:15–6:6

REFLECTION

The season of Pentecost is upon us. If we believe the Holy
Spirit moves on the earth and indwells the church, then we are
confident that we have tremendous power available to us.

MARY ALICE MULLIGAN

Psalm 50:7–15

REFLECTION

To approach God is to be exposed to One who knows the
secrets of the heart, who discerns our thoughts from far away,
and who, while welcoming worshipers, does not leave them
as they came. What a blessing to have texts such as this one
that help to keep clear and clean and morally significant our
worship of God!

WALTER J. HARRELSON

Romans 4:13–25

REFLECTION

This faith is not passive; it requires a behavioral response. This
text calls hearers to move from walking by sight to walking by
faith. It requires not spiritual blindness but spiritual courage
to move forward when all evidence tells you to stand still or
turn away. It invites hearers to walk alongside or in the faith
footsteps of Abraham by stepping out and acting upon what
they believe.

DIANE TURNER-SHARAZZ

Matthew 9:9–13, 18–26

REFLECTION

Can Jesus heal like this today? Can he raise the dead? Healing may be physical, but it is also relational and social, restoring the marginalized into community, where they can be lovingly touched again. Nothing can replace a restorative healing touch to those who need to know they are not alone, even in death. What kind of God will go all the way to touch death in order to destroy it for us? A God whose ministry is one of mercy.

LUKE A. POWERY

RESPONSE

As you meditate on these reflections, what do you most want to remember?

PRAYER

Healing God, I am prone to want to walk by sight. Help me to remember to order my steps by faith. Amen.

🌿 *Proper 6* 🌿

Exodus 19:2–8a

"Now therefore, if you obey my voice and keep
my covenant, you shall be my treasured possession out
of all the peoples. Indeed, the whole earth is mine, but you
shall be for me a priestly kingdom and a holy nation." (vv. 5–6)

Psalm 100

Make a joyful noise to the LORD, all the earth.
Worship the LORD with gladness;
come into his presence with singing. (vv. 1–2)

Romans 5:1–8

But God proves his love for us in that while
we still were sinners Christ died for us. (v. 8)

Matthew 9:35–10:8 (9–23)

Then he said to his disciples, "The harvest is plentiful,
but the laborers are few; therefore ask the Lord of the
harvest to send out laborers into his harvest." (9:37–38)

→ MONDAY ←

Exodus 19:2–8a

REFLECTION

The form scholars discern biblical writers to be using when they
discuss desert travails is called a "murmuring story." . . .
. . . Though we can read on in the story, this is a good place
to pause. It is easy to concentrate generally on the failure of
God's people to obey, to accept what God offers them, since the
preponderance of narratives stress that failing. Here, however,
they do well, indicating a wholehearted desire to move into
relationship with God distinctively. That is well done.

BARBARA GREEN

RESPONSE

What is your murmuring story?

PRAYER

God, you travel with me through life, hearing my murmuring
stories. Thank you for your abiding presence. Amen.

✦ TUESDAY ✦

Exodus 19:2–8a

REFLECTION

As pastor and people there are questions that confront us:

1. Do we talk as much about our responsibilities as about the blessings we are promised?
2. In inviting others to join our congregation, do we promise that their needs will be met, or do we focus on our mission of meeting the needs of the larger community?
3. If we wax eloquent about the ways we are carried by the wings of God, do we acknowledge that those wings carry us not only to vistas of splendor but also to points of great need?

H. JAMES HOPKINS

RESPONSE

What is your response to these questions?

PRAYER

I am both comforted and challenged by your wings, O God. Amen.

✦ WEDNESDAY ✦

Psalm 100

REFLECTION

This psalm is not primarily about the responsibilities associated with belonging to God, but rather about the joy—joy in God that the psalmist believed should be expressed with great fervor, zeal. Words like "gladness," "singing," "thanksgiving," and "praise" indicate that the people of God should worship God with everything they have—their bodies, voices, spirits, and minds. Worship of God should be a celebration.

DEBRA J. MUMFORD

RESPONSE

This day, how will you worship God with your voice, your spirit, your mind, and your body?

PRAYER

With joy and praise, I lift my thanks to you, God of my life. Amen.

✦ THURSDAY ✦

Psalm 100

REFLECTION

This psalm begins by inviting all the earth to make a joyful noise to God. However, one may ask how that can be possible, given so much misery in life. It is almost a call to revolution. Let all the earth rejoice in God the Creator, in spite of murder, war, and frightening climate change. Let us be glad in the presence of the Divine, in spite of depression and debilitating illness. Let us sing thanksgiving, in spite of poverty, hunger, and AIDS. Look death in the eye and make a joyful noise. Grab evil by the neck and shout loud hosannas!

Why? Because God still is God.

STEVEN D. MILLER

RESPONSE

What evils would you add to the list?

PRAYER

God of all life, a teenager was killed after a basketball game. It was a needless death. An elderly woman died from the heat in her apartment. It was a needless death. In life and in death, we belong to you. Amen.

✦ FRIDAY ✦

Romans 5:1–8

REFLECTION

Many African slaves endured the suffering of slavery because
they knew the present power of God's love and the future glory
that awaited them. What Christians know about the future
inspires us to act appropriately in the present. The future glory
is not to be used as an anesthesia or opiate to make us passively
accept pain. Rather, the love of God is so powerful that it
sustains us through suffering and empowers us to act according
to our faith.

DIANE GIVENS MOFFETT

RESPONSE

How have you experienced the power of God's love?

PRAYER

Loving God, empower me to act responsibly in your world, as I
live my faith. Amen.

⁜ SATURDAY ⁜

Matthew 9:35–10:8 (9–23)

REFLECTION

This is good news, because the movement of this passage reveals that when there is a need, Jesus shows compassion, and his compassion causes him to send out others on a mission to serve those in need. God provides avenues to meeting human needs, and this compassionate ministry is free for the "lost sheep." All Jesus desires is that the lost be found.

LUKE A. POWERY

RESPONSE

What compassionate ministry is God calling you to be involved in?

PRAYER

Compassionate God, show me the mission you want me to do. Amen.

✦ SUNDAY ✦

Exodus 19:2–8a

REFLECTION

Perhaps someday, in the fullness of time, all humanity, chosen by God, may answer God's call as one: "Everything that the LORD has spoken we will do."

BARBARA G. WHEELER

Psalm 100

REFLECTION

Praise is thanksgiving. Worship is being truly present to God. As we bask in God's presence, let the glad noise begin.

STEVEN D. MILLER

Romans 5:1–8

REFLECTION

Humanity in its most sinful, weakened state is the least deserving of God's mercy and goodness. Then, at the right time, when humanity needs God the most, Christ dies for the ungodly. Humanity would rarely die for a good or righteous person, but Christ died for us while we were yet sinners. Paul reminds us that this is proof of God's magnanimous love.

DIANE TURNER-SHARAZZ

Matthew 9:35–10:8 (9–23)

REFLECTION

Due in part to the efforts made by faithful Christians, diseases thought to be incurable have been eradicated, unjust laws have been overturned, and individuals who thought some doors would never open have seen them swing wide. Perhaps most humbling of all is the fact that in many parts of the world where Christians are persecuted today, Christianity not only survives but thrives.

ALEXANDER WIMBERLY

RESPONSE

As you consider these reflections, what common theological themes are evident to you?

PRAYER

As I lift my songs of praise and thanksgiving, O God, I am humbled to be in your presence. Amen.

❧ *Proper 7* ❦

Jeremiah 20:7–13

Sing to the LORD;
    praise the LORD!
For he has delivered the life of the needy
    from the hands of evildoers. (v. 13)

Psalm 69:7–10 (11–15), 16–18

Answer me, O LORD, for your steadfast love is good;
    according to your abundant mercy, turn to me.
Do not hide your face from your servant,
    for I am in distress—make haste to answer me.
Draw near to me, redeem me,
    set me free because of my enemies. (vv. 16–18)

Romans 6:1b–11

So you also must consider yourselves dead to
    sin and alive to God in Christ Jesus. (v. 11)

Matthew 10:24–39

"Those who find their life will lose it, and those
who lose their life for my sake will find it." (v. 39)

✦ MONDAY ✦

Jeremiah 20:7–13

REFLECTION

God is always and already enticing us. God can and will overwhelm us, sometimes for a moment, sometimes for a lifetime. In those moments, it is rare that those who know and love us will cheer us on, but the fire in our bones will find its way out, even if it must exhaust our defenses to get there.

TRACE HAYTHORN

RESPONSE

How has God enticed you? How has God overwhelmed you?

PRAYER

God of fire and water, fill me, nourish me, sustain me for the work you call me to do. Amen.

→ TUESDAY ←

Jeremiah 20:7–13

REFLECTION

The accusation against God we encounter here is therefore an expression of faith! It is not the antithesis of spirituality; it is part of it. Lament, and even anger at God, is not the opposite of faith in God. . . .

. . . The life of faith is not always serene. It is not simply quiet submission to God's will. It is, rather, a life of struggle with God and God's will.

RACHEL SOPHIA BAARD

RESPONSE

With the psalmist, name your lament, the places where you struggle.

PRAYER

God of my life, this day I commit again my life to your causes in this world. Amen.

⇴ WEDNESDAY ⇴

Psalm 69:7–10 (11–15), 16–18

REFLECTION

Psalm 69 is a prayer for help when one is rejected by one's own family and community, when one is feeling like the stranger or the alien, for doing nothing more than seeking to do what God has called us to do or to be, whether that is to preach the gospel, teach, serve, or carry out any other vocation that calls to us in our lives.

KATE COLUSSY-ESTES

RESPONSE

Write your own prayer for help and reflect on it in light of Psalm 69.

PRAYER

Thank you, God, for your steadfast love, which surrounds me this day and every day. Amen.

✢ THURSDAY ✢

Romans 6:1b–11

REFLECTION

Paul understands baptism as a type of exodus. As Israel once labored under Pharaoh, so humanity labored in bondage to sin. As Pharaoh's power was broken once when Israel passed through the waters of the Red Sea, so sin's power over us was broken when we passed through the waters of baptism.

TED A. SMITH

RESPONSE

In what ways has your baptism been an exodus for you?

PRAYER

Spirit of God who hovers over my baptism, I know the reality of sin and am grateful for the renewing power of your healing water. Amen.

→ FRIDAY ←

Matthew 10:24–39

REFLECTION

It is important to note that discipleship is a journey that includes learning, which is distinct from being an apostle or a messenger, who is sent to declare a message. The focus for us now is to try to understand what Jesus is seeking to teach us and what we are to learn from it. In this passage, our task is not to be the ones who deliver the teachings. Rather, we are to pause and learn from Jesus who we are to be, what we are to say, and how we are to communicate this with others. This pause is crucial as we consider one aspect of discipleship that is found in today's passage from Matthew: obedience.

EMILIE M. TOWNES

RESPONSE

What is the most important thing you have learned as a disciple of Jesus?

PRAYER

In this world that demands all speed, all immediacy, slow me down, Lord, help me to pause—to listen, to wait, to be. Amen.

✦ SATURDAY ✦

Matthew 10:24–39

REFLECTION

Throughout this passage, obedience implies responsibility. A disciple of Jesus is one who first listens closely to the teachings of Jesus and then decides on the appropriate response. This response is found in a discipleship that summons us to develop our capacity for learning and growing in faith. . . . Jesus requires a discerning obedience that has its eyes wide open, as we accept responsibility for the order of the world and engage in transforming it.

EMILIE M. TOWNES

RESPONSE

Which teachings of Jesus are easiest for you to follow? Which are harder?

PRAYER

Open the eyes of my heart, Lord, that I may see the places in the world to which you are calling me. Amen.

⇥ SUNDAY ⇤

Jeremiah 20:7–13

REFLECTION

Responding to God's call sometimes leads to poor grammar.
Like Jeremiah, we find ourselves using double negatives to
get to the heart of the matter. We do not respond to God's call
simply because it is exciting and intriguing and full of promise.
We respond to God's call because we cannot *not* respond.

TRACE HAYTHORN

Psalm 69:7–10 (11–15), 16–18

REFLECTION

The psalmist reminds us that on those days when life has hit
us hard, we are not alone, because people have been railing
and angry at God throughout history, and God can take our
anger. On those days when we feel far away from God, we are
reminded that we are not alone, and God can take our distance.
When we feel that all around us have turned their backs, the
psalmist reminds us that God calls us to live into what is right
in front of us. This is all God asks.

KATE COLUSSY-ESTES

Romans 6:1b–11

REFLECTION

Baptism brings about a radical change in our identity, a change
that has implications for every aspect of our lives. It is not a
demand, but a glorious possibility—to be alive to God. That
good news should be music to our ears.

SHAWNTHEA MONROE

Matthew 10:24–39

REFLECTION

Those who live by the light of faith challenge the evil powers of this world with the certainty of believers, knowing that the way of God will prevail against every hurt and every challenge.

WILLIAM GOETTLER

RESPONSE

Recall a time when you felt very far away from God. Now recall a time when you felt God's presence in your life to be very near.

PRAYER

All you ask, all you ever ask, God of love, is that we see with your eyes what is right in front of us. Help me see better. Amen.

❧ *Proper 8* ☙

Jeremiah 28:5–9

"As for the prophet who prophesies peace, when the word of that prophet comes true, then it will be known that the LORD has truly sent the prophet." (v. 9)

Psalm 89:1–4, 15–18

I will sing of your steadfast love, O LORD, forever;
with my mouth I will proclaim your faithfulness
to all generations.
I declare that your steadfast love is established forever;
your faithfulness is as firm as the heavens. (vv. 1–2)

Romans 6:12–23

But now that you have been freed from sin and enslaved to God, the advantage you get is sanctification. The end is eternal life. For the wages of sin is death, but the free gift of God is eternal life in Christ Jesus our Lord. (vv. 22–23)

Matthew 10:40–42

"Whoever welcomes you welcomes me, and whoever welcomes me welcomes the one who sent me." (v. 40)

Jeremiah 28:5–9

REFLECTION

Whenever we are faced with such either/or decisions, real discernment begins not with more debate or panel discussions, not with another book read or another task force established. Discernment begins on our knees, perhaps even prostrate on the floor. Discernment begins in the posture of humility, because it is all too easy for us to assume that our certainty is born of God and that those who disagree are most certainly not of God.

TRACE HAYTHORN

RESPONSE

Of what are you most certain? With whom are you in most disagreement? What discernment do you seek?

PRAYER

Humble me, as I remember the discerning work ahead of me. Amen.

Psalm 89:1–4, 15–18

REFLECTION

For us the idea of *hesed* is overwhelming. We cannot fathom such loving-kindness as coming from God. We liken it to the love of a parent for a child, but human parents struggle, not necessarily with loving their children, but certainly with the constancy and faithfulness that is often tested.

KATE COLUSSY-ESTES

RESPONSE

How will you live in response to God's steadfast love?

PRAYER

God, your *hesed* is more than I can understand. It surrounds me and sustains me all my days. Amen.

✦ WEDNESDAY ✦

Psalm 89:1–4, 15–18

REFLECTION

As Christians who live in hope that justice and righteousness
will ultimately prevail, we also believe that in spite of the
condition of the economy, in spite of joblessness, in spite of
the stress and distress that engulf us, in spite of the dark pall
of clouds that like smoke have obstructed our view of the sun's
bright rays of a new day on the horizon, we still have something
to shout about.

JAMES HENRY HARRIS

RESPONSE

What do you want to shout out to God this day?

PRAYER

Without your hope, O God, our days are dark. With your hope,
I live in the sunlight of your abiding love. Amen.

✤ THURSDAY ✤

Romans 6:12–23

REFLECTION

What does Paul mean when he says we are slaves? He is
really driving toward the idea of ultimate allegiance, loyalty,
obedience, and service. To be a slave, as Paul understands it, is
to surrender your life to the control of another. When slavery is
defined in this way, it turns out we are all slaves of one sort or
another.

SHAWNTHEA MONROE

RESPONSE

What enslaves you?

PRAYER

Your free gift of life eternal is sometimes beyond my ability to
understand, O God. Thank you. Amen.

✦ FRIDAY ✦

Romans 6:12–23

REFLECTION

Many young people have become disillusioned with organized religion because the church seems hypocritical—we say one thing and do another. It is a fair criticism. There is no lack of examples of good Christians who profess a faith that does not influence their lives. As a confirmation student told me, "They talk the talk but don't walk the walk."

SHAWNTHEA MONROE

RESPONSE

Whom have you noticed this week who does "walk the walk"?

PRAYER

Loving God, help our church find ways to be in ministry with our young people. Amen.

⇸ SATURDAY ⇷

Matthew 10:40–42

REFLECTION

The hospitality rooted in compassionate welcome is both a
practice and a spiritual discipline in which we discover that
by offering hospitality we may be welcoming something or
someone new, unfamiliar, and unknown into our lives. This
requires us to recognize another's gifts and vulnerabilities, the
need for shelter and sustenance, and encourages us to open up
our worldviews and perspectives as well as our hearts and souls.

EMILIE M. TOWNES

RESPONSE

Recall a story of your own experience of receiving hospitality
from another.

PRAYER

As I have received hospitality, so may I offer it to another. Open
my heart and soul to all of this possibility. Amen.

✦ SUNDAY ✦

Jeremiah 28:5–9

REFLECTION

Jeremiah does not offer us a recipe for avoiding disaster and ultimately leaves it to history to decide. He does, however, help us to understand that the quick and easy answer, the popular position, the position held by the charming prophet, is not necessarily the true one. His message still rings true: beware of easy answers and simple solutions; and beware of resting on God's grace as if we own it.

RACHEL SOPHIA BAARD

Psalm 89:1–4, 15–18

REFLECTION

Because God is God, we can shout. God's sovereignty alone gives us hope, and that hope alone is reason to shout and celebrate.

JAMES HENRY HARRIS

Romans 6:12–23

REFLECTION

If you want to know who your master is, pay attention to what occupies your thoughts and how you spend your time and money. We are all serving something or someone. This passage invites us to ask the question, whom do you serve?

SHAWNTHEA MONROE

Matthew 10:40–42

REFLECTION

God's hospitality teaches us that close, loving, enduring
relationships are to be valued along with distant, occasional,
and abrasive ones—as difficult as the latter ones may be. This
lively, and sometimes maddening, dynamic is the welcome
Jesus speaks of in today's passage. Further, if we live into this
welcome with each other, we will find the rich rewards of
discipleship found in God.

EMILIE M. TOWNES

RESPONSE

Pause with these four reflections. Which ones affirm what you
believe? Which challenge what you believe?

PRAYER

This journey in faith requires my close examination as well as
my affirmation that you are the God of my life. And I shout and
celebrate this. Amen.

❧ *Proper 9* ❧

Zechariah 9:9–12

Return to your stronghold, O prisoners of hope;
today I declare that I will restore to you double. (v. 12)

Psalm 145:8–14

The LORD is faithful in all his words,
and gracious in all his deeds.
The LORD upholds all who are falling,
and raises up all who are bowed down. (vv. 13b–14)

Romans 7:15–25a

For I do not do the good I want, but the
evil I do not want is what I do. Now if I do what
I do not want, it is no longer I that do it, but sin
that dwells within me. (vv. 19–20)

Matthew 11:16–19, 25–30

"Come to me, all you that are weary and are
carrying heavy burdens, and I will give you rest.
Take my yoke upon you, and learn from me; for I
am gentle and humble in heart, and you will
find rest for your souls. For my yoke is easy,
and my burden is light." (vv. 28–30)

❧ MONDAY ❧

Zechariah 9:9–12

REFLECTION

Zechariah's promise is in the plural: it is for those who are
imprisoned and those who long for the prisoners' release. It
is a promise of restoration, of wholeness. As children of the
covenant, we yoke our hearts to the promise of such new life,
and we live for its realization: the new Jerusalem, the new
Gilead, indeed, even the new (insert the name of your town
here).

TRACE HAYTHORN

RESPONSE

What in your community needs restoration?

PRAYER

Today I lift up my church and my community and pray for
continuing wholeness, health, and transformation. Amen.

✦ TUESDAY ✦

Zechariah 9:9–12

REFLECTION

Franciscan spirituality teaches us that we cannot be *of* the poor and the oppressed, because many of us are not poor or oppressed. We cannot be *for* the poor and the oppressed, because that is just another form of control. Nevertheless, we must stand *with* the poor and the oppressed. Our salvation, our wholeness, and our peace are found finally in the authentic justice and wholeness of all others. Show us a peace-giving and foot-washing congregation, and we will show you a changing neighborhood around it. Show us a justice-driven congregation, and we will show you a changing city.

DOUGLASS M. BAILEY

RESPONSE

With whom do you and your congregation stand?

PRAYER

Show me the ways of peace, merciful God, and the places where your justice is needed. Amen.

✣ WEDNESDAY ✣

Psalm 145:8–14

REFLECTION

In recognizing the sovereignty of God, we as believers are called to act as God's representative and to be part of lifting up those who are bowed down. As people of faith who live in the reign of God and its many blessings, we are reminded that those blessings are for the least among us. In this life we cannot sing praise to our God unless we also recognize all the gifts we have been given and raise up all who are bowed down.

KATE COLUSSY-ESTES

RESPONSE

How have you been blessed? Who needs your blessing?

PRAYER

God of my life, help me as I join you in lifting up those who are bowed down. Amen.

→ THURSDAY ←

Psalm 145:8–14

REFLECTION

The works of God in nature and God's mighty acts in the history of his people are the subject matter of God's self-revelation, not secrets of esoteric wisdom reserved for spiritual elites. The knowledge of this Sovereign should lead us to the practical work of prayer and praise in the company of God's people.

ROBERT A. CATHEY

RESPONSE

What examples of God's faithfulness have you experienced?

PRAYER

Loving God, I pray this day for all who stumble, for those who have fallen, for those whose heads are so bowed down they cannot see. Surround them with your care. Amen.

✧ FRIDAY ✧

Romans 7:15–25a

REFLECTION

Looking out at my congregation on a Sunday morning, I see
people who embody the motto "Never let 'em see you sweat";
but God knows the truth and so does Paul: we are all sweating.

SHAWNTHEA MONROE

RESPONSE

Pause and reflect on the good things you want to do and the
evil things you do.

PRAYER

Thank you, God, for your forgiving love, which keeps me going.
Amen.

✦ SATURDAY ✦

Matthew 11:16–19, 25–30

REFLECTION

The vital discipleship to which Jesus calls us in this passage
means that we must not place ourselves in the role of host or
hostess in churches whose ministries are concerned only with
when to do the next maintenance task, rather than how to
construct places of welcome and sustenance. The discipleship
to which Jesus invites us in this passage requires that we stretch
into our ministries by focusing on his message and realizing
that we will find rest for carrying the burden of the gospel by
living out the unique mission to which Jesus calls each of us.

EMILIE M. TOWNES

RESPONSE

How is God stretching your congregation's understanding of
mission and ministry?

PRAYER

Give me your rest, loving God. Amen.

✦ SUNDAY ✦

Zechariah 9:9–12

REFLECTION

Let us be honest. Are we not changed much more by a movement than by an organization? Organizations and institutions conjure up perceptions that are fixed in form, devoid of urgency, lacking in a "Way" that invites us to become engaged, and, more often than not, imagined as structures rather than as souls. On the other hand, movements lend themselves to being oriented to people; they are energetic, fluid, and visionary; they connect us to a cause on which our very life may well depend.

A friend of mine often remarked, "People do not engage themselves in causes that are feasible; we commit ourselves to movements that are irresistible." Show us a congregation that understands its ministry in terms of a movement, and we will show you a congregation that is making an irresistible presence and witness in its neighborhood and its world.

DOUGLASS M. BAILEY

Psalm 145:8–14

REFLECTION

To uphold is to support against an opponent. In the language of the masses, the Lord "ain't gonna" let us totally fall. No one knows what opponents you face today or the desires that engulf you; but the psalmist reminds us that there is a God whose greatness is unsearchable, whose power is infinite, who can calm our fears and release our burdens.

JAMES HENRY HARRIS

Romans 7:15–25a

REFLECTION

God does not just give individual humans the willpower to live our best lives now, or say that it does not matter if we do not. In Jesus Christ, God sets the cosmos free from bondage, redeeming the law and opening the way to life, and life abundant.

TED A. SMITH

Matthew 11:16–19, 25–30

REFLECTION

To accept the yoke of the gentle and humble Lord is to embrace the worthy task that puts the soul at ease.

LANCE PAPE

RESPONSE

In what ways has God released your burdens and put your soul at ease?

PRAYER

God, your greatness is known in your power and also in your presence in my life, calming my fears and easing my burdens. Amen.

❧ *Proper 10* ❦

Isaiah 55:10–13

For you shall go out in joy,
　　and be led back in peace;
the mountains and the hills before you
　　shall burst into song,
　　and all the trees of the field shall clap their hands.
　　　　　　　　　　　　　　　　　　　　　(v. 12)

Psalm 65:(1–8) 9–13

You visit the earth and water it,
　　you greatly enrich it;
the river of God is full of water;
　　you provide the people with grain,
　　for so you have prepared it. (v. 9)

Romans 8:1–11

But you are not in the flesh; you are in the Spirit,
　　since the Spirit of God dwells in you. (v. 9a)

Matthew 13:1–9, 18–23

"But as for what was sown on good soil, this is
the one who hears the word and understands it, who
indeed bears fruit and yields, in one case a hundredfold,
in another sixty, and in another thirty." (v. 23)

⇝ MONDAY ⇜

Isaiah 55:10–13

REFLECTION

Spring does not just arrive because the earth's axis tilts toward the sun. The warmth of God's presence arrives because God turns toward us in love. Forgiveness arrives because of the wideness of God's mercy. Joy arrives because we see a glimmer of our new life in God in our own. As Isaiah proclaimed so long ago, the word that goes out from the mouth of the Lord will not return empty, but shall accomplish its purpose and succeed in just the thing for which it was sent.

THOMAS W. BLAIR

RESPONSE

Where is the warmth of God's love needed in your community?

PRAYER

God, as you lead me out into your world in joy, help me be one who lives as your peacemaker. Amen.

✦ TUESDAY ✦

Psalm 65:(1–8) 9–13

REFLECTION

Whenever I wonder *whether or not God understands* the human struggle, I read a psalm. The description of the human condition in the psalms is astonishingly honest and accurate. If we think we need to keep secrets from God to be loved, the psalms remind us that God knows us better than we know ourselves and still loves us.

HERBERT ANDERSON

RESPONSE

What psalms do you read as you seek to understand the human struggle?

PRAYER

Thank you, God, for knowing us all and loving us all. Amen.

✦ WEDNESDAY ✦

Psalm 65:(1–8) 9–13

REFLECTION

Whenever I wonder *why I should be grateful*, I read a psalm.
Psalms that give thanks and praise for the abundance of God's
gifts through creation remind us again and again that God's
care is not limited by human need or even determined by
what we request. As creator, God established the order in the
universe, setting up the mountains and triumphing over chaotic
cosmic waters. However, God is not only the creator of the
world. God is the one who sustains the life brought forth.

HERBERT ANDERSON

RESPONSE

What psalms do you read when you wonder about being
grateful?

PRAYER

Creator God, today I am a grateful person. Thank you for . . .
Amen.

✦ THURSDAY ✦

Romans 8:1–11

REFLECTION

The Spirit dwells in those baptized in Jesus' name and keeps their minds on the things of God and life, rather than the ways of death. The Spirit is their assurance of God's promises, the person of the Trinity who will guide them as they navigate the challenges of this life. The Spirit will give Jesus' followers peace, come what may.

BLAIR ALISON POGUE

RESPONSE

How have you experienced the peace of God's indwelling Spirit?

PRAYER

Spirit of the living God, lead me in the ways of peace. Amen.

✢ FRIDAY ✢

Matthew 13:1–9, 18–23

REFLECTION

The parable's ending is its greatest challenge. Jesus goes beyond simply encouraging his listeners to "keep on keeping on" in the face of rejection. Instead, his parable challenges them—and us—to believe in God's abundance.

TALITHA J. ARNOLD

RESPONSE

Where is God challenging your notions of scarcity and abundance?

PRAYER

God who is the gardener of my soul, help me to be the bearer of the fruits of your Spirit in this world. Amen.

Matthew 13:1–9, 18–23

REFLECTION

Novelist Bebe Moore Campbell writes, "Some of us have that empty-barrel faith. Walking around expecting things to run out. Expecting that there isn't enough air, enough water. Expecting that someone is going to do you wrong. The God I serve told me to expect the best, that there is enough for everybody."* That is the God this parable calls us to trust. Jesus knows the hard ways of this world. He also knows the abundant ways of God.

TALITHA J. ARNOLD

RESPONSE

On your "empty-barrel faith" days, what do you most fear?

PRAYER

God of abundance, help me remember there is always enough to sustain my life of faith. Amen.

*Bebe Moore Campbell, *Singing in the Comeback Choir* (New York: Putnam, 1998), 131.

⊹ SUNDAY ⊹

Isaiah 55:10–13

REFLECTION

Is the text sacred only because it survived, or is its survival
actually the everlasting sign? God means what God says.
The Word engages the world through the language and life
of the prophets and the people of God again and again. Then
the Word becomes flesh and dwells among us.

HEATHER MURRAY ELKINS

Psalm 65:(1–8) 9–13

REFLECTION

Psalm 65 invites us to be newly overwhelmed—no longer by
transgression and failure, but by the limitless resources of grace,
flowing in a never-ending, ever-rejoicing cycle of abundance.

JO BAILEY WELLS

Romans 8:1–11

REFLECTION

As long as our minds are "on the flesh," sin will drive us; but if
our minds are set on the Spirit—our will and our lives are in
God—then life is not only a possibility, but a promise. This is
the hope in which we live: that God who raised Christ from the
dead will give life to us—body, mind, and spirit—through the
power of the Spirit dwelling in us.

KAREN CHAKOIAN

Matthew 13:1–9, 18–23

REFLECTION

This sower is a high-risk sower, relentless in indiscriminately throwing seed on all soil—as if it were *all* potentially good soil. On the rocks, amid the thorns, on the well-worn path, maybe even in a jail!

Which leaves us to wonder if there is any place or circumstance in which God's seed cannot sprout and take root.

THEODORE J. WARDLAW

RESPONSE

How might you be a "high-risk sower"?

PRAYER

God, your Spirit empowers my living and sowing. Thank you. Amen.

❧ *Proper 11* ☙

Isaiah 44:6–8

Do not fear, or be afraid;
> have I not told you from of old and declared it?
> You are my witnesses!
Is there any god besides me?
> There is no other rock; I know not one. (v. 8)

Psalm 86:11–17

For great is your steadfast love toward me;
> you have delivered my soul from the depths of Sheol.
O God, the insolent rise up against me;
> a band of ruffians seeks my life,
> and they do not set you before them.
But you, O Lord, are a God merciful and gracious,
> slow to anger and abounding in steadfast love
> > and faithfulness. (vv. 13–15)

Romans 8:12–25

> But if we hope for what we do not see,
> we wait for it with patience. (v. 25)

Matthew 13:24–30, 36–43

"Then the righteous will shine like the sun in the
kingdom of their Father. Let anyone with ears listen!" (v. 43)

✦ MONDAY ✦

Isaiah 44:6–8

REFLECTION

God's mercy is as steady as a heartbeat; God's faithfulness is as solid as a rock. Just as grace is a sheer gift of God, so also is the gift of being open to the possibilities of an unexpected future, trusting that all will be well when events are out of our control.

THOMAS W. BLAIR

RESPONSE

God's mercy . . . God's faithfulness . . . God's grace—Pause and reflect on these in light of the Isaiah text.

PRAYER

Merciful God, as I face a day and a future that sometimes seems beyond my control, I give thanks for your grace and steady presence in my life. Amen.

⤖ TUESDAY ⤔

Isaiah 44:6–8

REFLECTION

Sometimes God demands to be heard, but that does not always mean enveloping the hearer with bright lights and thunder. Sometimes God speaks words that are uninvited, unanticipated, and unexpected. Sometimes God puts us on edge or—better said—our anticipation of what God's message to us might be brings us to the edge.

THOMAS W. BLAIR

RESPONSE

What words have you heard from God that came to you uninvited, unanticipated, or unexpected?

PRAYER

Open my ears, O God, to hear the words you are speaking. Amen.

✦ WEDNESDAY ✦

Psalm 86:11–17

REFLECTION

The practice of lament and arguing with God is an unsettling
tradition of prayer because it includes the expression of
complaint, anger, grief, despair, and protest to God. What
makes lament such a bold practice of faith is that arguing with
God is predicated on the belief that my protest or argument
will change God or at least get God's attention. We are free to
lament because we believe it is not God's intent to be absent
permanently. We can protest against God and trust God at the
same time.

HERBERT ANDERSON

RESPONSE

What is your lament this day? What is your cry to God?

PRAYER

God who is present in both pain and happiness, hear my
prayers of complaint and lament this day. Amen.

✥ THURSDAY ✥

Psalm 86:11–17

REFLECTION

There is no hint of self-sufficiency here. The life of faith is constant receiving and letting go, never holding or possessing. We look to God for strength and not to ourselves. The request for strength is a countercultural word, because it acknowledges our neediness before God, who is "merciful and gracious . . . abounding in steadfast love and faithfulness" (v. 15).

HERBERT ANDERSON

RESPONSE

What in this psalm and this reflection do you most need to hear and wrestle with this day?

PRAYER

God, for your mercy, your gracious care, your faithfulness to your people, and your love that is always surrounding me, I am indeed grateful. Amen.

✦ FRIDAY ✦

Romans 8:12–25

REFLECTION

In the meantime, while we wait, we live in the already-and
not-yet, where here-and-now and there-and-then overlap
and intersect. Christians fall far from God's intention when
they hold one without the other. We have the first fruits of the
Spirit—here, already—and we groan for redemption, which is
not yet complete. If we fail to see the redemption that is already
here, we will lose heart. If we fail to understand that there is
more glory to be revealed to us, we will have lost hope. If we
hope, however, for what we do not yet see, we will wait with the
tension of eager patience.

KAREN CHAKOIAN

RESPONSE

For what do you hope? In what ways are you living in the
intersection of the "here-and-now and there-and-then"?

PRAYER

I know that sometimes my waiting is impatient, O God. Help
me learn to wait in your time. Amen.

✦ SATURDAY ✦

Matthew 13:24–30, 36–43

REFLECTION

In our time, though, we hear this parable as an amazing insight into the life of the church. Like that field in which there grow both healthy wheat and destructive weeds, the church is a mixed-bag reality. . . . Elements within each of our different churchly communions are forever troubled by how broadly or narrowly we should draw the boundaries of the contemporary church. Whom can we afford to let in, and who must remain out? Who is accepted by God, and why? Who is not accepted by God, and why not? In the very act of asking such questions, we so often assume that it is our job to draw up the specifications regarding the wideness of the church's welcome. How wide, really, can it be, and still be the church?

THEODORE J. WARDLAW

RESPONSE

As you pause with this parable from Matthew today, consider the question that is asked here and your response: How wide, really, is the church's welcome?

PRAYER

Help me, God of all, as I walk in your world and represent you and your expansive hospitality. Amen.

☩ SUNDAY ☩

Isaiah 44:6–8

REFLECTION

If you have been lost and now you are found, you are a witness. Are there any no-people who long to be now-people of the holy, living God? If you were nobody and now you are somebody, you are a witness. If you think God is not listening; if you have given up your dreams of finding a home. If you need shelter in the wilderness, trust your life to the Rock. Listen and live, as God is your witness.

HEATHER MURRAY ELKINS

Psalm 86:11–17

REFLECTION

If we connect the dots theologically, however, we find that the salvation that God has given and that we really seek in every situation is to be formed by God's steadfast, saving love, instead of by the circumstances of temporal, mortal existence. In other words, God's providential care is less about changing our circumstances and more about changing us.

O. WESLEY ALLEN JR.

Romans 8:12–25

REFLECTION

Suffering and hope hold no contradiction, for they are deeply connected in Christ, the One whose glory we have seen, the One who gives this creation life.

KAREN CHAKOIAN

Matthew 13:24–30, 36–43

REFLECTION

The parable's ending affirms that there is One who is stronger and smarter than the weed-sowing enemy. God will sort out the good from the bad. Again, that may sound harsh to our tolerant, enlightened ears, but this harvesttime judgment is the ultimate good news, be it for the person facing corruption in their workplace or those living in times and places of oppression. In a world where seeds of hatred and injustice are daily sown, the parable affirms unequivocally that God is still in charge.

TALITHA J. ARNOLD

RESPONSE

What "theological dots" connect these lectionary texts and these reflections?

PRAYER

With the prophets, I claim my place as a somebody, a witness to the love and care of you, holy, living God. Amen.

🌱 *Proper 12* 🌿

1 Kings 3:5–12

"Give your servant therefore an understanding mind
to govern your people, able to discern between good and evil;
for who can govern this your great people?" (v. 9)

Psalm 119:129–136

Keep my steps steady according to your promise,
and never let iniquity have dominion over me. (v. 133)

Romans 8:26–39

For I am convinced that neither death, nor life,
nor angels, nor rulers, nor things present, nor things
to come, nor powers, nor height, nor depth, nor anything
else in all creation, will be able to separate us from the
love of God in Christ Jesus our Lord. (vv. 38–39)

Matthew 13:31–33, 44–52

He put before them another parable: "The kingdom
of heaven is like a mustard seed that someone took and
sowed in his field; it is the smallest of all the seeds, but
when it has grown it is the greatest of shrubs and
becomes a tree, so that the birds of the air come
and make nests in its branches." (vv. 31–32)

⇢ MONDAY ⇠

1 Kings 3:5–12

REFLECTION

Orienting ourselves according to our *burdens* makes responding to situations more difficult. Orienting ourselves according to our *resources* helps us take on situations creatively and positively. Of course, in order to bring out our best resources, we need to know both what they are and how to appropriate them for use in any given situation.

THOMAS W. BLAIR

RESPONSE

How have you oriented yourself, according to your burdens or according to your resources?

PRAYER

O Lord, my God, orient me to all that I am and all that I have so that I may be one of your faithful leaders. Amen.

⇥ TUESDAY ⇤

1 Kings 3:5–12

REFLECTION

Wisdom arrives when the soul discerns its destiny, when life
aligns in sync with the soul. Wisdom pleases the Lord when it is
not self serving, but other serving.

THOMAS W. BLAIR

RESPONSE

What other ways would you describe wisdom as you reflect on
leaders you have known?

PRAYER

Give me a wise heart, O God. Amen.

✢ WEDNESDAY ✢

Psalm 119:129–136

REFLECTION

Rather than driving a wedge between spirituality and ethics, Psalm 119 forges a bond between them. It unites a life of "keeping" God's teachings with a life lived in sustaining and nourishing relationship to God. It is in keeping the decrees that the psalmist experiences the wonder of being in community with God (v. 129).

D. CAMERON MURCHISON

RESPONSE

What spiritual practices are most essential in supporting your living of a life of faith?

PRAYER

I pray, O God, that each day my keeping of your teaching will be seen in my living. Amen.

✣ THURSDAY ✣

Psalm 119:129–136

REFLECTION

For people of faith living on the other side of a century of war, death camps, apartheid, sexism, heterosexism, the social devastation of economic greed, and the lingering terror of 9/11, the psalmist echoes the ongoing desire of any believer and any community of faith, imploring God to "turn to me and be gracious to me" (v. 132). This petition is not an appeal for special privilege, but an expression of profound trust in God, who is more worthy of trust than any person, institution, organization, or government.

GARY W. CHARLES

RESPONSE

What is your petition to God this day?

PRAYER

Keep my steps steady, O God, as I turn to you and am surrounded by your gracious love. Amen.

✦ FRIDAY ✦

Romans 8:26–39

REFLECTION

If God's promises are true, if Paul is correct, we will never be separated from God's companionship and community. God will always have the last word.

BLAIR ALISON POGUE

RESPONSE

As you move through this day, keep this verse near to you, on your heart, in your mind. Let it be your breath prayer.

PRAYER

God of amazing love, thank you that I am never separated from your love and care. Amen.

☩ SATURDAY ☩

Matthew 13:31–33, 44–52

REFLECTION

The kingdom of heaven, like the mustard seed, invades the cultivated soil of our certainties and our boundaries and creates out of it all something new—"the better of the deal." Hidden within what we think we see so clearly, it is subversive and grows up in unexpected ways until what we thought we knew is transformed and redeemed by our surprising, invasive God.

THEODORE J. WARDLAW

RESPONSE

Consider how God has surprised you recently.

PRAYER

Sometimes I think I know so clearly where you are at work, O God. I have it all figured out, and then you surprise me and open my eyes to a new thing, a new growth. Thank you. Amen.

✤ SUNDAY ✤

1 Kings 3:5–12

REFLECTION

To be human is above all to have a story. To be holy is to be part of God's story. Our sense of self and community and world is relational and storied. This story of a dreaming king gathers up the history of a people of God past and present. It is a way for them and for us to remember into the future.

HEATHER MURRAY ELKINS

Psalm 119:129–136

REFLECTION

The God to whom too many pray today is more like a personal assistant than the great God Almighty, Creator of heaven and earth. This God to whom too many pray is one whom we dare not ask too much of, because this God is either too tired, too busy, or too impotent to attend to our prayers. Maybe the church could deepen its faith, expand its theology, and enrich its worship by spending a season listening to the entirety of Psalm 119, learning anew to pray with the sheer confidence of the psalmist, "Make your face shine upon your servant, and teach me your statutes" (v. 135).

GARY W. CHARLES

Romans 8:26–39

REFLECTION

Jesus' followers are called to participate in God's work of companioning others, walking alongside them as equals. We are to reach out to the world God so loved, the world far outside our church doors, the world that may not know the story of Jesus and of God's unconditional love for humanity. We are also to tell the world of God's power over death and all that separates us from the life abundant God offers. There is no reason to fear, and every reason to rejoice.

BLAIR ALISON POGUE

Matthew 13:31–33, 44–52

REFLECTION

So find new parables. What in your world produces the abundance of a mustard seed? In our time, what is like leaven, disdained as corrupt, but actually an agent of God's transforming power? Like the man plowing a field or the merchant searching for the pearl, what would your congregation give up everything to possess?

TALITHA J. ARNOLD

RESPONSE

In what ways does your story connect with these reflections? What new parables need to be written?

PRAYER

God of light and love, shine your face in all the dark places in your world, places that need our attention and our love. Amen.

❦ *Proper 13* ❦

Isaiah 55:1–5

Ho, everyone who thirsts,
    come to the waters;
and you that have no money,
    come, buy and eat!
Come, buy wine and milk
    without money and without price. (v. 1)

Psalm 145:8–9, 14–21

The LORD is gracious and merciful,
    slow to anger and abounding in steadfast love.
The LORD is good to all,
    and his compassion is over all that
      he has made. (vv. 8–9)

Romans 9:1–5

I am speaking the truth in Christ—I am
not lying; my conscience confirms it by the
Holy Spirit—I have great sorrow and unceasing
anguish in my heart. (vv. 1–2)

Matthew 14:13–21

Then he ordered the crowds to sit down
on the grass. Taking the five loaves and the two fish,
he looked up to heaven, and blessed and broke the
loaves, and gave them to the disciples, and the
disciples gave them to the crowds. (v. 19)

Isaiah 55:1–5

REFLECTION

This insignificant, humiliated people will not just survive; they will be a light to others. Surrounded by more powerful and richer countries, YHWH's people will be looked to by many other nations for the kind of society they create in covenant with God.

DAVID MAXWELL

RESPONSE

As you read this text from the prophet Isaiah, consider the ways in which your congregation serves as a light to others.

PRAYER

God, I name the dry places in my life knowing that you quench all thirsts and satisfy all hungers. Amen.

⇥ TUESDAY ⇤

Isaiah 55:1–5

REFLECTION

This covenant will be based on protecting the weakest members
of society, controlling greed and usury among the more
powerful, and breaking down the walls that divide rich and
poor. Those with money and those without money will sit
together and worship the same God who created them. It is the
way they live and treat one another—not how many oxcarts
they can fill—that makes them a light to others. That is God's
definition of life in abundance.

DAVID MAXWELL

RESPONSE

What is your definition of life in abundance?

PRAYER

Thank you for those who have been lights to me. They have
come from many unexpected places in your world. Amen.

✧ WEDNESDAY ✧

Psalm 145:8–9, 14–21

REFLECTION

No fruit is sweeter and more fulfilling than knowing the
holy and graceful truth of this psalm: we are not prisoners
to our appetites, no matter how virtuous or profane our
hungers might be.

KATIE GIVENS KIME

RESPONSE

Reflect on your own experience of God's graciousness, mercy,
and compassion in your life.

PRAYER

God of compassionate love, help me to love others as you love
me. Amen.

✦ THURSDAY ✦

Romans 9:1–5

REFLECTION

The rabbis note that God writes the word, the law, on the heart
rather than in it (Jer. 31:33). They say this is so that, when the
heart breaks, the word falls into it. Absent the heartbreak, the
word is never internalized as completely. Maybe this is how
we come to know God, when God enters our hearts as fully as
we have entered God's, and we share some of the pain of
God's love rejected. Because surely God, embodied in the
Messiah (v. 5), grieves at our refusal to be part of the blessed
community (Matt. 23:37; Luke 13:34).

MARTHA C. HIGHSMITH

RESPONSE

Take some time this day to reflect on your experience of
coming to know God.

PRAYER

Enter my heart, O God, so your word may be written there.
Amen.

✦ FRIDAY ✦

Matthew 14:13–21

REFLECTION

God has entrusted us to be the body of Christ—the hands and feet through which God's work is done in the world. God does not work alone, but through people, you and me. To follow Jesus is to express our faith in concrete acts of love, justice, and compassion toward others. It is no accident that Matthew tells us that we will meet Jesus in reaching out to the "least" of our brothers and sisters—the hungry, the thirsty, the imprisoned.

CLIFTON KIRKPATRICK

RESPONSE

In what ways is your life an expression of following Jesus? What acts of love, justice, and compassion have formed you in faith?

PRAYER

Guide my feet and use my hands for your work in this world. Amen.

⇥ SATURDAY ⇤

Matthew 14:13–21

REFLECTION

The promise of the story of the feeding of the five thousand is that if we join together in unity and faithfulness, God will be with us. It is not a promise of the absence of struggle and pain—Jesus even had to go the way of the cross—but a promise that God will be with us and that God's intention for love, peace, and justice in the world will ultimately prevail.

CLIFTON KIRKPATRICK

RESPONSE

What stories can you recall of people of faith joining together in unity and faithfulness?

PRAYER

Mothering God, you feed me with the bread of life and in the community of the faithful who surround my life. I am indeed grateful. Amen.

✦ SUNDAY ✦

Isaiah 55:1–5

REFLECTION

The abundance of life beyond water and bread is given to this covenanted people, even when they are exiled and oppressed by political powers; indeed, God makes a way out of no way. Believing and trusting God's power and love are integral to a genuine faith for individuals and communities.

God's power, love, and generosity, then, underline the hope for the future where the exiled community stood as witness to these things. The cost for the community was not money but a loving commitment to a covenant with God. This covenant is the true feast, the full satisfaction to which the Israelite community is invited.

STEPHANIE Y. MITCHEM

Psalm 145:8–9, 14–21

REFLECTION

Not only does God uphold and sustain, not only does God govern, but God also watches with kindness (v. 17) and concern (v. 19). In other words, God is attentive; God notices. This characteristic of God expands the classical affirmations of providence by underlining God's deep connection with all the details. God knows the details, cares about them, and includes them in all divine actions and intentions.

LEANNE VAN DYK

Romans 9:1–5

REFLECTION

Day by day, week after week, we witness to the life of the one whose love redeems, sustains, and shapes us. In our words and in our actions, we must seek to live as Christ commands, follow his way, and share the love and hope that is in us. Finally, at the end of the day, we must entrust all to God, who so graciously loves and cares for all of us.

MARY BETH ANTON

Matthew 14:13–21

REFLECTION

The events that took place on that hillside in Galilee two thousand years ago were a miracle to the five thousand people assembled that day. However, the deeper message is the miracle of God's love for the six billion people on our planet today and the miracle that we are called to be partners with God in making fullness of life become a reality today for the world that God loves.

CLIFTON KIRKPATRICK

RESPONSE

As you read these reflections, what characteristics of God do you see? God is . . .

PRAYER

God of miracles, God who watches over all creation with generosity and kindness, help me to be one who extends this care to others. Amen.

❧ *Proper 14* ❦

1 Kings 19:9–18

He said, "Go out and stand on the mountain before the LORD, for the LORD is about to pass by." Now there was a great wind, so strong that it was splitting mountains and breaking rocks in pieces before the LORD, but the LORD was not in the wind; and after the wind an earthquake, but the LORD was not in the earthquake; and after the earthquake a fire, but the LORD was not in the fire; and after the fire a sound of sheer silence. (vv. 11–12)

Psalm 85:8–13

Steadfast love and faithfulness will meet;
    righteousness and peace will kiss each other.
Faithfulness will spring up from the ground,
    and righteousness will look down from the sky.
                    (vv. 10–11)

Romans 10:5–15

But what does it say?
  "The word is near you,
    on your lips and in your heart"
(that is, the word of faith that we proclaim). (v. 8)

Matthew 14:22–33

Peter answered him, "Lord, if it is you, command me to come to you on the water." He said, "Come." So Peter got out of the boat, started walking on the water, and came toward Jesus. But when he noticed the strong wind, he became frightened, and beginning to sink, he cried out, "Lord, save me!" (vv. 28–30)

1 Kings 19:9–18

REFLECTION

While neither Che [Guevara] nor Fidel [Castro] claimed to be a prophet of God, the revolutionary project they promoted—envisioning a world where widows, orphans, and strangers were protected against the cruel demands of a market economy gone wild—resonates with many who understand the divine connection. Elijah's picture certainly hung on the walls of many of the original hearers of today's text, much as pictures of Jesus and Che hang in the living rooms of today's shantytowns throughout Latin America, giving hope that God's justice will ultimately prevail.

DAVID MAXWELL

RESPONSE

What prophet's picture hangs on your wall?

PRAYER

I wait to hear your voice, ever-present God, in the sound of sheer silence. Amen.

✣ TUESDAY ✣

1 Kings 19:9–18

REFLECTION

For many, Sunday worship is the time we gather with others
on the same path, practicing Sabbath and listening for the
still small voice that reminds us of the project of life we are
constructing together.

DAVID MAXWELL

RESPONSE

What project of life is your congregation constructing?

PRAYER

Help me to be at the center of Sabbath life in my congregation,
listening for your voice and helping to construct life-giving
projects. Amen.

→ WEDNESDAY ←

Psalm 85:8–13

REFLECTION

We cannot see the entire path, or how God's grace will
intervene and make good from the pain of our lives; but even in
our unknowing, God is with us on that path, and when we need
to see the bend in the road ahead, the mist will clear enough for
our visibility.

KATIE GIVENS KIME

RESPONSE

Recall a time in your journey in the life of faith when the path
was not clear. What enabled you to continue walking?

PRAYER

God of my life, there are days when I need to be reminded
that my path is surrounded by your love and that your faithful
presence will spring up before me. Amen.

✦ THURSDAY ✦

Psalm 85:8–13

REFLECTION

Shalom means wholeness, completeness, fullness, balance, as well as peace in the sense of an absence of hostility or brokenness. A peace like this in our context today means not only that guns and bombs will fall silent, but also that gardens will be planted, houses rebuilt, and schools repaired.

LEANNE VAN DYK

RESPONSE

What does *shalom* mean to you?

PRAYER

Show me the seeds of *shalom* that you would have me plant. Amen.

⤳ FRIDAY ⤶

Romans 10:5–15

REFLECTION

In its broadest sense, evangelism is the work of those who are messengers of good news. The word itself has the same roots as "angel." No matter what the times are like, we could all use a little good news; we could all benefit from more angels around us.

MARTHA C. HIGHSMITH

RESPONSE

You are a messenger of God. What is your good news?

PRAYER

Surround me with your abiding presence, O God, so that your word is always near me, on my lips and in my heart. Amen.

✣ SATURDAY ✣

Matthew 14:22–33

REFLECTION

Stepping out in faith is not a guarantee that we will not
face troubled waters or be filled with fear, but it is always
accompanied by the assurance that Jesus will not abandon us,
that when we need it most, he will extend his arm to lift us up
and get us back in the boat.

CLIFTON KIRKPATRICK

RESPONSE

What do you most remember from a time when you stepped
out in faith?

PRAYER

Like Peter, I am sometimes afraid to step out in faith. Help me
remember you are there. Amen.

⚜ SUNDAY ⚜

1 Kings 19:9–18

REFLECTION

The most important lesson in this text is the twofold message of hope and challenge. God will prevail, but our knees must not bow to Baal. Defining Baal in our consumerist baalistic culture is very easy. Resisting and not bending has always been the challenge.

DAVID MAXWELL

Psalm 85:8–13

REFLECTION

It seems worth naming the longings of the hearts before you, without suggesting that God promises to tie up our long lists of requests with neat bows. While we do not fully grasp what God's arrangement of the kiss of justice and peace will look like—we know it may not be our vision—surely we have tasted that meal, and want more. Unpacking that desire might be a first move.

KATIE GIVENS KIME

Romans 10:5–15

REFLECTION

For these questioning Christians, it is important to understand that neither private piety nor street-corner sermons will do. What the apostle is urging is a life of interior and exterior authenticity, a life based on faith. We may not be able to change anything, but faith can change everything.

MARTHA C. HIGHSMITH

Matthew 14:22–33

Getting out of the boat with Jesus is the most risky, most exciting, and most fulfilling way to live life to the fullest. Matthew 14:22–33 invites us to do just that!

CLIFTON KIRKPATRICK

RESPONSE

What in these reflections is most comforting? What is most challenging? What do you most need to hear this day?

PRAYER

Hear the longings of my heart, this day and tomorrow and the next. Amen.

❧ *Proper 15* ☙

Isaiah 56:1, 6–8

For my house shall be called a house of prayer
    for all peoples.
Thus says the Lord GOD,
    who gathers the outcasts of Israel,
I will gather others to them
    besides those already gathered. (vv. 7c–8)

Psalm 67

May God be gracious to us and bless us
    and make his face to shine upon us, Selah
that your way may be known upon earth,
    your saving power among all nations. (vv. 1–2)

Romans 11:1–2a, 29–32

For the gifts and the calling of God are irrevocable. (v. 29)

Matthew 15:(10–20) 21–28

Then Jesus answered her, "Woman, great
is your faith! Let it be done for you as you wish."
And her daughter was healed instantly. (v. 28)

Isaiah 56:1, 6–8

REFLECTION

What defines a faithful person is not his or her sexual condition, nationality, or religion, says Isaiah. The faithful person is the one who loves the name of the Lord, keeps the Sabbath, and holds fast God's covenant. These things do not have to do with church affiliation but with a way of life that honors and protects every single creature created by God.

DAVID MAXWELL

RESPONSE

In conversations (personally or digitally) ask people you know to answer this question: What defines a faithful person?

PRAYER

God, you gather to you an amazing group of people. Open my eyes and ears to all who are close to you. Amen.

⟶ TUESDAY ⟵

Isaiah 56:1, 6–8

REFLECTION

This text is great news for the hurricane or tsunami survivors
who never left, scavenging a living while slowly rebuilding
their home and community. It is good news for the Mexican
day laborer who moved into the abandoned house next door
with his wife and children. It is good news for the Palestinian
Muslim refugee who was just placed in an apartment across
the street. It is good news for the neighbor who is a drag-
queen performer in the tourist district downtown. All these are
gathered by the God who gathers the outcasts of Israel. Given
an equal opportunity to embody goodness, justice, and caring
for one another, they will be joyful in God's house of prayer.

DAVID MAXWELL

RESPONSE

Who else do you know for whom this text is good news?

PRAYER

God of all, help me to be the bearer of goodness, justice, and
caring for all those I meet this day. Amen.

✦ WEDNESDAY ✦

Psalm 67

REFLECTION

Psalm 67 challenges modern communities of faith to apply ancient words of blessing in contemporary settings, as the psalmist did. In a culture where sharp lines are often drawn between "sacred" and "secular," rituals that are both ancient and new serve to unmask this division, revealing it as a false distinction.

ELIZABETH MCGREGOR SIMMONS

RESPONSE

What are some ways that ancient or new rituals can bridge the gap between sacred and secular?

PRAYER

God, be gracious to me, bless me, and shine your face on all I meet this day. Amen.

→ THURSDAY ←

Psalm 67

REFLECTION

A church in Maryland begins each school year with a *Blessing of the Backpacks*. On a Sunday in early September, the children and teens of the church bring their backpacks to worship. They are invited to come forward and to sit on the floor of the chancel. Each student is given a prayer pull that has been lovingly crafted by an adult member of the congregation. This prayer pull can be attached to a zipper on a backpack, a computer case, or a coat. The students are told, "The zipper pull is a reminder of God's presence with you at all times. God walks beside you when things are going well; God walks with you when you are facing the most challenging of situations. God is your strength when you are joyful and when you are grieving. Each zip is a prayer—God is with me. God is with you." The service of blessing concludes with a prayer for students, teachers, aides, bus drivers, administrators, custodians, and cafeteria workers.

ELIZABETH MCGREGOR SIMMONS

RESPONSE

In addition to zip prayers, what other kinds of prayers can you imagine saying with others in response to your reading of this psalm?

PRAYER

God is with me. God is with you, this I know. Amen.

✦ FRIDAY ✦

Romans 11:1–2a, 29–32

REFLECTION

There is no one beyond the reach of grace. God's call is also inescapable. Those who have received the gift of grace are also to accept the call of the Giver. Grace, then, is a call to discipleship. God no more rescinds the call than God revokes the grace.

MARTHA C. HIGHSMITH

RESPONSE

How are you being called to be God's disciple?

PRAYER

The gifts you have given me, Creator God, are amazing. Help me use them wisely. Amen.

✧ SATURDAY ✧

Matthew 15:(10–20) 21–28

REFLECTION

Again and again she violates boundaries, boundaries set up because of ethnicity, heritage, religion, gender, and demon possession. She must even contend with Jesus' reluctance to violate the ethnic boundary; but contend she does. In the grand scheme of Matthew, she believes that she and her daughter are people who should benefit from God's ruling activity (God's kingdom). So she is willing to break through the barriers, and breaking through the barriers dramatizes her faith. When the Canaanite believes that she and her daughter should receive mercy from the ruling activity of God, this is what Jesus calls faith.

JAE WON LEE

RESPONSE

Whom have you met recently who has a persistent faith like this?

PRAYER

Give me persistent faith, like that of the Canaanite woman. Amen.

⟶ SUNDAY ⟵

Isaiah 56:1, 6–8

REFLECTION

Upon their return, the former exiles are reminded of God's
immeasurable generosity through the divine invitation to
others. At the same time, they are called to do what is right,
acting in justice, and—implicitly—remaining faithful to the
covenant. The demands placed upon idol worshipers, which
they witnessed during exile, are contrasted with the hallmark
of God's loving-kindness. The former exiles themselves are
challenged to remain open, reflecting God's own loving-
kindness. This is how they will "maintain justice and do what is
right," as stated in the first verse. This is the true "return" of the
exiles.

STEPHANIE Y. MITCHEM

Psalm 67

REFLECTION

In modern cultures that vigorously propose alternate
frameworks, the affirmation that all good gifts come from God
steadies and orients the believer to the true source of life and
being. No, the stock market is not the source of all good things;
the marketplace is not the source of all good things; human
ingenuity and will is not the source of all good things; certainly
human power and control is not the source of all good things. It
is God who is the source of all that is good.

LEANNE VAN DYK

Romans 11:1–2a, 29–32

REFLECTION

These twin constants, gift and call, are signs of God's unbounded faithfulness, which is unaffected by anything we do and, at the same time, never ceases to call us back to our own faithfulness. The gift, the grace, is irrevocable, and so is the call.

MARTHA C. HIGHSMITH

Matthew 15:(10–20) 21–28

REFLECTION

Kyrie eleison—"*Lord, have mercy.*" The prayer rings down through the centuries, chanted in cloisters, whispered in hospitals, screamed out on battlefields. It is the cry of the soul in extremis, a raw witness to the depth and the misery of the human condition. On this occasion, Jesus is silent in the face of it. Remarkably, the woman is undeterred by Jesus' indifference. Still she keeps shouting.

IWAN RUSSELL-JONES

RESPONSE

What common threads do you hear in these reflections?

PRAYER

God, source of all that is good, have mercy on me this day. Amen.

❧ *Proper 16* ❧

Isaiah 51:1–6

Listen to me, my people,
and give heed to me, my nation;
for a teaching will go out from me,
and my justice for a light to the peoples. (v. 4)

Psalm 138

Though I walk in the midst of trouble,
you preserve me against the wrath of my enemies;
you stretch out your hand,
and your right hand delivers me.
The LORD will fulfill his purpose for me;
your steadfast love, O LORD, endures forever.
Do not forsake the work of your hands. (vv. 7–8)

Romans 12:1–8

I appeal to you therefore, brothers and sisters, by the mercies
of God, to present your bodies as a living sacrifice, holy and
acceptable to God, which is your spiritual worship. Do not be
conformed to this world, but be transformed by the renewing
of your minds, so that you may discern what is the will of God—
what is good and acceptable and perfect. (vv. 1–2)

Matthew 16:13–20

He said to them, "But who do you say that I am?"
Simon Peter answered, "You are the
Messiah, the Son of the living God." (vv. 15–16)

⤖ MONDAY ⤛

Isaiah 51:1–6

REFLECTION

The garden of joy, gladness, thanksgiving, and song that has
been prepared for the redeemed *will* endure. Hearers pressing
forward through barren, wasted lands can indeed find strength
in the temporary gardens God planted in the deserts of our
forebears, but even more in the expansive horizon of the garden
that will finally, unshakably, perennially thrive.

What do we do here in between?

Listen. Look. Give heed. Remind one another of what
has been and what will be when present circumstances look
hopeless.

ANGELA DIENHART HANCOCK

RESPONSE

Where are the barren places, places in your community where
hope is diminished?

PRAYER

Even in the desert, you are there, O God. Shine your light on
the places where your justice is needed. Amen.

✤ TUESDAY ✦

Isaiah 51:1–6

REFLECTION

Rather than seeking to fit non-Western worldviews of time (and therefore of eschatology) into a Western/Christian/modern framework, it is possible to see how this text creates an organic web that links memory, experience, and expectation at mutually enriching rather than progressive/linear points. The intertwining of these three keeps the meaning of life and the restoration of faith connected to the multifaceted journey of a communal faith. In other words, the faith of my ancestors and the promises of God to my ancestors belong not to me, but to those who share the same ancestry and embrace the same hope.

The Western/modern theological constructs of past, present, and future collapse in this wonderful text as God's promises *flow* through any human concept of time. God's salvation for all creation *flows* through us as we "do" memory, as we experience hope, and as we expect divine deliverance that never ends.

CARLOS F. CARDOZA-ORLANDI

RESPONSE

Where do you experience hope in your life, your church, and your community this week?

PRAYER

God of all, help me to remember the small part that I play in helping your saving work flow through me. Amen.

✢ WEDNESDAY ✢

Psalm 138

REFLECTION

We are not made whole simply so that we can feel better. We are restored, renewed, and lifted up so that we may rejoin God's great design and give thanks. A grateful, redeemed community is one that can face anything in trust. A grateful, redeemed community is charged to be a living witness to the steadfast care of the Almighty. In time, even the halls of power will recognize and give thanks to the one true Power.

JULIE PEEPLES

RESPONSE

What is your experience of being restored, renewed, or lifted up this day?

PRAYER

For your preserving and abiding presence in my life, I am grateful this day, O God. Amen.

→ THURSDAY ←

Romans 12:1–8

REFLECTION

When the Spirit dwells in the community of believers, a new
vitality will be its expression and various charisms will be its
gift. Then a new way of thinking, dwelling, relating, and acting
will reign in the community that stands in contrast to the ways
of the world—to the ways of the global domination system and
its myriad expressions.

ELEAZAR S. FERNANDEZ

RESPONSE

What evidence do you see of the Spirit's dwelling in your
community of believers?

PRAYER

Loving God, keep me in your transforming presence so I may
discern your will for my life. Amen.

✦ FRIDAY ✦

Matthew 16:13–20

REFLECTION

Scripture is not static; it must be reapplied to new situations.
Just as Jesus applies the teachings of the Torah in fresh and
creative ways, the church must be emboldened to interpret the
teachings of Jesus in new and inspired ways, attempting both
to be faithful to the teachings of Jesus as found in Matthew's
Gospel (and the rest of the New Testament) and to be open
to the voice of Jesus that speaks through the church to new
situations and problems.

MITCHELL G. REDDISH

RESPONSE

Think about situations and problems that are being faced by
your church and by your community. How is the voice of Jesus
speaking?

PRAYER

Jesus, help me be as bold as Peter as I interpret your life in new
ways. Amen.

☩ SATURDAY ☩

Matthew 16:13–20

REFLECTION

Peter's confession is distinctive in that Jesus presses him for it and then rewards him with a powerful blessing. This suggests that there is urgency in the theological enterprise; doctrine is not an add-on to what is essentially spiritual, but integral to religious experience itself. Theology and spirituality are two sides of the same divine encounter.

CHARLES E. HAMBRICK-STOWE

RESPONSE

What is your confession this day?

PRAYER

Bless me this day, O God, as I live in response to my confession of faith. Amen.

✦ SUNDAY ✦

Isaiah 51:1–6

REFLECTION

To "look" hard at our ancestors is a generative reminder that God's deliverance is swift and extends to the ends of creation. Heaven and earth will vanish, but salvation is forever. For Isaiah, the past is agency and energy; it is memory that shapes the current experience of the exile and generates new expectations for renewal and salvation.

CARLOS F. CARDOZA-ORLANDI

Psalm 138

REFLECTION

Where is there new strength of soul, a swelling of energy, new light breaking forth? How have challenging times in the past served to usher in unexpected blessings? Can we see God's hand sustaining, guiding us through to a better day? As individuals and as communities of faith, when we look back, we are amazed at the clear signs of YHWH's help, signs we could not detect when the suffering was at its worst. "We called you, and you answered us, you increased our strength of soul" (v. 3, adapted).

JULIE PEEPLES

Romans 12:1–8

REFLECTION

In the world, the faithful will need to engage as those who seek what is good and acceptable to God, and this will surely mean witnessing with their whole selves (presenting their bodies as a living sacrifice) against injustice and advocating for anyone who is marginalized because of matters such as the color of their

skin, their gender, their sexual orientation, their poverty, and/
or their immigrant status. In the church, the faithful will need
to let go of value systems that order relationships hierarchically
and embrace instead a value system that honors diversity
without destroying distinctly and equally valuable persons
("many members, and not all the members have the same
function," v. 4).

KIRK BYRON JONES

Matthew 16:13–20

REFLECTION
Jesus' question to each of us is, "Who do *you* say that I am?
What is *your* testimony of me? What is *your* experience of the
living God through my witness and presence?"

JIN S. KIM

RESPONSE
Where can you see a "new strength of soul, a swelling of energy,
new light breaking forth" from the voices and witness of the
lives of children, youth, and young adults in your church?

PRAYER
God, your guiding hand leads me into places I could never
imagine. Help me to continue to live my life as a testimony to
you. Amen.

❧ *Proper 17* ❧

Jeremiah 15:15–21

Your words were found, and I ate them,
   and your words became to me a joy
   and the delight of my heart;
for I am called by your name,
   O LORD, God of hosts. (v. 16)

Psalm 26:1–8

Prove me, O LORD, and try me;
   test my heart and mind.
For your steadfast love is before my eyes,
   and I walk in faithfulness to you. (vv. 2–3)

Romans 12:9–21

Live in harmony with one another; do not
be haughty, but associate with the lowly; do not claim to be
wiser than you are. Do not repay anyone evil for evil, but take
thought for what is noble in the sight of all. (vv. 16–17)

Matthew 16:21–28

From that time on, Jesus began to show his disciples that he
must go to Jerusalem and undergo great suffering at the hands
of the elders and chief priests and scribes, and be killed, and on the
third day be raised. And Peter took him aside and began to rebuke
him, saying, "God forbid it, Lord! This must never happen to you."
But he turned and said to Peter, "Get behind me, Satan! You
are a stumbling block to me; for you are setting your mind
not on divine things but on human things." (vv. 21–23)

⤞ MONDAY ⤝

Jeremiah 15:15–21

REFLECTION

Everybody has "a bad day" from time to time: moments when
things just do not turn out the way we would like them to turn
out. It is natural to expect that when we try to do our best or,
at least, when we have not intentionally or knowingly done
anything wrong, ordinarily, things will work out all right in
the end. Nevertheless, in spite of good intentions and best
efforts, there are times when plans fail, friends disappoint,
relatives do not understand, health falters, calamity strikes, or
stresses mount. Not surprisingly, we often ask ourselves and
God, *why*? In seminaries, students examine issues in what is
called *theodicy*—exploration of the reality that in spite of God's
goodness and omnipotence, evil exists. In popular culture the
question is framed more simply: *Why do bad things happen to
good people*?

RONALD E. PETERS

RESPONSE

Why do bad things happen to good people? In light of the
existence of evil, a more relevant question for the believer in
God might be, *how do I survive this mess*?

RONALD E. PETERS

PRAYER

For those who are struggling this day, I offer my heartfelt
prayer. Amen.

→ TUESDAY ←

Jeremiah 15:15–21

REFLECTION

The promise of God to the prophet and to all believers regarding *how to survive* unpleasant realities is clear: "If you turn back, I will take you back. . . . And I will make you . . . a fortified wall of bronze; . . . they shall not prevail over you, for I am with you to save you and deliver you" (vv. 19–20). When Christians follow the example of Christ, who prayed, "Not what I want but what you want" (Mark 14:36), self-centeredness is replaced by a God-centeredness that enables not only survival, but a sense of God's presence in the struggle that brings the best from us all, even the promise of overcoming struggle and tribulation.

RONALD E. PETERS

RESPONSE

In what area of your life do you need to turn back to God?

PRAYER

Give me the courage and grace to admit where I have strayed in my faith, and to offer that part of my life back to you. Amen.

✦ WEDNESDAY ✦

Psalm 26:1–8

REFLECTION

In verses 9 and 10, the innocence of the believer is contrasted with the sins of those who are called worthless, hypocrites, evildoers, and wicked. The first time one reads these verses it is natural to wish that the psalmist had been more precise. Exactly who is worthless or a hypocrite? Upon more reflection, it seems there is wisdom in the psalmist's brevity, because it makes it easier for us to think of the people we know who struggle with these sins, as well as the times when we ourselves wrestle with hypocrisy and sinful behavior. Even the most famous biblical characters sinned and were later declared innocent.

MARY ELISE LOWE

RESPONSE

When you think of someone whom you consider to be a hypocrite, do you think of another person—or yourself?

PRAYER

Before I point the finger at someone else for their sins, let me look deep within myself for my own, and ask your forgiveness. Amen.

✦ THURSDAY ✦

Romans 12:9–21

REFLECTION

Hospitality does not mean simply welcoming newcomers into our congregations and doing charitable acts, important as they are. We must move beyond hospitality as charity to hospitality as an act of justice. Hospitality as charity offers crumbs from our tables; hospitality as justice offers a place at the table. In the context of our predatory global market, hospitality involves transformation of the system that is inhospitable to many.

ELEAZAR S. FERNANDEZ

RESPONSE

What is distinctive about the community called church? What is the character and narrative of this community? What are the norms that guide and the practices that sustain this community?

ELEAZAR S. FERNANDEZ

PRAYER

May I do my part to make the church a place of hospitality for all. Amen.

Romans 12:9–21

REFLECTION

Then a few verses later Paul gives a closely related example of how we worship bodily, actively: "Do not repay anyone evil for evil. . . . if your enemies are hungry, feed them; if they are thirsty, give them something to drink" (vv. 17, 20). This is a tough injunction when we are dealing with enemies close at hand—that annoying person in the neighborhood, that recalcitrant elder at church. It is even harder to help the congregation think about how we embody love for the enemy when our whole political system seems to depend on identifying those whom we should fear and even those whom we should hate. What on earth would it mean to feed the Taliban or give Al-Qaeda something to drink? When can Christians think of public policy not just as prudential self-protection but as an expression of what we owe God—right worship?

DAVID L. BARTLETT

RESPONSE

Who are the people you consider to be "enemies" and why?

PRAYER

Let me find it in my heart to forgive even those whom I consider to be my enemies. Amen.

✣ SATURDAY ✣

Matthew 16:21–28

REFLECTION

Jesus is clearly not the professor or scribe who teaches
about the church from a distance, but the good shepherd
who lives with, leads, and feeds his sheep, heals their wounds,
protects them from their enemies, sleeps in the same fold as
them, and is willing to lay down his life for them. He is to
undergo great suffering at the hands of elders, chief priests,
and scribes because he desires to be the shepherd of the real,
messy, flesh-and-blood church instead of the invisible, pure,
and undefiled church, thereby exposing the gnostic lie for what
it is. If we want to follow him, then we are also going to have to
bleed, weep, sweat, and die, "for those who want to save their
life will lose it, and those who lose their life for my sake will
find it" (v. 25).

JIN S. KIM

RESPONSE

Upon reading this Scripture, what is the first concern that
comes into your mind?

PRAYER

I ask to be aware of my fears, so that I can confront them, with
your help. Amen.

✦ SUNDAY ✦

Jeremiah 15:15–21

REFLECTION

God, in love, has repeatedly relented from judging this people (Jer. 15:6). All the same, God will not stoop to their level and refuses to leave them in denial. God accepts the tension in this conflict, feels impelled to live it, refraining from judgment, persisting in the hope that "they . . . will turn" (v. 19). Jeremiah's public display of God's agony might provoke such a turning. For this reason, God wills that Jeremiah persist in inner turmoil, torn, like the divine self, between loving the people and hating their sin.

STEPHEN L. COOK

Psalm 26:1–8

REFLECTION

The psalmist cries out for vindication, for some acknowledgment from God. The psalmist clings to the hope that the Holy One, who knows the minds and hearts of all, will set things right. God is the only source of true and ultimate justice; this is the ground, the foundation, that offers support and sustenance. The sanctuary, the dwelling of the Almighty, has been exactly that: a sanctuary, a place where peace is restored, where right relationships are honored. To lose that would leave the petitioner bereft. God is the last and only hope for the unjustly accused.

JULIE PEEPLES

Romans 12:9–21

REFLECTION

Unquestionably, when visitors attend worship for the first time in a congregation rent with conflict, they are unlikely to return.

Growing churches often report that those who joined after a time of visiting did so because they found in the community a spirit that attracted them by its power of love and hospitality, not just in the way the members treated visitors, but also in the way they treated each other. Churches are practice fields for living the covenant of love Paul describes.

ROCHELLE A. STACKHOUSE

Matthew 16:21–28

REFLECTION

Our concern is not first and foremost the purity of the church or the rightness of our doctrine, but our willingness to follow Jesus into the world and onto the cross. We do not control God or give Jesus the conditions to our discipleship; instead, we risk contamination and insecurity by releasing the need to protect our own lives and institutions.

JIN S. KIM

RESPONSE

The concept of "loving the person but hating the sin" is a difficult one to implement in daily life. How do you do this? What makes it possible—or impossible—for you?

PRAYER

Lord, only by your mercy am I able to live as you have called me to do. Only by your grace am I forgiven for my sins. I pray that in my own life, I may reflect the love you have for me in the way that I approach others. Amen.

❧ *Proper 18* ❧

Ezekiel 33:7–11

Say to them, As I live, says the Lord God, I have
no pleasure in the death of the wicked, but that the wicked
turn from their ways and live; turn back, turn back from your
evil ways; for why will you die, O house of Israel? (v. 11)

Psalm 119:33–40

Lead me in the path of your commandments,
    for I delight in it.
Turn my heart to your decrees,
    and not to selfish gain.
Turn my eyes from looking at vanities;
    give me life in your ways. (vv. 35–37)

Romans 13:8–14

Owe no one anything, except to love one another; for the
one who loves another has fulfilled the law. The commandments,
"You shall not commit adultery; You shall not murder; You shall
not steal; You shall not covet"; and any other commandment, are
summed up in this word, "Love your neighbor as yourself."
Love does no wrong to a neighbor; therefore, love is the
fulfilling of the law. (vv. 8–10)

Matthew 18:15–20

"Again, truly I tell you, if two of you agree on earth
about anything you ask, it will be done for you by my
Father in heaven. For where two or three are gathered
in my name, I am there among them." (vv. 19–20)

⤙ MONDAY ⤚

Ezekiel 33:7–11

REFLECTION

The word "integrity" typically refers to the quality of inner moral and ethical character or strength. Integrity also calls to mind other words, like "reliability," "accountability," "genuineness," and even "legitimacy." A crucial point about faith in God is that the integrity or quality of the believer's relationship to God is always contingent upon the integrity or quality of the believer's relationship to others.

RONALD E. PETERS

RESPONSE

Do you consider yourself to be a person of integrity? How does this affect the way you conduct yourself in your daily life?

PRAYER

I long to be a person of integrity, to live a life worthy of your love. Amen.

⇥ TUESDAY ⇤

Ezekiel 33:7–11

REFLECTION

Our individual freedom to grasp life from God is the meaning of Ezekiel's metaphor of the sentinel. There exists an exit from the fast track to death; no one is trapped by collective guilt. To complain, "We're wasting away, we're wasting away," is ridiculous. If citizens listen to the warnings of a sentinel, they save their lives. The oracles of Ezekiel the sentinel aim not at despondency, but at transformed hearts and a transformed world.

Each 'adam is a unique, created subject of God, intended for life in relationship with God and neighbor. To will to exist as an 'adam is to choose to live into God's purpose in creating humanity. Both resolution and action are vital in this regard. To be oriented toward God, to bask in God's holiness, is to feel obliged to work for interconnection, mutuality, and wholeness in the world. To imagine that our will and work can mean nothing in this life is to remain captive to the defeatist and cowardly thinking that ensnared Ezekiel's audience.

STEPHEN L. COOK

RESPONSE

What work have you done that you are most proud of doing?

PRAYER

I choose to live my life in a healthy relationship with you and with my neighbor. Amen.

⇥ WEDNESDAY ⇤

Psalm 119:33–40

REFLECTION

Psalm 119:33–40 in particular offers two gifts to modern-day
seekers, gifts both timely and much in demand. The first of
these is to lift up the quality of wholeheartedness. Verse 34
asks, "Give me understanding, that I may keep your law and
observe it with my whole heart." Verses 36 and 37 invite God to
"turn my heart . . . [and] turn my eyes," in order to give them
their proper focus. Studying and living in God's way engages
the whole person, and when a person can give his or her whole
heart to such a path, the rewards include a greater depth for life,
a peace that cannot be destroyed by any of life's circumstances.

JULIE PEEPLES

RESPONSE

How does God reveal the divine self in my life? What is it
that has the power in my life that the law has in the life of the
psalmist, the power to keep me in relationship with God?

ELIZABETH P. RANDALL

PRAYER

Give me understanding, that I may keep your law and observe
it with my whole heart. Amen.

☙ THURSDAY ❧

Romans 13:8–14

REFLECTION

Love builds communities. It is more than a sentimental feeling. The love that does what is good to the neighbor is a love incarnate in the form of justice or right relation; it is a love that establishes egalitarian practices; it is a love that subverts covetousness and greed. Without forgetting ecological right relation, it is not far off to say that the earth provides enough for the needs of all, but not for the insatiable greed of the few. In its more rapacious form, this greed has assumed the cloak of savvy business practices under the aegis of the global market. In contrast, however, to the practices that dominate the wider sociopolitical atmosphere, faith communities are characterized by practices of radical love and generous hospitality.

ELEAZAR S. FERNANDEZ

RESPONSE

Choose five different words that define the word "love" for you.

PRAYER

I love you with my whole heart, O God—at least, that is my desire. Amen.

✢ FRIDAY ✢

Matthew 18:15–20

REFLECTION

The nature of the church of which Jesus speaks resonates with Paul's image of the body of Christ. Christ is in the church: "Whoever welcomes one such child in my name welcomes me" (18:5) and "where two or three are gathered in my name, I am there among them" (18:20). Each member is of great value, and no member may be considered superior to any others. Thus the church is not a voluntary association of like-minded individuals that regulates its corporate life by the will of the elite, the powerful, or the majority; it is a fellowship of believers united with one another in Jesus Christ under his headship.

CHARLES E. HAMBRICK-STOWE

RESPONSE

What part of the body of Christ are you?

PRAYER

Whatever it is you call me to do for the sake of the whole body of Christ, let me be faithful. Amen.

✦ SATURDAY ✦

Matthew 18:15–20

REFLECTION

The church is not fundamentally an institution or a denomination, but any place where two or three or more people live together in mutual interdependence under Christ. This requires casting off the yoke of individualism, which results in alienation, loneliness, anxiety, and distrust, into a profound trust of and commitment to people different from ourselves. This means that there will be conflict, but it is precisely through conflict that we model for the world how to bind and loose one another appropriately. Thereby we witness to the world Christ's ministry of reconciliation, which overcomes all divisions through the power of the cross. In this way, the body of Christ prefigures the eschatological healing and reconciliation of the whole groaning creation.

JIN S. KIM

RESPONSE

What makes it difficult for you to trust others?

PRAYER

Even when it is risky to trust another person, may I always put my trust in you. Amen.

✦ SUNDAY ✦

Ezekiel 33:7–11

REFLECTION

In verse 11 we find the center of gravity, and it is a glimmer
of hope. God's wish, purpose, and longing are that those who
wither among the dead will return to the land of the living.
God delights in the return of prodigals, in the prayers of tax
collectors, in the sole sheep who are recovered. For all the
conditional language at work in Ezekiel's prophecy, here is a
trace of a deeper theme: God desires to embrace human beings,
to show them what is good, and to enjoy them forever.

ANGELA DIENHART HANCOCK

Psalm 19:33–40

REFLECTION

In a most countercultural fashion, the psalmist speaks of
finding happiness, not as life's highest priority, but rather as a
byproduct of pursuing understanding of God's law. The freeing
discipline of such study and the subsequent ordering of life
afford new depths of joy, for these bring one closer to God.
Do you want to find greater happiness? Refrain from focusing
solely on the self; seek God and God's reign. You will find
greater happiness than you thought possible. Such a valuable
lesson emerges from the words of the psalmist. This is a lesson
that offers a needed corrective to our current way of life.

JULIE PEEPLES

Romans 13:8–14

REFLECTION

Paul, however, makes clear that love has very little to do
with emotion. The examples of love to which he refers have
to do with behavior rather than feelings. Love fulfills the

commandments not to break marriage vows and not to murder, steal, or covet. With the possible exception of the last in the list, these commandments concern action, not emotion. Our neighbors will know that we love them by how we treat them, not by greeting card aphorisms.

ROCHELLE A. STACKHOUSE

Matthew 18:15–20

REFLECTION

What makes us Christian is not *whether* or not we fight, disagree, or wound one another, but *how* we go about addressing and resolving these issues.

JIN S. KIM

RESPONSE

What are your highest priorities in life, as an individual, as part of a family, and as part of the church?

PRAYER

As I seek to discover and use my own gifts, I ask to be aware of and to encourage the gifts of others, so that together we may be your body in this time and place. Amen.

❧ *Proper 19* ☙

Genesis 50:15–21

But Joseph said to them, "Do not be afraid!
Am I in the place of God? Even though you intended to do
harm to me, God intended it for good, in order to preserve
a numerous people, as he is doing today." (vv. 19–20)

Psalm 103:(1–7) 8–13

For as the heavens are high above the earth,
    so great is his steadfast love toward those who fear him;
as far as the east is from the west,
    so far he removes our transgressions from us.
As a father has compassion for his children,
    so the LORD has compassion for those who fear him.

(vv. 11–13)

Romans 14:1–12

We do not live to ourselves, and we do not die
to ourselves. If we live, we live to the Lord, and if we die,
we die to the Lord; so then, whether we live or whether
we die, we are the Lord's. For to this end Christ died
and lived again, so that he might be Lord of
both the dead and the living. (vv. 7–9)

Matthew 18:21–35

Then Peter came and said to him, "Lord, if another
member of the church sins against me, how often should
I forgive? As many as seven times?" Jesus said to him, "Not
seven times, but, I tell you, seventy-seven times." (vv. 21–22)

✦ MONDAY ✦

Genesis 50:15–21

REFLECTION

Forgiveness is costly. It demands repentance and it should not happen without a long critical engagement between victims and perpetrators. Forgiveness goes hand in hand with issues of justice. Joseph's brothers talk about justice as a matter of simple reciprocity. Joseph changes this perspective and offers a new model of justice by way of forgiveness. How does our sense of forgiveness shape our understanding of justice? For us, as for Joseph and his brothers, forgiveness never comes without weeping.

CLAUDIO CARVALHAES

RESPONSE

Too often, we try to force forgiveness before we, or the one with whom there is an issue, are ready. What allows you to take the needed time for forgiveness to be honest?

PRAYER

Forgive me, allow me to forgive, and remind me to let your presence infuse the process of forgiveness with truth. Amen.

✣ TUESDAY ✣

Psalm 103:(1–7) 8–13

REFLECTION

Worship, after all, catches us up in both the promise and
threat of recognizing that the Holy and the profane can share a
common space. Far from removing us from ourselves in order
to find God, we become aware of ourselves before God when we
worship. In such a context, the complex relationships between
love and justice are less likely to be shaped by oppositions than
sublimations: love and justice touch in holiness. That is to say,
the demands of love and justice do not so much compete with
each other as complete each other.

MARK DOUGLAS

RESPONSE

Do you belong to or support specific organizations that fight for
justice? If not, consider finding one to which you can offer your
time and talents.

PRAYER

Inspire me to work to eliminate injustice in your world, O Lord.
Amen.

✣ WEDNESDAY ✣

Psalm 103:(1–7) 8–13

REFLECTION

We are told that God "redeems your life from the Pit" (v. 4).
Sin has a way of trapping us in just such a place of darkness
and confinement, from which we cannot hope to extricate
ourselves. By God's grace, the psalmist is lifted up from
that place into a whole new world—a world where God's
steadfast love stretches high overhead like the canopy of
heaven (v. 11), where sin has been removed "as far as the
east is from the west" (v. 12).

WALLACE W. BUBAR

RESPONSE

Think of a time when God redeemed your life from "the Pit,"
and give thanks.

PRAYER

As far as the east is from the west, so remove my sins from me.
Amen.

→ THURSDAY ←

Romans 14:1–12

REFLECTION

Once we stop seeing another person as a child of God and
view him or her instead as the personification of a sin, it
becomes easy to enjoy the energy of disdain and self-righteous
opposition. It becomes easy to lose oneself to opposition to
oppression, to define oneself in terms of one's opposition to sin.
The child of God before one is effaced as the enemy becomes
the personification of sin, and the child of God within one's self
is simultaneously and proportionally effaced as one identifies
one's self in terms of one's fight against oppression, against sin.

WILLIAM GREENWAY

RESPONSE

As easy as it is to see the sin in another person, consider that
there has probably been an instance (or instances) when
another person has seen the sin in you, when you have been the
enemy. How do you feel as you think of this?

PRAYER

If I have offended another of your children in any way, may
they find the grace to forgive me. Amen.

→ FRIDAY ←

Romans 14:1–12

REFLECTION

God invites us into an experience that has significance and purpose for our lives. That does not mean the same thing for every member of our faith community. Sometimes discovering or rediscovering that joy requires that we come out of our comfort zones, into a willingness to try new things. With this comes the responsibility of tolerance. Our spiritual practices, as well as our daily living, must grow from our own convictions, not the convictions of others. Otherwise our spiritual practices become empty rituals, devoid of significance and the power to transform.

GILBERTO COLLAZO

RESPONSE

What does it mean to observe the Sabbath? Are just certain days holy, or are all days holy?

JEANETTE A. GOOD

PRAYER

This is the day that you have made, O God; I rejoice and am glad in it! Amen.

⇥ SATURDAY ⇤

Matthew 18:21–35

REFLECTION

In order for there to be forgiveness, there must first be sin or debt. The servant who is brought before the king owes an outrageous sum that he has no chance of repaying. The king's first reaction, to sell this servant and his family, puts utter fear into the heart of the servant, such that he begs for mercy. Readers surmise that God is likewise ready and able to mete out cruel punishments in response to great debts. Traditional sources quickly reassure Christians, however, that it is never the king's desire to punish the servant, nor is it God's desire to punish sinners. Quite the contrary—the king's threat, like God's law, is a mirror that brings the servant/sinner to self-knowledge and repentance. Only when debtors acknowledge the overwhelming weight of their debt can they see the true greatness of God's mercy.

KATHRYN D. BLANCHARD

RESPONSE

List at least two ways in which you have owed a debt, either literally or figuratively. Were you able to get out of debt? What made that happen (or will make that happen)?

PRAYER

I am in your debt, but that is a debt that brings me new life. Thank you! Amen.

Genesis 50:15–21

REFLECTION

This insight into God's activities may be the final twist in this wonderfully deep story. In the end, it may not matter whether the repentance of the brothers is motivated by a desire for reconciliation or escape from retribution. It may not matter whether Joseph has been able to completely put behind him a desire to be lord over those who have treated him so unjustly. At the end of the story, as all through its many twists and turns, God is at work to bring about the redemption of Joseph and his brothers, to bring reconciliation to this shattered family. God is still busy imputing goodness in the midst of all the intentional and unintentional harm that we do.

TIMOTHY B. CARGAL

Psalm 103:(1–7) 8–13

REFLECTION

The collective memory of what God has done—of God's "benefits"—can give shape to our experiences of suffering. That memory binds us to God and God to us, and it binds us to one another so that when we do suffer, we may know that we do not bear our pain alone, that together we wait for redemption.

AMY ERICKSON

Romans 14:1–12

REFLECTION

The fundamental reason that believers cannot lord it over each other is that there is one Lord—and to that Lord, and that Lord alone, weak and strong alike owe allegiance. From that Lord, and that Lord alone, weak and strong alike receive welcome.

DAVID L. BARTLETT

Matthew 18:21–35

REFLECTION

Forgiveness means to release, to let go of the other.
Forgiveness is not denying our hurt. When we minimize what
has happened to us, gloss over it, tell ourselves that it was
not really that bad, we cannot really forgive. Forgiveness is a
possibility only when we acknowledge the negative impact
of another person's actions or attitudes in our lives, for
example, when children who have been abused by parents can
acknowledge what their parents did.

CHARLOTTE DUDLEY CLEGHORN

RESPONSE

In a time of suffering, who are the people and what are the
places that have brought relief to you or to a larger group (such
as those who have suffered the effects of a natural or human-
caused disaster)?

PRAYER

When I am weak, and when I am strong, you receive me into
your presence. Amen.

❧ *Proper 20* ❧

Jonah 3:10–4:11

Then the LORD said, "You are concerned about the bush, for which you did not labor and which you did not grow; it came into being in a night and perished in a night. And should I not be concerned about Nineveh, that great city, in which there are more than a hundred and twenty thousand persons who do not know their right hand from their left, and also many animals?" (4:10–11)

Psalm 145:1–8

I will extol you, my God and King,
    and bless your name forever and ever.
Every day I will bless you,
    and praise your name forever and ever.
Great is the LORD, and greatly to be praised;
    his greatness is unsearchable. (vv. 1–3)

Philippians 1:21–30

For to me, living is Christ and dying is gain. If I am to live in the flesh, that means fruitful labor for me; and I do not know which I prefer. I am hard pressed between the two: my desire is to depart and be with Christ, for that is far better; but to remain in the flesh is more necessary for you. (vv. 21–24)

Matthew 20:1–16

"'Take what belongs to you and go; I choose to give to this last the same as I give to you. Am I not allowed to do what I choose with what belongs to me? Or are you envious because I am generous?' So the last will be first, and the first will be last." (vv. 14–16)

✦ MONDAY ✦

Jonah 3:10–4:11

REFLECTION

We have to consider the ways in which God speaks to us and the ways we listen, for it is in this in-between space that our lives and the mission of the church come together. Jonah hears God's call and tries to flee. He does not want to do God's work—not only because it is dangerous and consuming, but also because he knows who God is.

CLAUDIO CARVALHAES

RESPONSE

How do we know God's mercy, and where do we discern the marks of God's wrath in the world?

CLAUDIO CARVALHAES

PRAYER

Push me to go to those places where I am reluctant to go, where I am called to do your will. Amen.

Psalm 145:1–8

REFLECTION

Perhaps it is a good thing that praise is not entirely natural.
Were it too natural, we might forget to question what we were
doing while offering praise. Asking who and why and how (and
where and when and by whom) keeps us alert to meaning and,
along the way, may train us in the very habits of discernment
that we will have to rely on if we are to gain a better sense of
how God has acted and is acting in the world so that we may
offer praise.

MARK DOUGLAS

RESPONSE

Does it matter who does this praising? Should praise be offered
only by those who feel they have benefited from God's work? If
so, what is the difference between offering praise and offering
thanks? Does the act of offering praise help train one in feeling
as if she has benefited from God's work? Should those who do
not feel like offering praise do so anyway, in order to change
their attitudes?

MARK DOUGLAS

PRAYER

I both praise you and give you thanks, for all that you have
done, for all that you are. Amen.

Psalm 145:1–8

REFLECTION

For those for whom praise comes slowly and who come to worship with heavy hearts, there is an invitation to offer a quieter response. The worshiper may "meditate" on God's "wondrous works" (v. 5) that at present lie outside the grasp of an individual's understanding but help to fashion a hope. For such people there is an assurance. The God praised in the psalm is "gracious and merciful, slow to anger and abounding in steadfast love" (v. 8).

RICHARD F. WARD

RESPONSE

What, for instance, makes someone or something praiseworthy? Is it something she does? Something he resists doing?

MARK DOUGLAS

PRAYER

Merciful God, you are indeed "gracious and merciful, slow to anger and abounding in steadfast love." Amen.

✦ THURSDAY ✦

Philippians 1:21–30

REFLECTION

Sometimes our eyes are so focused on the sky, waiting for our resurrection and "true life," that we miss in our present life the opportunities for the abundant life to which Christ calls us. We know that tomorrow holds promises of hope and joy. Our God, though, is also in our present, challenging us to look at life and its circumstances through the lens of hope that will bring a song of joy into our life. God has already spoken a word of life on our behalf. This spoken word will help us find hope in the midst of the most difficult situations life will lob at us.

GILBERTO COLLAZO

RESPONSE

Do we dare believe God's promises that we will experience life and life in abundance if we learn to live a life that trusts God even in the face of our greatest challenges?

GILBERTO COLLAZO

PRAYER

My life is already abundant in grace. Let that grace continue to overflow! Amen.

✦ FRIDAY ✦

Matthew 20:1–16

REFLECTION

How easily we can relate to the grumbling of the laborers who assumed that because they went into the vineyard early in the day, they would be paid more. Such dangerous assumptions can be in our closest relationships, within our work settings, within our congregations, within our national thinking. There is a saying, "Assumptions are planned resentments." Whenever we assume anything, we set ourselves up for possible disappointment or even worse, as we set the other person, place, or thing up as the object of our disappointment, anger, or resentment.

CHARLOTTE DUDLEY CLEGHORN

RESPONSE

Do we find ourselves envious of another's gifts, talents, abilities, possessions, social status, and so forth? How often am I envious of others' good fortune?

CHARLOTTE DUDLEY CLEGHORN

PRAYER

Free me from the envy I may have for the abundance in the lives of others. Amen.

⇥ SATURDAY ⇤

Matthew 20:1–16

REFLECTION

It would be wonderful if these were the only assumptions we made:

—God loves me and all of creation deeply and profoundly.
—I and all others are made in the image of God.
—God's generosity is beyond our wildest imagination.
—There is nothing I can do to earn or deserve God's generosity.

How different our lives would be if we lived from those assumptions!

CHARLOTTE DUDLEY CLEGHORN

RESPONSE

Are we unable to celebrate another's good fortune because we have not celebrated our own? How often am I ungrateful for God's graciousness and mercy? How often do I deny God's love and forgiveness in my own life?

CHARLOTTE DUDLEY CLEGHORN

PRAYER

Sometimes my heart is hardened; in this moment, I ask for release. Amen.

✦ SUNDAY ✦

Jonah 3:10–4:11

REFLECTION

Like many people, Jonah not only thankfully receives God's acts of deliverance and grace directed toward him (2:9) but even seems to develop a sense of entitlement toward them. However, when it comes to extending that same longing for God's grace to others, he is slow to make the connection. Maybe one can hope for God's nurture for those who are themselves the conduit for God's grace to us.

TIMOTHY B. CARGAL

Psalm 145:1–8

REFLECTION

Most of the verbs used throughout the psalm's first eight verses reflect a certain joyful exuberance: "extol" (v. 1), "praise" (v. 2), "laud" (v. 4), "declare" (v. 4), "proclaim" (v. 6), "celebrate" (v. 7), "sing aloud" (v. 7). There is no room here for keeping one's faith quietly to oneself. There is something about the grandeur of God that evokes a response, calling forth our gladdest praise and prompting us to stand up and shout from the rooftops about the mighty works of God.

WALLACE W. BUBAR

Philippians 1:21–30

REFLECTION

To be clear, the classic Christian hope in the reality of heaven is not in question—there are some contexts where, qualified carefully, one might perhaps say lovingly, "Dying is/was gain." The problem Paul discerns concerns the typically dangerous dynamics of that hope vis-à-vis oneself, namely, that it facilitates pseudospirituality (wholly of this world) that serves selfishness and delivers spiritual destruction.

WILLIAM GREENWAY

Matthew 20:1–16

REFLECTION

This parable is essentially about the generosity of God. It is not about equity or proper disbursement of wages but about a gracious and undeserved gift. It is not about an economic exchange but, rather, about a bestowing of grace and mercy to all, no matter what time they have put in or how deserving or undeserving we may think them to be. God's generosity often violates our own sense of right and wrong, our sense of how things would be if we ran the world.

CHARLOTTE DUDLEY CLEGHORN

RESPONSE

Is God looking merely for obedience, or does God desire actions that arise from hearts conformed to God's own heart?

TIMOTHY B. CARGAL

PRAYER

I long to have a heart like yours, O God. May my life be spent in that quest. Amen.

❧ *Proper 21* ❦

Ezekiel 18:1–4, 25–32

Cast away from you all the transgressions that you have committed against me, and get yourselves a new heart and a new spirit! Why will you die, O house of Israel? For I have no pleasure in the death of anyone, says the Lord GOD. Turn, then, and live. (vv. 31–32)

Psalm 25:1–9

Make me to know your ways, O LORD;
    teach me your paths.
Lead me in your truth, and teach me,
    for you are the God of my salvation;
    for you I wait all day long. (vv. 4–5)

Philippians 2:1–13

If then there is any encouragement in Christ, any consolation from love, any sharing in the Spirit, any compassion and sympathy, make my joy complete: be of the same mind, having the same love, being in full accord and of one mind. Do nothing from selfish ambition or conceit, but in humility regard others as better than yourselves. Let each of you look not to your own interests, but to the interests of others. Let the same mind be in you that was in Christ Jesus. (vv. 1–5)

Matthew 21:23–32

"For John came to you in the way of righteousness
and you did not believe him, but the tax collectors and
the prostitutes believed him; and even after you saw it, you
did not change your minds and believe him." (v. 32)

✦ MONDAY ✦

Ezekiel 18:1–4, 25–32

REFLECTION

What is at stake here in the voice of God is not the dismissal of the rolling effect that one generation's deeds and thoughts has over the next, but rather rejecting a specific theological view on sinful behaviors that ends up creating a cascading effect of blaming people for their parents' behaviors instead of for their own actions.

CLAUDIO CARVALHAES

RESPONSE

Is God fair or more than fair? How is "God's Word" different from an everyday proverb?

TODD M. HOBBIE

PRAYER

Your word is a lamp to my feet and a light to my path. Amen.

→ TUESDAY ←

Psalm 25:1–9

REFLECTION

Psalms may be full of praise but they are not simply "praise music," meant to carry us up out of the human condition into the realm of glory. They ask, instead, for God to be present in this condition—to engage enemies, to respond to tears, to take care of the faithful. As jarring as it may be in the rarified and tolerant air of comfortable contemporary Western liberalism, avoiding defeat in front of one's enemies and shaming them instead is a prayer that makes sense in the context of a life in which pain and suffering are regular occurrences, real enemies are nearby, and misfortune is only a day or a season away.

MARK DOUGLAS

RESPONSE

Is it ever right to shame another person, and if so, in what circumstances?

PRAYER

Be present in the lives of those who live in danger. Amen.

☙ WEDNESDAY ❧

Psalm 25:1–9

REFLECTION

Prayer frequently involves both petition and praise, and in this specific case the speaker offers his brokenness to God at the outset, in the hopes of being protected and reformed. This dynamic is apparent in verse 2: "O my God, in you I trust; do not let me be put to shame." This line indicates the psalmist's absolute dependence on God and need to be reformed and constantly taught. It also reflects the complex relationship between confidence and brokenness throughout the Psalter. An individual expresses complete trust in God's ability to make all things possible, including human redemption, but Psalm 25 and other psalms like it also acknowledge the human tendency to make poor choices and the fear that this will lead to terrible consequences, such as isolation, defeat at the hands of one's enemies, even death.

SAMUEL L. ADAMS

RESPONSE

Acknowledge a time when you have made a poor choice. What were the consequences? Would you respond differently now?

PRAYER

May I learn wisdom from my errors, and allow your good to shine through my darker days. Amen.

✣ THURSDAY ✣

Philippians 2:1–13

REFLECTION

This passion empties one of self. One does not "self-empty" by focusing upon oneself. One is emptied of self to the degree one is overcome by the needs, pains, hopes, and desires of others. When concern for others takes one utterly beyond self-interest, beyond obsession with achievements and self-obsessing guilt over failures, beyond self, then one receives the comfort of an Easter "yes" so overwhelming, unconditional, undeniable, and absolute that it is experienced as unfailing and forever—a yes more potent and enduring than any imaginable no.

WILLIAM GREENWAY

RESPONSE

Take an inventory of the concerns that are troubling you right now. Which are important and which should you let go?

PRAYER

Empty me of concerns that crowd my spirit when I ought to be more aware of concerns that deserve my attention. Amen.

⤳ FRIDAY ⤳

Philippians 2:1–13

REFLECTION

We are called to be imitators of Christ, to live in a way that allows other people to see Christ in us. What is an imitator? There is a great difference between an impersonator and an imitator. Impersonators take great pains to make people believe they are who they are not. On the other hand, imitators are clearly aware that they strive to live up to the challenge of being a reflection of the person they look up to. It is so hard to walk in the footsteps of others. Many younger siblings for years wither in the shadow of an overachieving older sibling, who sets the standard so high that it is a constant frustration to try to be like him or her. We look up to those people in church whom we consider spiritual giants and wonder if we will ever be as spiritual as they appear. At work there is always that coworker who is the top salesperson, who makes us wonder if we really have what it takes to live up to those high standards, no matter how hard we try.

GILBERTO COLLAZO

RESPONSE

When is imitation of another something that provides spiritual growth, and when does it cause the opposite effect?

PRAYER

Even as I value the gifts of others, I long to be an imitator of the qualities I find in the risen Christ. Amen.

✦ SATURDAY ✦

Matthew 21:23–32

REFLECTION

The tax collectors and prostitutes believed him; the chief priests and elders did not. The question is not first of all between saying and doing but between believing John and not believing John. Of course, the authority and status of John the Baptist and Jesus of Nazareth are intertwined. Both come in the way of righteousness; both come, by implication, with authority from heaven. Thus one's status in the kingdom depends upon one's reaction to Jesus and John. It is by this act of believing that those of lowest social rank acquire higher status than those of highest social rank. The real failure of the chief priests and elders is that they do not receive Jesus. . . .

. . . Thus, to believe John and Jesus is to walk in the way of righteousness in both words and deeds.

LEWIS R. DONELSON

RESPONSE

What is it like to answer a question to which you know the correct answer but that you do not want to hear? What is it like to be asked a question that may call you to change your mind, your ways of being and doing?

CHARLOTTE DUDLEY CLEGHORN

PRAYER

Lord, I believe; help my unbelief! Amen.

✦ SUNDAY ✦

Ezekiel 18:1–4, 25–32

REFLECTION

God's answer is grace. God is willing to remove the consequence of death from those who have "considered and turned away from all the transgressions that they had committed" (v. 28). There does seem to be one nonnegotiable in God's position: those who would receive grace must admit their need for it. They must, as God puts it, "Turn, then, and live" (v. 32). Life is available to all who admit their ultimate reliance upon grace.

TIMOTHY B. CARGAL

Psalm 25:1–9

REFLECTION

The psalmist's personal experience of God's mercy leads her to declare that this divine mercy knows no bounds. God will lead the humble in what is right and teach the humble God's way. All who are willing will be taught to live in a way that honors a merciful and just God. With a good and merciful God in the lead, there will be no more cause for anxiety about how to live a good life, no more questions about which path is the right path, for "all the paths of YHWH are steadfast love and faithfulness" (v. 10).

AMY ERICKSON

Philippians 2:1–13

REFLECTION

Deep down inside, many of us have the clear understanding that we will fall short of a perfect imitation. That is all right. Ultimately Paul's admonition is not about impersonating

Christ, but about adopting Christlike attitudes in all aspects of our life. When we try to live up to God's standards on our own, we become impersonators. That is a tall order and an unrealistic expectation on our part, and it is not what God expects of us.

GILBERTO COLLAZO

Matthew 21:23–32

REFLECTION

In this exchange, the interviewee becomes the interviewer; the one questioned becomes the questioner. Jesus not only avoids the religious leaders' trap; more importantly, he places the question of his authority back on them. Moreover, his question not only outwits the religious leaders; it also unmasks their deepest priorities and concerns. They are not primarily interested in Jesus' true identity or in discovering how God would have them respond to Jesus.

CHARLES CAMPBELL

RESPONSE

Which Christlike attributes do you most long to have in your life?

PRAYER

I pray that even when I fall short, I will never fall from your grace. Amen.

❧ *Proper 22* ❧

Isaiah 5:1–7

What more was there to do for my vineyard
    that I have not done in it?
When I expected it to yield grapes,
    why did it yield wild grapes? (v. 4)

Psalm 80:7–15

Turn again, O God of hosts;
    look down from heaven, and see;
have regard for this vine,
    the stock that your right hand planted.
                (vv. 14–15)

Philippians 3:4b–14

Beloved, I do not consider that I have made
it my own; but this one thing I do: forgetting what
lies behind and straining forward to what lies ahead,
I press on toward the goal for the prize of the heavenly
call of God in Christ Jesus. (vv. 13–14)

Matthew 21:33–46

Jesus said to them, "Have you never read in the scriptures:

    'The stone that the builders rejected
        has become the cornerstone;
    this was the Lord's doing,
        and it is amazing in our eyes'? (v. 42)

✦ MONDAY ✦

Isaiah 5:1–7

REFLECTION

It is difficult to live with the consequences when a child reared in a loving home makes unwise choices and dashes the hopes and dreams of his or her parents; when regular and prudent investments fall prey to difficult economic times and retirement is placed on hold; when a longtime loyalty to one employer is met with an ill-timed layoff in the face of a plant closure. In times like these we are forced to reevaluate our identity, goals, and relationships. It is difficult when we do the right thing yet are forced to live with the consequences of other people's poor decisions. We can plow under the garden, but what do we do with relationships that matter? How do we judge ourselves in light of such relationships?

JEFFRY W. CARTER

RESPONSE

What does it mean to say that God "feels"? What are the relative risks of anthropomorphism and abstraction? When we say that we are created in God's image, does that mean that the very things we believe make us most human, such as emotion, are also true of God?

JAMES BURNS

PRAYER

How am I made in your image? May my life give honor to you. Amen.

⇸ TUESDAY ⇷

Psalm 80:7–15

REFLECTION

As humans, we cannot treat God as merely the projection of
our needs for security. If God is God, then God is far more
than we hope. Perhaps we discover this fact most clearly when
our prayers go unanswered and our hopes remain unfulfilled,
for then we are faced with a reality that dispels our aspirations.
We encounter experiences that reveal our projections. In those
moments, how do we respond? Do we continue to impose
on God conditions for our faith and obedience, as did the
psalmist? Do we accept the new reality that is encountering
us and continue to have faith in the midst of our doubts and
questions?

STEPHANIE MAR SMITH

RESPONSE

Reflecting on the reality of your life, what questions or doubts
have challenged your faith? What conditions for faith have you
imposed on God?

PRAYER

With no demands or requests, I only offer my praise and thanks
for your loving-kindness. Amen.

Psalm 80:7–15

REFLECTION

God is portrayed as both the problem—God has not cared for or protected the people from calamity (probably a defeat of some kind)—and the solution. The psalm expresses the pain of the calamity and anger at God for allowing it to happen; at the same time it includes a repetitive refrain containing the people's cry to God for help.

Underlying the entire psalm is a foundation of faith and trust that, even though God is the source of the problem, God will nonetheless save and restore the people. This psalm goes well with the other Old Testament lection (Isa. 5:1–7). In times of community or national or even international distress, this psalm allows for the expression of true feelings in the context of an ongoing faith relationship.

MARY E. SHIELDS

RESPONSE

Does God ever seem a problem to you? Has there been a time when you blamed God for a difficulty in your life, or in the world?

PRAYER

How grateful I am that you can absorb my anger and accusations, and that you love me still. Amen.

✦ THURSDAY ✦

Philippians 3:4b–14

REFLECTION

Paul uses personal testimony and other examples to authenticate and energize his call to action. What is that call? Paul encourages the believers at Philippi to hold on to and live out core Christian values. The primary goal of faith, in Paul's view, is to know or experience Christ. Communal life is to be centered on attaining this ultimate prize. None of the identity markers that say we are people of faith is more important than a community's heart-centered desire to know and to be like Christ.

JILL Y. CRAINSHAW

RESPONSE

Write down the Christian values that guide the way you live your life.

PRAYER

I have a heart-centered desire to know and be like you, my Savior! Amen.

❧ FRIDAY ❧

Matthew 21:33–46

REFLECTION

Embedded within this parable of rejection of and deadly violence against the landowner's son is the reminder that the heart of faith is relationship with Jesus. The tenants did not seize and kill an idea, a principle, or a system of doctrine. They seized and killed the landowner's son. The gospel comes to us as a person.

ANDREW PURVES

RESPONSE

Pause and give thanks for the sacrifices Christ made for you.

PRAYER

Jesus, I thank you with my whole heart and soul and mind and strength. Amen.

✢ SATURDAY ✦

Matthew 21:33–46

REFLECTION

The idea of Israel rejecting God stands at the heart of this parable. This same problem of rejecting God takes many forms today. First, there are those people who simply declare that there is no God. They see the beauty and order of creation. They acknowledge the power and splendor of the universe. They do not deny the perfectly designed "vineyard" in which they are allowed to live. They simply deny that they have any obligation to whoever is responsible for this arrangement. They attribute creation to random chance and unregulated circumstances. We reject God when we reject the work of God as creator and sustainer of the universe.

MARVIN A. MCMICKLE

RESPONSE

Begin and end your day—every day—by taking a few moments to look at the sky and give thanks for the beauty of the universe.

PRAYER

You created the heavens and the earth, and how beautiful is your creation! Amen.

✦ SUNDAY ✦

Isaiah 5:1–7

REFLECTION

It is a hard lesson to learn that even our most diligent preparations do not always lead to desired results. Parents understand this feeling. Pouring every possible bit of care, protection, and nurture into another person may not be enough. You can set a good example, take your child to church, and move to a better neighborhood, but the child may still go astray. What does it mean that God feels that same pain?

JAMES BURNS

Psalm 80:7–15

REFLECTION

Too often religious practice differentiates between piety and practice, spirituality and social responsibility. True religion, the psalmist seems to suggest, is more integrated than that. Since God is about the business of integrating all of the aspects of human life, including the here and now and the yet to come, we should be committed to that business as well.

JOHN WILKINSON

Philippians 3:4b–14

REFLECTION

The stories of success and failure that we tell of our churches, our communities, and ourselves are open to revision in light of God's astounding action in Christ. The story is not yet finished; but, although we have glimpsed the ending, letting God revise the plot requires new habits of perception. One imagines that Paul's initial audit, sprung on him by God, was subsequently bolstered by such habits. It is remarkable enough to sit in a prison cell and write encouraging letters to others, more remarkable yet to offer a sincere invitation to "rejoice in the Lord always" (Phil. 4:4).

NATHAN EDDY

Matthew 21:33–46

REFLECTION

Another way in which we reject God occurs when we reject some of God's people for reasons of our own. Human beings are capable of doing terrible things to other people whom they are somehow able to define as less worthy, less human, less valuable than themselves. If we can manage to turn another human being into the "other," there is no limit to what we will do or will allow to be done to them. We can be as brutal to one another as were the men who beat, stoned, and killed people in Matthew 21:35–37.

MARVIN A. MCMICKLE

RESPONSE

What does such brokenness look like? What are the postures and activities that lead us to seek God? What does salvation look like? What does restoration look like? What does it look like and feel like when God's face shines on us and on our broken and fearful world? How do we respond to this good news of salvation?

JOHN WILKINSON

PRAYER

Heal my broken places, restore my soul, fill me with gratitude, and make me an instrument of your peace. Amen.

❧ *Proper 23* ❧

Isaiah 25:1–9

And he will destroy on this mountain
    the shroud that is cast over all peoples,
    the sheet that is spread over all nations;
    he will swallow up death forever. (vv. 7–8a)

Psalm 23

Even though I walk through the darkest valley,
    I fear no evil;
for you are with me;
    your rod and your staff—
    they comfort me. (v. 4)

Philippians 4:1–9

Rejoice in the Lord always; again I will say, Rejoice. Let your gentleness be known to everyone. The Lord is near. Do not worry about anything, but in everything by prayer and supplication with thanksgiving let your requests be made known to God. And the peace of God, which surpasses all understanding, will guard your hearts and your minds in Christ Jesus. (vv. 4–7)

Matthew 22:1–14

"Then the king said to the attendants, 'Bind him hand and foot, and throw him into the outer darkness, where there will be weeping and gnashing of teeth.' For many are called, but few are chosen." (vv. 13–14)

✦ MONDAY ✦

Isaiah 25:1–9

REFLECTION

No one should take divine judgment lightly—not least God's chosen people. The chosen ones, more than anyone else, should recognize what such judgment finally reveals. In Isaiah 25's retrospective vision, Israel's sojourn through exile and return bears witness to the God of reversals, prompting a prospective vision for the entire human race, the hope for an end to humanity's cosmic exile. The strength of this claim matches and then surpasses the severity of the diagnosis that preceded it: God will destroy death itself, the pall hanging over all people, and wipe away the tears from every eye (vv. 7–8).

JAY EMERSON JOHNSON

RESPONSE

Does our hope take us only as far as our own backyard? Is the God on whom we wait too small?

JAY EMERSON JOHNSON

PRAYER

Even in the darkest valleys, you are my hope and salvation. Amen.

✦ TUESDAY ✦

Isaiah 25:1–9

REFLECTION

Thus the table is set for friend and foreigner, strong and weak, wealthy and needy. Together they are reconciled and share in a common meal, and in keeping with Isaiah's larger theme, the meal gives occasion to share the promise of God's salvation. "He will destroy on this mountain the shroud that is cast over all peoples, the sheet that is spread over all nations; he will swallow up death forever. Then the Lord GOD will wipe away the tears from all faces, and the disgrace of his people he will take away from all the earth" (vv. 7–8). Amid the memory of death, ruin, and disgrace, and during a banquet that speaks of God's activity and purpose, Isaiah proclaims that God is a God of life and not of death—a God who ends war, slavery, and exile, not by political power or military might, but by upholding past promises.

JEFFRY W. CARTER

RESPONSE

Invite a friend or family member into your home for a meal. Enjoy a time of gathering around a table in friendship and peace.

PRAYER

Remove the shroud around me, open my eyes, and let your light shine! Amen.

Psalm 23

REFLECTION

Fear is the opposite of love. Our friendship with God is not based on fear. In fact, many of us must overcome fear of God as we begin our friendship with God. When we overcome our fear of God and enter into friendship with God, no other fear may conquer us. We become fearless with God at our side. We trust God. We have experienced God's discipline and support. We know God will defend us from all evil. The Good Shepherd imparts courage and comfort in times of need.

JON BURNHAM

RESPONSE

Do you think of God as a friend? How can that help or inhibit your faith?

PRAYER

You are a friend in whom I can confide, who loves me as I am, and who encourages me to be all that I can be. Amen.

→ THURSDAY ←

Philippians 4:1–9

REFLECTION

As Jesus' mother Mary and his foster father Joseph assisted one another in the commonest of human tasks, so Paul engaged in a panoply of tasks to help forge a family of followers of Jesus. So it has ever been: beyond the ever-present forbearance toward one another, what followers of Jesus consistently enjoy is the gift of following one another along the path offered. That has of course been the witness of holy women and men throughout the history of this community, as those who are forbearing toward one another also call each other forth to live faithfully to the call of the "God of peace," who is ever living in their midst, recognizable in their fellow travelers.

DAVID B. BURRELL

RESPONSE

Think of the people who are on the faith journey with you, and write a few of them notes of thanks.

PRAYER

I am not on this journey of faith alone. I give thanks for those who walk the path with me. Amen.

✦ FRIDAY ✦

Philippians 4:1–9

REFLECTION

Seasons of identity exploration and maturing hold the potential to remind communities of the profound extraordinariness of what seems merely ordinary. Keep on with your everyday works of gentleness and prayerful living, Paul counsels the Philippians (v. 4). Bake a loaf of bread for the woman down the street whose husband just died, Paul might say to contemporary believers. Take a bag of groceries to the food closet. Visit a church member in the nursing home. Seemingly ordinary acts bear extraordinary gifts of God's love. Ordinary Time, through Scripture and gospel acts of caring, teaches communities about the persistent, everyday powerful, promises of God's grace in Christ.

JILL Y. CRAINSHAW

RESPONSE

Choose one of the options in the reflection above—bake a loaf of bread for someone, visit a church member in a nursing home—and put it on your agenda, at the top of the list.

PRAYER

Expand my awareness to seek out and find another person to whom I can show kindness and Christian compassion. Amen.

SATURDAY ←

Matthew 22:1–14

REFLECTION

Within the Christian community there are those members like the ones in the parable who refuse the invitation from God in one way or another. They want the safe, soft side of discipleship, but they shy away from the more difficult work of outreach and social justice. They want blessings from God, but they cannot be found when it is time to share in the work of ministry. They can always be counted on to share in a free dinner at the church, but they are not willing to serve a meal in the hunger center or hand out a bag of groceries at the food pantry. They want peace on earth, but they do not want to work toward that end. They want to end world hunger, but they do not want to miss a meal themselves or make a contribution to work toward that end.

MARVIN A. MCMICKLE

RESPONSE

Are you like the people in the parable who ignore God's invitation to serve?

PRAYER

In service to you, I find wholeness and joy. Amen.

Isaiah 25:1–9

REFLECTION

No matter how desperate the circumstances one starts from, a powerful vision for a better tomorrow can take hold. First, simply offer praise and acknowledge who God is. Then, remember God's faithfulness in the past. Next, look for signs of God at work in the present, and finally expect to see God move in the lives of others, even enemies. This creates a foundation upon which even the loftiest promises can be heard and believed.

JAMES BURNS

Psalm 23

REFLECTION

When churches celebrate the Eucharist, we celebrate this hospitality of God, who is both the host and the meal. We witness to this aspect of divine character by providing in ourselves and in our churches a merciful and compassionate space for others to encounter God.

STEPHANIE MAR SMITH

Philippians 4:1–9

REFLECTION

Our anxiously ironic, spiritually seeking age needs God's good news in this text. Unaffected, childlike rejoicing in the Lord is the hallmark of the Christian life. Soaring over everything else that fills church calendars, joy is the command to all who know Christ. For Paul, joy and life beyond constant worry come not when one has mastered this or that spirituality, or when they arrive "special delivery" from God, but when one perceives God's action even amid difficulty and pain.

NATHAN EDDY

Matthew 22:1–14

REFLECTION

Gospel living only begins with the invitation. It cannot remain a mere idea; its sine qua non is a transformed life. Though many have been called, the ones who are to be chosen are those who are living in a new way—who have put on life in Christ, as Paul will exhort "God's chosen ones, holy and beloved," in the church at Colossae to "clothe yourselves with compassion, kindness, humility, meekness, and patience. Bear with one another and, if anyone has a complaint against another, forgive each other" (Col. 3:12–13)—as the rebellious tenants in the vineyard could not bring themselves to do.

RICHARD E. SPALDING

RESPONSE

What garment of faith are you currently wearing, and which do you need to add to your closet? Compassion, kindness, humility, meekness, patience, forgiveness?

PRAYER

I clothe myself in the garments of faith. May I wear them well! Amen.

✤ *Proper 24* ✤

Isaiah 45:1–7

I call you by your name,
　　I surname you, though you do not know me.
I am the LORD, and there is no other;
　　besides me there is no god. (vv. 4b–5)

Psalm 96:1–9 (10–13)

Ascribe to the LORD the glory due his name;
　　bring an offering, and come into his courts.
Worship the LORD in holy splendor;
　　tremble before him, all the earth. (vv. 8–9)

1 Thessalonians 1:1–10

We always give thanks to God for all of you and
mention you in our prayers, constantly remembering before
our God and Father your work of faith and labor of love and
steadfastness of hope in our Lord Jesus Christ. (vv. 2–3)

Matthew 22:15–22

Then he said to them, "Give therefore to the emperor
the things that are the emperor's, and to God the things
that are God's." When they heard this, they were amazed;
and they left him and went away. (vv. 21b–22)

✣ MONDAY ✣

Isaiah 45:1–7

REFLECTION

The world is filled with friendly churches. Friendly churches have room in their pews for new people; willingly welcome visitors with smiles, warm greetings, and welcome gifts; and make it a point to host invite-a-friend Sundays with zest and zeal. The world is filled with friendly churches, but *what the world needs is open churches*. Churches open to new people are open to their gifts, needs, and wants. Churches that are simply friendly make use of an informal and covert vetting process, one that moves through a series of questions regarding a new person's past church affiliation, family background, and personal interests. Open churches seek to hear how God might be calling them to widen their circle of discipleship as they embrace the new person. For open churches, two questions live in concert: How will we share God with others? How is God sharing others with us?

JEFFRY W. CARTER

RESPONSE

How and where do we discern divine action in the world? Does God micromanage historical events, even shaping the decisions of political leaders who have no knowledge of God at all? If not in every sociopolitical movement, then in which ones do we wish to claim evidence of God's purposes for the world? Who decides? How do we faithfully "interpret the signs of the times," as Matthew's Jesus urged (16:3)?

JAY EMERSON JOHNSON

PRAYER

If I am missing the signs of your activity in the world, let me become more aware. Amen.

✦ TUESDAY ✦

Psalm 96:1–9 (10–13)

REFLECTION

The psalm promotes a form of witness that is portrayed as a playful celebration of life. The fields exult and the trees of the forest shout for joy (v. 12). Their very existence displays the greatness of the Lord. By implication, witness may be viewed as not only a pointing beyond ourselves but as being and becoming ourselves. For instance, the sea is one of the "marvelous works" (v. 3) of God, and simply by being its roaring self, it witnesses to God's glory. Likewise, humans witness to the "marvelous works" of a creator God by being themselves.

STEPHANIE MAR SMITH

RESPONSE

In what ways do you witness to God's glory by being yourself? What attributes allow you to be a reflection of God?

PRAYER

What a joy it is to be a witness to your wonderful works! Thank you for the person you created me to be. Amen.

☀ WEDNESDAY ☀

Psalm 96:1–9 (10–13)

REFLECTION

Every living thing that squirms on the ground, flies in the air, roots in the ground, and swims in the sea will sing a jubilant song, because God comes to judge the earth in righteousness and the peoples in truth (v. 13). God's judgment brings rejoicing because the evil powers that currently wage war on the earth and its peoples will finally be restrained. The evil that we too often deny is the dark backdrop against which the psalmist paints his joyful canvas of a jubilant creation, finally freed from the dominating and intimidating power of evil. After that evil is finally destroyed, we will sing a new song to the Lord, and we will not be singing a solo. The whole earth, all of creation, and all God's people will join us in that joyful redemption song.

JON BURNHAM

RESPONSE

Listen to a piece of music that brings you joy.

PRAYER

"Worship the Lord in holy splendor; tremble before him, all the earth." Amen.

✦ THURSDAY ✦

1 Thessalonians 1:1–10

REFLECTION

Paul's handwritten and snail-mailed words of greeting to the church at Thessalonica continue to offer wisdom for today's faith communities and their leaders. Congregations are to be bonded to one another in Christ by a spirit of thanksgiving for one another. What are the gifts of such a spirit? A spirit of thanksgiving can motivate us as believers to be more intentional and thoughtful in all of the ways we communicate with one another. A spirit of thanksgiving can motivate us toward greater communal intimacy. A spirit of thanksgiving can motivate us to forgive and seek forgiveness, especially as each of us works to be understood and to understand. Finally, a spirit of thanksgiving can and should motivate us toward collaborative ministries that spin out threads of relational authenticity and depth.

JILL Y. CRAINSHAW

RESPONSE

When was the last time you wrote an actual letter to another person? Set aside some stationery and a pen that bring you joy, and write one letter each week to a different individual or family.

PRAYER

Write your name on my heart, O God. Amen.

⤖ FRIDAY ⤖

Matthew 22:15–22

REFLECTION

True, the image can sometimes be difficult to recognize. When we look at each other, or in the mirror, we tend to see the inscriptions that our business with the world has left on us: you are what you look like, what you have, what you wear, what you do, the company you keep. Nevertheless, underneath all those inscriptions is a much deeper mark: the kiss of light in the eyes, the watery sign of a cross made once upon a time on the forehead, the image of all those children in the arms of their mothers, and the little ember of resolve to remember them. All those faces are a part of your face, when you begin to see the image that God sees, the image engraved in the palm of the hand of the God who, in Jesus, stands behind us with full faith and credit.

RICHARD E. SPALDING

RESPONSE

Look at yourself in the mirror, and instead of being critical, see yourself as God sees you.

PRAYER

You love me inside and out. Help me to love myself in the same ways. Amen.

❖ SATURDAY ❖

Matthew 22:15–22

REFLECTION

"Is it lawful to pay taxes to Caesar?" (v. 17 RSV). This is not simply a question of economics or politics or dual citizenship; it is essentially a question of conscience. It is a question of what to do when allegiance to Caesar conflicts with our allegiance to Christ. It is a question of what Christians should do when the God they serve and the government to which they have sworn allegiance are pulling them into a situation of divided loyalties.

MARVIN A. MCMICKLE

RESPONSE

Set aside a special jar or bank in which to collect your change each day, and when the jar is full, donate it to a charity of your choice. Make this a year-round habit.

PRAYER

It is so easy to make a difference in another's life. Thank you for the many opportunities I have to do so. Amen.

⟶ SUNDAY ⟵

Isaiah 45:1–7

REFLECTION

We get in trouble when we attempt to domesticate God—that is, when we dare to speak of God as part of our household. Such an exclusive relationship means that God not only acts on behalf of our particular household, but works within the household for the benefit of those related.

JEFFRY W. CARTER

Psalm 96:1–9 (10–13)

REFLECTION

This creator God possesses splendor and majesty, yet chose to become a human who was born in a cow stall in an obscure Jewish village. "Strength and beauty are in God's sanctuary" (v. 6), yet God took on human form as a helpless infant in a smelly, dark place. This God is unpredictable and beyond control. We must sing a new song if we are to stay current with what this creative God continues to do. God is never stagnant.

JON BURNHAM

1 Thessalonians 1:1–10

REFLECTION

God in the Holy Spirit is especially active in this passage. Paul has seen not simply a cooperative "spirit," but the Holy Spirit in their life (vv. 4–5a): something beyond Paul's doing or theirs, something sacred in which they share. The "message of the gospel" comes not in word only, but in power in the Holy Spirit (v. 5).

NATHAN EDDY

Matthew 22:15–22

REFLECTION

Union with Christ in his coming again creates in the present
a restless, forward-looking way of life in which trust in God's
promises motivates discipleship for action in such a way that
every area of the world's life is seen in terms of Christ's rule.

ANDREW PURVES

RESPONSE

As the passage in 1 Thessalonians suggests, keep in your prayers
those who are part of the sharing of the gospel with you.

PRAYER

Bless all those who work together for your good. Amen.

❧ *Proper 25* ❧

Leviticus 19:1–2, 15–18

You shall not hate in your heart anyone of your kin;
you shall reprove your neighbor, or you will incur guilt
yourself. You shall not take vengeance or bear a grudge
against any of your people, but you shall love your
neighbor as yourself: I am the LORD. (vv. 17–18)

Psalm 1

Happy are those
   who do not follow the advice of the wicked,
or take the path that sinners tread,
   or sit in the seat of scoffers;
but their delight is in the law of the LORD,
   and on his law they meditate day and night. (vv. 1–2)

1 Thessalonians 2:1–8

For our appeal does not spring from deceit
or impure motives or trickery, but just as we have
been approved by God to be entrusted with the message
of the gospel, even so we speak, not to please mortals,
but to please God who tests our hearts. (vv. 3–4)

Matthew 22:34–46

"Teacher, which commandment in the law is the greatest?"
He said to him, "'You shall love the Lord your God with all
your heart, and with all your soul, and with all your mind.'
This is the greatest and first commandment. And a second is
like it: 'You shall love your neighbor as yourself.' On these two
commandments hang all the law and the prophets." (vv. 36–40)

❖ MONDAY ❖

Leviticus 19:1–2, 15–18

REFLECTION

As part of its *pastoral* mission the congregation could
constantly seek to understand that being holy means acting
ethically with those around us. The first step in "holiness" is to
recognize that it is a term that properly belongs to God—God is
holy. God is set apart from everyone and everything else. God
is different. God is independent. However, God also chooses
to be with us (Immanuel) and to live among us (incarnation).
The second step is to recognize that God intends us to be holy
too. "As he who called you is holy, be holy yourselves in all your
conduct; for it is written, 'You shall be holy, for I am holy'"
(1 Pet. 1:15–16). The third step is love.

TOM TATE

RESPONSE

What words would you use to define "holy"?

PRAYER

Immanuel, be with us, in thought, word, and deed. Amen.

✦ TUESDAY ✦

Leviticus 19:1–2, 15–18

REFLECTION

Made in the image of God, human beings share in God's holiness. God has placed within them what they need to do God's will. God has furthermore placed them in communities of support, giving them teachings to guide them in their life together. Wherever sinfulness comes from and whatever drives it, it is less fundamental to human nature than holiness. People can be sinful, but the Lord their God is not sinful. People can be holy, for the Lord their God is holy.

BARBARA BROWN TAYLOR

RESPONSE

Have you ever thought of yourself as holy? What does that mean to you?

PRAYER

I am holy in your sight, a thought that amazes me! Amen.

✣ WEDNESDAY ✣

Psalm 1

REFLECTION

The psalmists knew better than anyone that turning from the advice of the wicked or walking hand in hand with goodness could be accomplished only with God's help. That may be the key to our disconnect with goodness and evil, with justice and judgment. We forget that we cannot live this life by ourselves. We cannot be the people God desires us to be and that we desire to be without complete surrender and dependence on God. It is not right behavior and action that win us God's favor. Rather, the realization of our need for God in our lives softens the places that wickedness comes from and empowers us to be a loving people. Blessed are those who find such a relationship with the Creator and one another!

CAROLYN R. WATERS

RESPONSE

Are you in a right relationship with God? What allows you to do so? What keeps you from doing so?

PRAYER

Blessed are we when we live in a right relationship with the One who created us! Amen.

✦ THURSDAY ✦

Psalm 1

REFLECTION

We live in a both/and world. We meditate on the teaching of
YHWH, yet we also experience the way of the world upon
us. The "wicked" often have their way. They seem to win even
in their losing. Furthermore, tragedy befalls all people—the
"happy" and the righteous, the "scoffers" and the wicked.
We cannot divide humanity into two types of people. We are
all at times the righteous as well as the wicked. We are all
sinners seeking righteousness—that is, seeking to be in right
relationship with God, self, and neighbor.

JANN CATHER WEAVER

RESPONSE

Scan the news for articles that report the goodness of human
beings, rather than just the ways in which we fail and cause
harm.

PRAYER

I thank you, God, for the people who make a difference in the
world for good. Amen.

⤳ FRIDAY ⤲

1 Thessalonians 2:1–8

REFLECTION

The question of church governance is also addressed in this passage. Paul does not approach the people using hierarchy and power, but rather persuasion. This says a lot about how Paul understands the church and its hierarchical structure; he models a form of discipleship that should be employed today. In certain ways, we become very concerned with order and hierarchy within the church. Those with power want to exert their authority upon the rest of the church members. Paul, however, paints a different picture, a picture of discipleship where all are equal and important. In this picture, we listen to everyone in the church, as all are part of the body of Christ and are accepted and loved.

GRACE JI-SUN KIM

RESPONSE

What should we do in the face of evil and in times of suffering?

GRACE JI-SUN KIM

PRAYER

May I have the courage to act when I see injustice. Amen.

→ SATURDAY ←

Matthew 22:34–46

REFLECTION

Our Lord's answer honors the question with two grand texts from the law—first from Deuteronomy 6:5, which is the great "Hear, O Israel" (*shema*) text that always begins worship in the synagogue. He then quotes the Leviticus expansion on the law (Lev. 19:18). Finally Jesus the Lord puts his own imprint upon these two sentences. "On these two commandments hang all the law and the prophets" (v. 40). In this final sentence Jesus asserts his own authority as the one who is privileged to unite these two commandments together as the theme of the whole. It is his final sentence that makes his answer messianic and in its own way becomes a witness to the fact that Jesus is the Messiah now in their presence.

EARL F. PALMER

RESPONSE

How does one love God?

ALLEN HILTON

PRAYER

Even though my love is imperfect, I do love you, my Redeemer. Amen.

Leviticus 19:1–2, 15–18

REFLECTION

As the matter is framed in Leviticus 19, incorrect conduct is not simply injurious to society; it is also an affront to the holiness of God. In the second place, it expands the duties under the law to include not only forms of service and worship (vv. 4–8), but also a kind of positive activity toward one's neighbor that is found nowhere in other ancient law codes: "You shall love your neighbor as yourself" (v. 18).

CHRISTOPHER B. HAYS

Psalm 1

REFLECTION

The First Psalm, besides being a beautiful example of poetry, is also the prologue or introduction to the book of Psalms as a whole. Its message is the door that grants us access to the message of the rest of the poems and songs included in the Psalms. In this sense, we may affirm that understanding correctly any other psalm is impossible if we do not understand the First Psalm.

PABLO A. JIMÉNEZ

1 Thessalonians 2:1–8

REFLECTION

Every step of faith and hope demands faithful obedience, commitment, and trust, despite all the trials and temptations we face. Risking, testing yourself, pushing out your limits, coloring outside the lines, trying new things, standing up for your faith, and accepting challenges are essential.

WILLIAM N. JACKSON

Matthew 22:34–46

REFLECTION

Love of oneself is neither praised nor condemned but merely taken for granted. Love of God and neighbor receive the primary emphasis. Insofar as Jesus gives no concrete instruction on how one is to love God, it is perhaps safe to infer on the basis of other ancient Jewish writings that it entails proper knowledge of God and obedience to God's law.

PATRICK GRAY

RESPONSE

Reread Psalm 1, replacing the plural pronouns with a singular, and imagine yourself as that tree planted by a stream of water.

PRAYER

Your word is a stream of living water, rushing through my soul. Amen.

❧ *All Saints' Day* ❦

Revelation 7:9–17

"For the Lamb at the center of the throne will be their shepherd,
  and he will guide them to springs of the water of life,
and God will wipe away every tear from their eyes." (v. 17)

REFLECTION

How might the reality of suffering, even martyrdom, be
recognized as the lived experience of many in a broken, unjust
world, but without slipping into a glorification of suffering?
Battered women, for example, need a theological response
to imposed suffering that calls for resistance and change, not
merely for endurance and patience. Moreover, they need to hear
that Christian hope is found, not in replicating crucifixions, but
in putting them to an end. How might atonement theologies
("washed in the blood of the Lamb"), which express the divine
project by accenting judgment, punishment, sacrifice, and
salvation through death, be juxtaposed to other Christian
theological frameworks that emphasize creation/creativity, new
life, and the flourishing of all humanity and the earth itself?

MARVIN M. ELLISON

Psalm 34:1–10, 22

The angel of the LORD encamps
  around those who fear him, and delivers them.
O taste and see that the LORD is good;
  happy are those who take refuge in him. (vv. 7–8)

REFLECTION

The God who delivered a people also intervenes to save
individual persons who fear God. The psalmist speaks from
his firsthand experience to all who find themselves in need of
help. One need only cry out. The ringing affirmation of this

psalm is that God is a responsive God who hears and intervenes to rescue those who turn to the Lord. In fact, God does not idly wait for us to call but proactively sends agents, such as the angels of verse 7, protectively to watch over and save those who fear the Lord.

LEAH MCKELL HORTON

1 John 3:1–3

See what love the Father has given us, that we should
    be called children of
God; and that is what we are. (v. 1)

REFLECTION

As children of God, we are born with a purpose in creation and need to carry out our purpose, which involves living a life similar to that of Jesus Christ. As 2:6 says, "Whoever says, 'I abide in him,' ought to walk just as he walked." This life requires us to examine ourselves and our intentions so that we can become the best possible creation of God. The love of God is a gift, which we do not have to earn; but as children of God, we must work toward doing good in order to honor God.

GRACE JI-SUN KIM

Matthew 5:1–12

"Blessed are the poor in spirit, for theirs is
    the kingdom of heaven.
"Blessed are those who mourn, for they
    will be comforted.
"Blessed are the meek, for they will
    inherit the earth.(vv 3–5)

REFLECTION

The Beatitudes are primarily about the character of God and only secondarily about the character of Christians.

Because God behaves in the way God does, a person would be foolish not to act in the way the Beatitudes recommend. That the behavior of Christians so often fails to conform to the Beatitudes is a sign not of moral weakness but of a lack of faith. We simply do not trust Jesus, his words, or his deeds. We do not really believe that God will bless the poor in spirit, those who mourn, the meek, those who hunger and thirst for righteousness, the merciful, the pure in heart, the peacemakers, and the persecuted. In other words, we do not think it is sensible to behave in the way Jesus did, because we do not believe that God is really the way he describes.

TIM BEACH-VERHEY

RESPONSE

How do you "bless the Lord, my soul" while listening to the traffic on one of the busiest streets in the United States just outside your office window? How do you "bless the Lord, my soul" when the preschool kids take over the gym outside your office door? How do you "bless the Lord, my soul" when there are more to-do items on the day's list than there are hours in the day? What is this thing called life that gets in the way of my relationship with God?

CAROLYN R. WATERS

PRAYER

Bless those who are poor in spirit, who mourn, who are meek, who hunger and thirst for righteousness, who are merciful, who are pure in heart, who are peacemakers, who are persecuted for your sake. Amen.

❧ *Proper 26* ❦

Micah 3:5–12

But as for me, I am filled with power,
   with the spirit of the LORD,
   and with justice and might (v. 8)

Psalm 43

Why are you cast down, O my soul,
   and why are you disquieted within me?
Hope in God; for I shall again praise him,
   my help and my God. (v. 5)

1 Thessalonians 2:9–13

We also constantly give thanks to God for this,
that when you received the word of God that you heard from
us, you accepted it not as a human word but as what it really is,
God's word, which is also at work in you believers. (v. 13)

Matthew 23:1–12

"The greatest among you will be your servant. All
who exalt themselves will be humbled, and all who
humble themselves will be exalted." (vv. 11–12)

Micah 3:5–12

REFLECTION

Not unlike Micah's false prophets, evildoers use religion for a purpose: to acquire ill-gotten gain. Often they succeed because wrongdoing is cloaked as virtuous and just, even loving. In the nineteenth century, Christian slave owners justified their complicity in evil by declaring that slavery was for the slaves' own good. Although evil surely resides in individual acts, evil also becomes routinized in everyday attitudes and systemic patterns that, over time, are taken for granted as "the way things are." Innocently or not, people "without vision," "without revelation" (v. 6), let their institutions do their sinning for them while they keep up the appearance of having "clean hands."

MARVIN M. ELLISON

RESPONSE

Are there ways, however subtle, in which your actions involve complicity in some kind of wrongdoing?

PRAYER

I ask forgiveness for any way in which I add to the darkness of the world, either by my actions or by my inactions. Amen.

Psalm 43

REFLECTION

The sense and belief that God is absent is a stark reality we all face during our lives. It is easy to say that God is always present and that we have exiled ourselves from God. This borders on the trite, however, especially to people with long suffering and painful experiences. The human condition is not so black and white. Our pain and suffering may make the presence of God, as we have known God, difficult to find. Finding God's presence anew amid our pain and suffering is a response of faith few of us can summon without the support of the community around us. The psalmist tells us to have hope amid our despair over God's absence and our pain, for in the future we will return from exile and find ourselves praising God.

JANN CATHER WEAVER

RESPONSE

Where is God? Why does God not rescue God's servant? How long will he be exiled from God's sanctuary?

LEAH MCKELL HORTON

PRAYER

In times of distress and despair, I cling to you, the one who can save me. Amen.

✦ WEDNESDAY ✦

1 Thessalonians 2:9–13

REFLECTION

In verse 10 Paul calls us to be pure, upright, and blameless. Sanctification is the act of setting apart for a special purpose, and we are made holy by fulfilling our purpose. It is important that we accept this calling and act accordingly. Grace makes a difference in our lives, and we are called to be different from this world as we are set aside to carry on a different task. We need to love people for who they are and try our best to do what is holy. This is a difficult calling to fulfill, but God's word is at work within us and can transform us to live a holy life. To be worthy of God, we must live in intimacy with God, which is secured through Christ. Jesus is God, and we can foster a fellowship with God through Jesus.

We sometimes think that we cannot be changed, but if God enters our lives, we will be transformed.

GRACE JI-SUN KIM

RESPONSE

None of us are blameless in every way. Where do you need transformation?

PRAYER

Form and reform me, as a potter with the clay. Amen.

✦ THURSDAY ✦

1 Thessalonians 2:9–13

REFLECTION

Paul's willingness to be vulnerable with the Thessalonians is further reminder that those who need encouraging include lurkers on the margins, youth, the aged, the suffering, regular stalwarts, and leaders (v. 9). Christian affection is the center of the faith and calls for celebrating, caring for, encouraging, guiding, and appreciating one another.

SUSAN MARIE SMITH

RESPONSE

"God's word" is "at work in you believers" (v. 13)—*all of you*. Do we believe it? Expect it? Anticipate it? Look for it? Recognize it? *Give thanks to God* for it, *constantly*? Do we allow ourselves the *joy* that results from God's word at work in our lives?

SUSAN MARIE SMITH

PRAYER

Fill my heart with joy, and let that joy spill into the lives of the people around me. Amen.

Matthew 23:1–12

REFLECTION

The true measure of faithfulness is found not in the words one
speaks or the doctrines one accepts but in the orientation of
one's heart. Is one's whole heart and life oriented toward God,
or is it aimed at something less than God (Matt. 6:19–34)? As
Augustine's words intimate, orienting one's whole self toward
God entails a radical form of egalitarianism. Though people
are unequal by many measures, from intelligence to physical
strength, from social standing to material wealth, they are all
equal before God.

TIM BEACH-VERHEY

RESPONSE

Place your hand over your heart; feel it beating. What a
wonderful gift, one that works so hard all the time, yet is rarely
appreciated unless there is a problem.

PRAYER

Thank you for my heart, which beats life into my veins. I offer
the heart of my spirit to you. Amen.

❖ SATURDAY ❖

Matthew 23:1–12

REFLECTION

The good news in this remarkable encounter is that we are
invited to know the God who knows us and loves us as a parent
knows children in the family. We are called by Jesus to be
brothers and sisters who do not need human masters to confer
worth upon us. We are set free pastorally by Jesus from that
organizational result of cultic entrapment that presses upon us
the desire to want to have power over other folks. We are set
free from that bondage of self-power and self-preoccupation by
the refreshing centeredness of these words that turn our eyes
toward the Lord of the Lord's Prayer and toward God whom we
are invited to call Father.

EARL F. PALMER

RESPONSE

There are people who have difficulty imagining God as Father,
and sometimes Mother as well. Be sensitive to this. Study the
many words that are used to personalize God.

PRAYER

God, you are Creator, Sustainer, Redeemer. You are Love,
Grace, Peace. You are Almighty and yet gentle. You are my God.
Amen.

Micah 3:5–12

REFLECTION

Micah 3 is a forceful threat against taking the Lord's name in vain. Understood in its historical context, it also serves as a warning against unjust exploitation by the wealthy and powerful. It also perceptively indicts the tendency of elites of various types to form a self-confirming, self-enriching power structure. Against these powerful ones who subvert the divine plan for justice, righteousness, and abundance, the Lord has a day of vengeance.

CHRISTOPHER B. HAYS

Psalm 43

REFLECTION

The language of this psalm is often very personal. "O God, *my* God," the psalmist cries (v. 4). The God who is addressed is not some remote, unengaged deity to be placated or obeyed. God is the God who is deeply committed to and involved with God's people as a whole, but who also relates and speaks to individuals. The psalmist is confident God will hear his prayers, not only because of the covenant, but also because of the intimate relationship he has experienced with God in the past.

LEAH MCKELL HORTON

1 Thessalonians 2:9–13

REFLECTION

The reign of God is the accomplishment of God's will for this world, which is marked primarily by liberation and consists of a world without slavery, poverty, or oppression. This reign of God is made manifest when God acts and becomes part of our

reality. As God is present in our lives, we live out our call to
holiness, and we join in God's work to bring the reign of God
into being.

GRACE JI-SUN KIM

Matthew 23:1–12

REFLECTION

Equality before God insists not only that the proud humble
themselves but that the marginalized take their place among
God's children. Not everyone has the same gifts or fulfills the
same role in the community, but all are children of the same
God and students of the same teacher. Everyone has a role to
play and gifts to contribute in God's kingdom.

TIM BEACH-VERHEY

RESPONSE

Are you confident that God hears your prayers?

PRAYER

You promise to be with me, to be my God, and I claim that
promise for myself, as well as for all who call upon your name.
Amen.

❧ *Proper 27* ☙

Amos 5:18–24

Take away from me the noise of your songs;
    I will not listen to the melody of your harps.
But let justice roll down like waters,
    and righteousness like an ever-flowing stream.
(vv. 23–24)

Psalm 70

Let all who seek you
    rejoice and be glad in you.
Let those who love your salvation
    say evermore, "God is great!" (v. 4)

1 Thessalonians 4:13–18

But we do not want you to be uninformed,
brothers and sisters, about those who have died, so that
you may not grieve as others do who have no hope. For since
we believe that Jesus died and rose again, even so, through Jesus,
God will bring with him those who have died. (vv. 13–14)

Matthew 25:1–13

"Keep awake therefore, for you know neither
the day nor the hour." (v. 13)

⇥ MONDAY ⇤

Amos 5:18–24

REFLECTION

Folks in our churches know all too well what it is like to be expecting a season of light, only to be overcome by darkness instead. They beat the lion of cancer but are mauled by the bear of depression. They shut the door on abuse and think they are safe, only to have the fangs of divorce pierce their flesh. "Spare us the scolding, Amos," we want to say, nursing our snakebites and fumbling for the light switch. "Sure, our festivals leave something to be desired, and our offerings are often pretty paltry, but are we not simply doing what God has asked us to do? We are all just doing the best we can."

MARYANN MCKIBBEN DANA

RESPONSE

Are you doing the best you can? When is it all right to let yourself off the hook, and when it is necessary to be tougher on yourself?

PRAYER

Help me to discern when I need to push myself a little more, and when I need to give myself a break. Amen.

✦ TUESDAY ✦

Psalm 70

REFLECTION

In prayer we are so often taught that the appropriate stance toward God is the accepting "Thy will be done." The psalmist, though, issues a demanding "Help me now." He is urgent in his plea, impatient even. The psalmist calls to God with an urgency born of authenticity. His cry is immediate, his fear is palpable, his pain is raw. His words are born out of honest feeling, hope, and experience. A reserved, polite prayer simply will not do.

JESSICA TATE

RESPONSE

Pray a heartfelt prayer for help, without reservation.

PRAYER

Lord, help me now. NOW! I ask you for . . . . Hear my prayer. Amen.

✛ WEDNESDAY ✛

Psalm 70

REFLECTION

Churchgoers can probably supply a parallel from their own lives
for each of the psalmist's laments. However, popular culture
today discourages individuals from voicing either personal
grief or outrage at social injustices. At work, churchgoers hear
about the value of being a team player. As evinced by media
presentations of tragic events such as school shootings, popular
culture asserts that "achieving closure" and "moving on with
life" should be quick, and that extensive reflection on negative
experiences is somehow unhealthy.

Psalm 70 suggests that faithful people may legitimately speak
up for themselves—perhaps against the "team"—and may voice
grief over death and catastrophe, frustration at hypocrisy, and
outrage over injustice.

HAYWOOD SPANGLER

RESPONSE

What arouses your anger? How do you use that anger for good?

PRAYER

Kindle within me a fiery spirit that engages my actions and
words for your service. Amen.

1 Thessalonians 4:13–18

REFLECTION

What does Christ's coming say about God's own identity?
Whether God descends from heaven and meets Christians in
the air, arrives in the Christ child, or continually breaks into
this-worldly living through the power of the Spirit, this passage
witnesses to the fact that God is a God on the move. God is
a dynamic God, never static, never stale, but always stirring,
always opening reality up to God's eschatological promises and
possibilities. Most fundamentally, God is a God who comes.

JENNIFER M. MCBRIDE

RESPONSE

Make a list of action words that describe God.

PRAYER

Stir in me the desire to embrace life with a spirit of energy and
action. Amen.

✤ FRIDAY ✤

Matthew 25:1–13

REFLECTION

Against claims that there will be nothing new under the sun,
that we live in the last age, and that from this time forward it
is only a matter of our working out the niceties of how to live
in the kingdom that is already here, the text reminds us that
this is not as good as it gets, that the bridegroom's delay does
not mean he will not come, and that the party will not really
start until he arrives. It asks us to live in hope for what has been
promised and what will be but is not yet. It reminds us that
knowledge, faith, and love are tools for living in the time before
eternity, not tools to gain entrance into it.

MARK DOUGLAS

RESPONSE

Assuming it does not look like stockpiling weapons, canned
goods, or canned answers to questions about Jesus' return
(which tend to be used as weapons anyway), what does being
prepared for that delay look like?

MARK DOUGLAS

PRAYER

Prepare me to be ready for whatever this day brings. Amen.

⭒ SATURDAY ⭒

Matthew 25:1–13

REFLECTION

The point is living expectantly and hopefully. Christian hope rests on trust that the God who created the world will continue to love the world with gentle providence, will continue the process of creation until the project is complete, and will continue to redeem and save the world by coming into it with love and grace, in Jesus Christ.

Christian hope is as big as the whole sweep of human history, but also as small as each individual. Ultimate issues have been resolved for the human race, but also for each of us individually. In every congregation are faithful people genuinely frightened about where human history seems to be headed. Freedom, justice, and compassion seem fragile in the face of the forces of oppression, injustice, violence, and torture. Living in hope does not mean immunity to the harsh realities of history. On the contrary, it means living confidently and expectantly, trusting that the Lord of history continues to come into life with compassion and redemption and hope.

JOHN M. BUCHANAN

RESPONSE

Write the word "hope" on several index cards, and place them in spots where you will come across this word in the course of your day (for example, the car, a dresser drawer, the bathroom mirror).

PRAYER

I am hopeful because you are the God who brings hope in every situation. Amen.

⟿ SUNDAY ⟿

Amos 5:18–24

REFLECTION

Amos focuses his ire on the people's festivals, assemblies, and offerings to God. Few things are more personal. How we worship, how we engage with one another, and what we give to God all speak volumes about who we are. It stings to be told that these are not right or good enough, so it is no wonder that we have learned to tune out the likes of Amos.

MARYANN MCKIBBEN DANA

Psalm 70

REFLECTION

The "poor and needy" known to the psalmist are those especially sensitive to God's love and care, those most inclined to offer genuine thanksgiving and praise to God. The petitioner prays God's blessing on all who seek God's presence and relish God's "salvation" that they may say evermore, "God is great!" (v. 4).

W. EUGENE MARCH

1 Thessalonians 4:13–18

REFLECTION

The world can seem to many a dangerous place, at war with God and God's people, where only the most dramatic actions by God can save. People feel pressed from every side by the forces opposed to God, their loyalties undermined by the endless compromises of earning, consuming, and recreating. They imagine that their lives as believers should move from glory to glory; instead, they find them going from crisis to crises. They are kept going by faith that God will vindicate God's people in the end and remedy the losses they have experienced—whether privations, or hunger, or death of their loved ones.

MARK B. LEE

Matthew 25:1–13

REFLECTION

Now is the time for active discipleship, and every moment we can sense the ticking of the clock or the closing of certain doors. The kingdom of heaven summons us to new life, improved commitment, casting away of false idols, active waiting in hope, and renewed vigor in faith. Jesus taught in parables in order to teach the secrets of the kingdom (Matt. 13:11). One of the secrets taught by Matthew 25:1–13 is that faithful action done now prepares us to weather the unexpected timing of God, even as it prepares us for a heavenly wedding celebration, when Jesus and his people, the bridegroom and his beloved bride, are joyfully joined together in celebration forever. The Messiah comes "at the right time" (Rom. 5:6)—which is altogether better than coming at the convenient time or on our time—and brings a party with him.

LINDSAY P. ARMSTRONG

RESPONSE

Set a timer for five minutes. Then as the timer keeps track of time, slowly breathe in and out, being conscious of each breath, and of God's Spirit filling every fiber of your being. End when the timer goes off.

PRAYER

You summon each of us to new life. Let us claim that life with all that is within us. Amen.

❧ *Proper 28* ❦

Zephaniah 1:7, 12–18

Be silent before the Lord GOD!
> For the day of the LORD is at hand;
the LORD has prepared a sacrifice,
> he has consecrated his guests. (v. 7)

Psalm 90:1–8 (9–11), 12

Lord, you have been our dwelling place
> in all generations.
Before the mountains were brought forth,
> or ever you had formed the earth and the world,
> from everlasting to everlasting you are God.
> (vv. 1–2)

1 Thessalonians 5:1–11

For God has destined us not for wrath but for
obtaining salvation through our Lord Jesus Christ,
who died for us, so that whether we are awake or asleep
we may live with him. Therefore encourage one another and
build up each other, as indeed you are doing. (vv. 9–11)

Matthew 25:14–30

"'For to all those who have, more will be given,
and they will have an abundance; but from those who have
nothing, even what they have will be taken away.'" (v. 29)

✢ MONDAY ✤

Zephaniah 1:7, 12–18

REFLECTION

Listen up! Zephaniah booms from the outset, and he does not let up for the rest of the passage. The text offers no righteous underdogs for us to hide behind to escape judgment, no freedom for the oppressed, no bit of hope lurking in the margins—unless you consider abject destruction of a self-indulgent, morally bankrupt, spiritually complacent way of life hopeful. Perhaps we should view it that way; but the fact is that we like our stuff and our way of life, and we are willing to submit our lives to God so long as God does not require too much in return. Into the tension between our wholehearted proclamation on Sunday and the halfhearted discipleship we typically pursue the rest of the week steps Zephaniah, with his warrior shrieks and blind stumblings and blood and feces (v. 17). "How inappropriate," we cluck to ourselves, clutching our Sunday bulletins. "How tacky."

MARYANN MCKIBBEN DANA

RESPONSE

What are you willing to give up—time, possessions, a grudge, an indulgence—in order to be more faithful?

PRAYER

I am reluctant to let go of my comforts, but give me the courage to let go of whatever it is that turns my allegiance from you. Amen.

✦ TUESDAY ✦

Psalm 90:1–8 (9–11), 12

REFLECTION

Yes, human life is fleeting. Yes, time measured in years is but
a blink of an eye to God. Yes, God's wrath is a consuming fire.
None of that need be of terrible concern, because humans are
not the center of things. For all the generations of humanity,
God has been the dwelling place. Throughout all of time, God
has been and will be God. Humanity often seems unable to
grasp that God's grandeur, God's limitlessness, God's eternity
are good news that places perspective on human existence.
The psalm issues a corrective to the aversion to human frailty.
Rather than asserting human authority, the psalmist asks, Why
not stand in awe and wonder at God's infinity and constancy?

JESSICA TATE

RESPONSE

Do you turn away from the sight of affliction, of pain?
Sometimes, it is necessary to do so, because the sight is more
than we can bear. In such a case, remember to hold the afflicted
in prayer: that much, we all can do.

PRAYER

I place myself in a proper reverence, with you at the center of
my life. Amen.

❧ WEDNESDAY ❧

Psalm 90:1–8 (9–11), 12

REFLECTION

Psalm 90 begins with the confession of faith that God is our dwelling place. The very fact that God stands outside of human time allows God to be a place of safety for each and every generation (v. 1). Moreover, because God stands outside of time (v. 2), the believer finds solace in a vision of things seen though God's eyes. The believer can relax in the knowledge that God was there long before his or her journey through this world and that God will be there long after it. Human life and efforts are significant, but ultimately not dependent on the brief period of time that humans live on this earth.

L. JULIANA CLAASSENS

RESPONSE

Try to get along without looking at your watch or clock for as many hours as you can. Be mindful of your dependence upon such!

PRAYER

Allow me the gift of stepping outside the restrictions of earthly time, if even for a moment. Amen.

⊹ THURSDAY ⊹

1 Thessalonians 5:1–11

REFLECTION

While the "signs of the time" might challenge us to rededicate our commitment to discipleship, hardship in life does not threaten our assurance of salvation. There is no need for believers to respond as advised by the bumper sticker that reads, "Jesus is coming—act busy!" Paul reassures them, "Of course you will be prepared. You already know. You live in the light, faith, and life of the resurrection." In a sense, it is as though the day of the Lord has already arrived for those who have received the gift of faith. These can be encouraging pastoral words for Christians today, who often still struggle to hold the assurance of eternal salvation amid worldly calamity. It is as if Paul is echoing the words of the psalmist: "Be still, and know that I am God" (Ps. 46:10). Believers should trust in the promises of God and be at peace.

JOHN E. COLE

RESPONSE

Be still, breathe deeply and slowly, and repeat the prayer below.

PRAYER

Be still . . . and know that God *is* God. Be still . . . and know that God is *God*. Be still . . . and know that God is God. Amen.

✦ FRIDAY ✦

Matthew 25:14–30

REFLECTION

The greatest risk of all, it turns out, is not to risk anything,
not to care deeply and profoundly enough about anything to
invest deeply, to give your heart away and in the process risk
everything. The greatest risk of all, it turns out, is to play it
safe, to live cautiously and prudently. Orthodox, conventional
theology identifies sin as pride and egotism. However, there
is an entire other lens through which to view the human
condition. It is called sloth, one of the ancient church's seven
deadly sins. Sloth means not caring, not loving, not rejoicing,
not living up to the full potential of our humanity, playing it
safe, investing nothing, being cautious and prudent, digging a
hole and burying the money in the ground.

JOHN M. BUCHANAN

RESPONSE

Are you prone to play it safe in a situation that calls for risk? Is
there something or someone who can encourage you to step
outside the safety zone?

PRAYER

I am reluctant to take risks, but with your courage I find my
strength. Amen.

⇢ SATURDAY ⇠

Matthew 25:14–30

REFLECTION

Now for most of us, religion, our personal faith, has not seemed like a high-risk venture. In fact, it has seemed to be something like the opposite. Faith has seemed to be a personal comfort zone. Faith, many of us think, is about personal security, here and in the hereafter. Faith, we think, is no more risky than believing ideas in our heads about God and Jesus, a list of beliefs to which we more or less subscribe intellectually. Faith, we think, because that is what we have been taught, is getting our personal theology right and then living a good life by avoiding bad things. Religion, we think, is a pretty timid, nonrisky venture.

Here Jesus invites us to be his disciples, to live our lives as fully as possible by investing them, by risking, by expanding the horizons of our responsibilities. To be his man or woman, he says, is not so much believing ideas about him as it is following him. It is to experience renewed responsibility for the use and investment of these precious lives of ours. It is to be bold and brave, to reach high and care deeply.

So the parable is the invitation to the adventure of faith: the high-risk venture of being a disciple of Jesus Christ.

JOHN M. BUCHANAN

RESPONSE

What talents do you bury out of sight and use?

PRAYER

Unearth the talents you have given me, that I may use them as you ask me to do. Amen.

Zephaniah 1:7, 12–18

REFLECTION

So what is to be made of a text in which God promises to destroy all people everywhere, including God's people by (very likely) serving them as food, and also promises to destroy the ecological systems of the planet at the same time? At its most basic level, this text is about the awesome power of God. God, who created and blessed this world, can and will destroy it, having judged it and found it lacking. A contemporary reading of this text may conclude that humanity is the destructive force on this earth. Human sin leads to God's judgment; humans are ultimately responsible for the destruction of human life and the dismantling of the ecological systems of this earth.

WIL GAFNEY

Psalm 90:1–8 (9–11), 12

REFLECTION

In many respects this refusal to accept limits and this desire for control are good. They allow people to take stands, to push harder than they thought they could, to accomplish what seemed impossible, to create and innovate beyond the wildest of dreams. In another light, however, this refusal to confront limitation and acknowledge human frailty is also a refusal to accept half of life. It is a refusal to see ourselves in our proper place.

JESSICA TATE

1 Thessalonians 5:1–11

REFLECTION

The best evidence believers have of the assurance of God's forgiveness and salvation is each other. The promise of

Christ's return sustains and upbuilds the church in whatever circumstance it finds itself. God has given us two great gifts for sustaining our faith in the midst of hardship: the promise of Christ's return and the mutual encouragement of the community of faith. According to Paul, we can step out into eternity on these two realities.

JOHN E. COLE

Matthew 25:14–30

REFLECTION

The point here is not really about doubling your money and accumulating wealth. It is about living. It is about investing. It is about taking risks. It is about Jesus himself and what he has done and what is about to happen to him. Mostly it is about what he hopes and expects of them after he is gone. It is about being a follower of Jesus and what it means to be faithful to him, and so, finally, it is about you and me.

JOHN M. BUCHANAN

RESPONSE

Make an investment in committing yourself to prayer and one form of outreach that is new to you.

PRAYER

These I give to you: my heart, my soul, my hands, my voice. Use them as you will. Amen.

❦ *Proper 29* ❦

(Reign of Christ)

Ezekiel 34:11–16, 20–24

For thus says the Lord GOD: I myself will search for my sheep, and will seek them out. As shepherds seek out their flocks when they are among their scattered sheep, so I will seek out my sheep. I will rescue them from all the places to which they have been scattered on a day of clouds and thick darkness. (vv. 11–12)

Psalm 95:1–7a

O come, let us worship and bow down,
  let us kneel before the LORD, our Maker!
For he is our God,
  and we are the people of his pasture,
  and the sheep of his hand. (vv. 6–7)

Ephesians 1:15–23

I pray that the God of our Lord Jesus Christ, the Father of glory, may give you a spirit of wisdom and revelation as you come to know him, so that, with the eyes of your heart enlightened, you may know what is the hope to which he has called you. (vv. 17–18)

Matthew 25:31–46

"When the Son of Man comes in his glory, and all the angels with him, then he will sit on the throne of his glory. All the nations will be gathered before him, and he will separate people one from another as a shepherd separates the sheep from the goats, and he will put the sheep at his right hand and the goats at the left." (vv. 31–33)

✦ MONDAY ✦

Ezekiel 34:11–16, 20–24

REFLECTION

Even with the judgment language, the image of God as the reconciler is present in this passage. God seeks to reconcile humanity in a divine/human relationship that results in salvation, redemption, safety, obedient discipleship, and divinely ordained leadership (vv. 22–24). That is what the shepherd does: care for the wounded, find the lost, nurture those that have been left behind. One of the reasons shepherds determine which sheep are fat and which are lean is to make sure the undernourished are provided better opportunities to be "fattened." However, God will also hold accountable those sheep who are predatorily taking more than their needs require, as well as the shepherds who are called to care for God's flock (v. 22).

KARYN L. WISEMAN

RESPONSE

Be mindful of what you eat today, and keep track of every item. Does this make you feel more accountable? Do you eat out of stress even when you are not hungry? Being aware of bad habits can help you overcome them.

PRAYER

I long to live each day in a mindful way, for every day is a gift. Amen.

✦ TUESDAY ✦

Psalm 95:1–7a

REFLECTION

This God who is sovereign over all the earth does not use that power to force the allegiance, worship, or obedience of God's people. Instead, this God invites us to worship. This God invites us to bow down. This God invites us to listen to God's voice. Our response to these invitations is to be given freely. God knows the risks involved: like the Israelites in the wilderness, we may harden our hearts. God nevertheless gives us the freedom to respond. As this psalm reminds us, the appropriate response to such a God is worship, gratitude, and obedience.

KRISTEN DEEDE JOHNSON

RESPONSE

Write an invitation: "You are invited to live a full and joyful life in Christ." Mail it to yourself. Note how you feel when you receive this message. Keep it where you can refer to it often.

PRAYER

Thank you for the invitation to live a full and joyful life. I accept! Amen.

✢ WEDNESDAY ✢

Psalm 95:1–7a

REFLECTION

To be sure, Psalm 95 does not indicate how God's power can be known in every situation, for instance, by commending particular rules or commandments. However, just as it encourages discernment about the differences between God's will and our own for the environment, it encourages a more general awareness that what we would plan for ourselves and what God may call us to do can be very different.

HAYWOOD SPANGLER

RESPONSE

How do you discern God's will from your own? When do the two intersect?

PRAYER

Grant me the clarity to know your will, to know when it intersects my own, and when it calls me to a new way of life. Amen.

✦ THURSDAY ✦

Ephesians 1:15–23

REFLECTION

Paul's prayer for the Ephesians is no mere assembly of pious sentiments. He asks for the Ephesians a "spirit of wisdom and revelation . . . so that, with the eyes of your heart enlightened, you may know what is the hope to which God has called you" (vv. 17–18). . . . This wisdom is the power of God, even that which raised Christ from the dead and has exalted him above all things. To receive a share of this wisdom is certainly an attractive prayer! While praying for abstract wisdom can be entirely appropriate, Paul has in mind something intensely concrete.

MARK B. LEE

RESPONSE

Have you ever asked God to give you a spirit of wisdom? There is no time like the present!

PRAYER

Open the eyes of my heart, Lord. Let me see you. Amen.

✢ FRIDAY ✢

Matthew 25:31–46

REFLECTION

God wants not only a new world modeled on the values of Jesus. God wants us—each of us. God is not a social engineer but a God of love who wants to save our souls, to use the language of the old revival meetings.

God wants to save our souls and redeem us and give us the gift of life—true, deep, authentic human life.

God wants to save us by touching our hearts with love. God wants to save us by persuading us to care and see other human beings who need us.

God wants to save us from obsessing about ourselves, our own needs, by persuading us to forget about ourselves and worry about others.

That is God's favorite project: to teach you and me the fundamental lesson, the secret, the truth—that to love is to live.

JOHN M. BUCHANAN

RESPONSE

Could any of us ever think of ourselves as among the least of these? Do desires, motives, or situations matter if judgment turns on actions alone?

MARK DOUGLAS

PRAYER

To love you is to live. I seek to live with your love as my foundation. Amen.

✦ SATURDAY ✦

Matthew 25:31–46

REFLECTION

God created the world out of an abundance of love. Like a
bubbling fountain, God is love and overflows with love. In
creation, God gives something of self, and in sending Jesus
and the Holy Spirit, God repeatedly and generously pours
love out upon all people, showing us God's own self as well
as who we are. Created in the image of this freely giving God,
we freely share, because this is what it means to be created
in God's image. In particular, we love those conventionally
considered unable to give back, and we do not do so to earn
God's love or anyone else's love, to curry favor, or to make sure
we are considered righteous at the end of time. We give as an
expression of the love that is inside of us bubbling up, spilling
over, and flowing out.

LINDSAY P. ARMSTRONG

RESPONSE

Do you include yourself in the group of those who are surprised
that they have ministered to Jesus through their care of others,
or those who have not?

PRAYER

May I be surprised in the ways I serve you without knowing,
and aware of the ways I need to do more. Amen.

✦ SUNDAY ✦

Ezekiel 34:11–16, 20–24

REFLECTION

Three of the first seven verses begin with the phrases, "Come, let us sing"; "Let us come into his presence with thanksgiving;" and "Come, let us . . . kneel," making Psalm 95 an appropriate opening to worship. The phrases "Come" and "Let us come" imply a choice—most simply the choice to pay attention to God, or not.

HAYWOOD SPANGLER

Psalm 95:1–7a

REFLECTION

Somewhere along the way, worship has become a solemn experience; but praise felt in the depth of one's being is anything but solemn. There is nothing in the psalm that suggests solemnity—quite the opposite, actually. Perhaps this psalm on Reign of Christ Sunday suggests that worship and praise of our Lord and King needs a shot of joy, particularly in this season in which there is so much else to distract us.

JESSICA TATE

Ephesians 1:15–23

REFLECTION

A closer look at this lyrical prayer reveals a biting irony for those who seek a faith grounded in individual triumph and cheap grace: the lordship of Jesus Christ may usher in a new age, but it is an age of communal witness, not solitary reward. To begin with, this prayer is an intercession not for an individual but for a church.

JOHN E. COLE

Matthew 25:31–46

REFLECTION

Thus this passage provides a wellness check and possibly even a warning to those living in unhealthy, self-centered ways. Akin to measuring weight or blood pressure, Matthew 25:31–46's emphasis on freely sharing with strangers; prisoners; and all who are hungry, thirsty, naked, and/or sick is a key diagnostic tool to help us assess our righteousness and health. If we cannot share freely and fully or if we do not make ourselves available to do so, this indicates that our relationship with God and the world is not as healthy and whole as Jesus' triumph on the cross makes possible. Loving those for whom Jesus gave his life, particularly those who are undervalued, is a primary expression of our love of God and of our experience of God's love for us.

LINDSAY P. ARMSTRONG

RESPONSE

This is the final week in the church calendar, before a new year begins with Advent. What resolutions do you make for the coming year, as a person of faith?

PRAYER

For the year that has come to completion, I give you thanks. Let me live this new year renewed each day by your Spirit. Allow me to serve others in your name. Fill me with joy, that I may be a channel of your grace and love. I sing to you, Lord, and come into your presence with thanksgiving every day. Amen.

Contributors

Numbers in italic are page numbers on which each contributor's refeclection can be found.

Charles L. Aaron, Pastor, First United Methodist Church, Farmersville, Texas; *63.* **P. Mark Achtemeier,** Associate Professor of Systematic Theology, Dubuque Theological Seminary, Dubuque, Iowa; *101.* **Harry B. Adams,** Professor Emeritus, Yale Divinity School, Hamden, Connecticut; *74, 84.* **Joanna M. Adams,** Retired Pastor, Morningside Presbyterian Church, Atlanta, Georgia; *9, 18, 24.* **Samuel L. Adams,** Assistant Professor of Biblical Studies, Union Presbyterian Seminary, Richmond, Virginia; *472.* **E. Lane Alderman Jr.,** Pastor, Roswell Presbyterian Church, Roswell, Georgia; *35, 38.* **O. Wesley Allen Jr.,** Associate Professor of Homiletics and Worship, Lexington Theological Seminary, Lexington, Kentucky; *386.* **Katherine E. Amos,** Resident Professor of Spirituality and the Arts, Wake Forest University School of Divinity, Winston-Salem, North Carolina; *200, 205, 211, 215.* **Herbert Anderson,** Research Professor in Practical Theology, Pacific Lutheran Theological Seminary, Berkeley, California; *372, 373, 382, 383.* **Maryetta Anschutz,** Founding Head, The Episcopal School of Los Angeles, California; *156, 165, 167, 168, 170.* **Mary Beth Anton,** Chaplain, Trinity School of Midland, and Parish Associate, First Presbyterian Church, Midland, Texas; *405.* **Thomas L. Are Jr.,** Pastor, Village Presbyterian Church, Prairie Village, Kansas; *265, 266, 274, 283.* **Lindsay P. Armstrong,** Associate Pastor of Christian Education, First Presbyterian Church, Atlanta, Georgia; *534, 550, 552.* **Talitha J. Arnold,** Senior Minister, United Church of Santa Fe, New Mexico; *375, 376, 387, 396.* **Emily Askew,** Associate Professor of Systematic Theology, Lexington Theological Seminary, Lexington, Kentucky; *50, 68.*

Rachel Sophia Baard, Lawrence C. Gallen Postdoctoral Fellow, Villanova University, Villanova, Pennsylvania; *345, 359.* **Douglass M. Bailey,** President, Center for Urban Ministry, Inc., and Assistant Professor of Urban Ministry, Wake Forest University School of Divinity, Winston-Salem, North Carolina; *363, 368.* **David L. Bartlett,** Professor Emeritus of New Testament, Columbia Theological Seminary, Decatur, Georgia; *18, 25, 59, 278, 438, 458.* **Michael Battle,** Rector, Church of Our Savior, San Gabriel, California; *278, 287.* **Tim Beach-Verhey,** Co-Pastor, Faison Presbyterian Church, Faison, North Carolina; *516, 522, 525.* **Christopher A. Beeley,** Walter H. Gray Associate Professor of Anglican Studies and Patristics, Yale Divinity School, New Haven, Connecticut; *164, 166, 169.* **David M. Bender,** Pastor, Faith Presbyterian Church, Indian Land, South Carolina; *306, 311.* **April Berends,** Rector, St. Mark's Episcopal Church, Milwaukee, Wisconsin; *132, 140, 145, 150.* **Jon L. Berquist,** President, Disciples Seminary Foundation, Claremont, California; *162, 169.* **Bruce C. Birch,** Dean and Miller Professor of Biblical Theology, Wesley Theological Seminary, Washington, D.C.; *8.* **Thomas W. Blair,** Pastor, Second Presbyterian Church, Baltimore, Maryland; *371, 380, 381, 389, 390.* **Barbara S. Blaisdell,** Pastor, United Community Church, Hilo, Hawaii; *109.* **Kathryn D. Blanchard,** Assistant Professor of Religious Studies, Alma College, Alma, Michigan; *457.* **Dave Bland,** Professor of Homiletics, Harding University Graduate School of Religion, Memphis, Tennessee; *31, 300, 305.* **Ellen J. Blue,** Mouzon Biggs Jr. Associate Professor of the History of Christianity and United Methodist Studies, Phillips Theological Seminary, Tulsa, Oklahoma; *128, 136.* **Kathleen Long Bostrom,** Co-Pastor, Wildwood Presbyterian Church, Grayslake, Illinois; *227, 228.* **Matthew Myer Boulton,** Associate Professor of Ministry Studies, Harvard Divinity School, Cambridge, Massachusetts; *139, 150.* **Wallace W. Bubar,** Pastor, Overbrook Presbyterian Church, Philadelphia, Pennsylvania; *454, 467.* **John M. Buchanan,** Pastor, Fourth Presbyterian Church, Chicago, Illinois; *532, 540,*

541, 543, 549. **Drew Bunting,** Musician and Homemaker, Milwaukee, Wisconsin; *100.* **John P. Burgess,** James Henry Snowden Professor of Systematic Theology, Pittsburgh Theological Seminary, Pittsburgh, Pennsylvania; *9, 16, 27.* **Jon Burnham,** Pastor, St. John's Presbyterian Church, Houston, Texas; *490, 499, 503.* **David M. Burns,** Executive Pastor/Acting Pastor, Trinity Presbyterian Church, Atlanta, Georgia; *174, 183, 187, 191.* **James Burns,** Pastor, Metropolitan Community Church of the Rockies, Denver, Colorado; *479, 485, 494.* **David B. Burrell,** Professor of Ethics and Development Studies, Uganda Martyrs University, Nkozi, Uganda; *491.* **Jason Byassee,** Executive Director of Leadership Education at Duke Divinity and Director of the Center for Theology, Writing, and Media, Duke Divinity School, Durham, North Carolina; *130, 138, 147.* **Gay L. Byron,** Baptist Missionary Training School Professor of New Testament and Christian Origins, Colgate Rochester Crozer Divinity School, Rochester, New York; *194.*

Charles Campbell, Professor of Homiletics, Duke University Divinity School, Durham, North Carolina; *477.* **Cynthia M. Campbell,** President, McCormick Theological Seminary, Chicago, Illinois; *5, 14, 23.* **Carlos F. Cardoza-Orlandi,** Professor of Global Christianities and Mission Studies, Perkins School of Theology, Southern Methodist University, Dallas, Texas; *426, 431.* **Timothy B. Cargal,** Interim Associate for Preparation for Ministry/Examinations, Office of the General Assembly of the Presbyterian Church (U.S.A.), Louisville, Kentucky; *458, 467, 468, 476.* **Jeffry W. Carter,** Pastor, Manassas Church of the Brethren, Manassas, Virginia; *479, 489, 497, 503.* **Claudio Carvalhaes,** Assistant Professor of Worship and Preaching, Louisville Presbyterian Theological Seminary, Louisville, Kentucky; *452, 461, 470.* **Robert A. Cathey,** Professor of Theology, McCormick Theological Seminary, Chicago, Illinois; *365.* **Karen Chakoian,** Pastor, First Presbyterian Church, Granville, Ohio; *377, 384, 386.* **Gary W. Charles,** Pastor, Central Presbyterian Church, Atlanta, Georgia; *44, 392, 395.* **Jana Childers,** Professor of Homiletics and Speech-Communication, San Francisco Theological Seminary, San Anselmo, California; *294, 296, 314.* **W. Michael Chittum,** Senior Minister, First Congregational Church, Salt Lake City, Utah; *146.* **L. Juliana Claassens,** Associate Professor of Old Testament, Faculty of Theology, University of Stellenbosch, Stellenbosch, South Africa; *538.* **Linda Lee Clader,** Dean of Academic Affairs and Professor of Homiletics, Church Divinity School of the Pacific, Berkeley, California; *270, 277, 285, 286.* **Kimberly L. Clayton,** Director of Contextual Education, Columbia Theological Seminary, Decatur, Georgia; *131, 140, 149.* **Charlotte Dudley Cleghorn,** Retired Executive Director, The Centers for Christian Studies, Cathedral of All Souls, Asheville, North Carolina; *459, 465, 466, 468, 475.* **Kelton Cobb,** Professor of Theology and Ethics, Hartford Seminary, Hartford, Connecticut; *199.* **John E. Cole,** Pastor, Christ Presbyterian Church, Ormond Beach, Florida; *539, 543, 551.* **Gilberto Collazo,** Vice President for Missional Development and Operations, Christian Church (Disciples of Christ), Indianapolis, Indiana; *456, 464, 474, 477.* **Kate Colussy-Estes,** Julia Thompson Smith Chaplain, Agnes Scott College, Decatur, Georgia; *346, 350, 354, 364.* **Andrew Foster Connors,** Pastor, Brown Memorial Park Avenue Presbyterian Church, Baltimore, Maryland; *107, 117, 122.* **Kate Foster Connors,** Parish Associate and Youth Director, Brown Memorial Park Avenue Presbyterian Church, Baltimore, Maryland; *129, 137, 141, 150.* **Charles James Cook,** Professor Emeritus of Pastoral Theology, Seminary of the Southwest, Austin, Texas; *102, 105, 112, 114, 123.* **Stephen L. Cook,** Catherine N. McBurney Professor of Old Testament Language and Literature, Virginia Theological Seminary, Alexandria, Virginia; *440, 444.* **Martin B. Copenhaver,** Pastor, Wellesley Congregational Church, United Church of Christ, Wellesley, Massachusetts; *225, 232.* **Barbara Cawthorne Crafton,** The Geranium Farm, Metuchen, New Jersey; *218.* **Jill Y. Crainshaw,** Associate Professor and Academic Dean, Wake Forest University Divinity School, Winston-Salem, North Carolina; *482, 492, 500.* **Carole A. Crumley,** Senior Program

Director, Shalem Institute for Spiritual Formation, Washington, D.C.; *290, 291, 296, 309.* **R. Alan Culpepper,** Dean, McAfee School of Theology, Atlanta, Georgia; *60.* **Michael B. Curry,** Bishop, Diocese of North Carolina, Raleigh, North Carolina; *127.*

Maryann McKibben Dana, Associate Pastor, Burke Presbyterian Church, Springfield, Virginia; *73, 90, 527, 533, 536.* **Lillian Daniel,** Senior Minister, First Congregational Church, United Church of Christ, Glen Ellyn, Illinois; *125, 135, 143.* **J. David Dark,** Adjunct Faculty, David Lipscomb University, Nashville, Tennessee; *239, 260.* **Linda Day,** Independent Scholar, Pittsburgh, Pennsylvania; *86.* **Miguel A. De La Torre,** Associate Professor, Iliff School of Theology, Denver, Colorado; *267, 269, 275.* **Carol J. Dempsey,** Professor of Theology (Biblical Studies), University of Portland, Oregon; *98, 113.* **Lewis R. Donelson,** Ruth A. Campbell Professor of New Testament Studies, Austin Presbyterian Theological Seminary, Austin, Texas; *475.* **Mark Douglas,** Associate Professor of Christian Ethics and Director of the MATS Program, Columbia Theological Seminary, Decatur, Georgia; *453, 462, 463, 471, 531, 549.* **Steven D. Driver,** Director of Formation, Immanuel Lutheran Church, Valparaiso, Indiana; *78.* **Paul Simpson Duke,** Co-Pastor, First Baptist Church, Ann Arbor, Michigan; *12, 21.* **Stacey Simpson Duke,** Co-Pastor, First Baptist Church, Ann Arbor, Michigan; *2, 11, 17, 20, 26.*

Steven P. Eason, Senior Pastor, Myers Park Presbyterian Church, Charlotte, North Carolina; *297, 304, 312.* **Nathan Eddy,** Chaplain, St. Peter's House Church, University Precinct Center, Manchester, United Kingdom; *486, 495, 503.* **Heather Murray Elkins,** Professor of Worship, Preaching, and the Arts, Drew University, Madison, New Jersey; *377, 386, 395.* **Marvin M. Ellison,** Willard S. Bass Professor of Christian Ethics, Bangor Theological Seminary, Portland, Maine; *514, 518.* **Amy Erickson,** Assistant Professor of Hebrew Bible, Iliff School of Theology, Denver, Colorado; *458, 476.* **Barbara J. Essex,** Minister for Higher Education and Theological Education, United Church of Christ, Cleveland, Ohio; *132, 141, 148.* **Ward B. Ewing,** Dean and President, The General Theological Seminary, New York, New York; *175, 188, 193.*

Stephen Farris, Dean, St. Andrew's Hall, and Professor of Homiletics, Vancouver School of Theology, Vancouver, British Columbia, Canada; *201, 215.* **Eleazar S. Fernandez,** Professor of Constructive Theology, United Theological Seminary of the Twin Cities, New Brighton, Minnesota; *428, 437, 446.* **Lisa G. Fischbeck,** Vicar, The Episcopal Church of the Advocate, Carrboro, North Carolina; *55, 56.* **Robert W. Fisher,** Associate Rector, All Saints-by-the-Sea Episcopal Church, Santa Barbara, California; *173, 178, 182, 191, 192, 196.* **Anna Carter Florence,** Peter Marshall Associate Professor of Preaching, Columbia Theological Seminary, Decatur, Georgia; *176, 177, 185, 186.*

Wil Gafney, Associate Professor of Old Testament and Hebrew, The Lutheran Theological Seminary at Philadelphia, Pennsylvania; *542.* **Nora Gallagher,** Writer, Preacher-in-Residence, Trinity Episcopal Church, Santa Barbara, California; *222.* **Greg Garrett,** Professor of English, Baylor University, Waco, Texas, and Writer in Residence, Seminary of the Southwest, Austin, Texas; *76.* **Roger J. Gench,** Pastor, The New York Avenue Presbyterian Church, Washington, D.C.; *110, 119, 123.* **William Goettler,** Co-Pastor, First Presbyterian Church, and Assistant Dean of Ministry Studies, Yale Divinity School, New Haven, Connecticut; *351.* **Jeanette A. Good,** Pastor, State Street Church United Church of Christ, Portland, Maine; *456.* **Patrick Gray,** Associate Professor of Religious Studies, Rhodes College, Memphis, Tennessee; *513.* **Barbara Green,** Professor of Biblical Studies, Dominican School of Philosophy and Theology, Berkeley, California; *317, 335.* **William Greenway,** Associate Professor of Philosophical Theology, Austin Presbyterian Theological Seminary, Austin, Texas; *455, 468, 473.* **Alan**

Gregory, Academic Dean and Associate Professor of Church History, Seminary of the Southwest, Austin, Texas; *83, 93, 96.* **Christopher Grundy,** Assistant Professor of Preaching and Worship, Eden Theological Seminary, St. Louis, Missouri; *155.* **David P. Gushee,** Distinguished University Professor of Christian Ethics, Mercer University, Atlanta, Georgia; *293, 303.*

Douglas John Hall, Professor Emeritus of Christian Theology, McGill University, Montreal, Quebec, Canada; *157.* **Charles E. Hambrick-Stowe,** Pastor, First Congregational Church of Ridgefield, Connecticut; *430, 447.* **Jin Hee Han,** Associate Professor of Biblical Studies, New York Theological Seminary, New York, New York; *134.* **Angela Dienhart Hancock,** Adjunct Faculty, PhD Candidate, Princeton Theological Seminary, Princeton, New Jersey; *425, 449.* **Gary Neal Hansen,** Assistant Professor of Church History, University of Dubuque Theological Seminary, Dubuque, Iowa; *236, 245.* **Timothy B. Hare,** Pastor, Huntington United Methodist Church, Shelton, Connecticut; *242, 254, 260.* **Walter J. Harrelson,** Professor Emeritus of Vanderbilt University, residing in Winston-Salem, North Carolina; *323, 328, 332.* **Daniel Harris,** Associate Professor of Homiletics, Aquinas Institute of Theology, St. Louis, Missouri; *34, 36, 39.* **James Henry Harris,** Professor of Homiletics and Pastoral Theology, Virginia Union University, School of Theology, Richmond, Virginia; *355, 359, 368.* **Christopher B. Hays,** D. Wilson Moore Assistant Professor of Ancient Near Eastern Studies, Fuller Theological Seminary, Pasadena, California; *512, 524.* **Trace Haythorn,** President, The Fund for Theological Education, Atlanta, Georgia; *344, 350, 353, 362.* **Susan Hedahl,** Herman G. Stuempfle Chair of Proclamation of the Word, Professor of Homiletics, Lutheran Theological Seminary at Gettysburg, Gettysburg, Pennsylvania; *67.* **William R. Herzog II,** Dean of Faculty, Professor of New Testament, Andover Newton Theological School, Newton Centre, Massachusetts; *6.* **Martha C. Highsmith,** Deputy Secretary of the University and Lecturer in Divinity, Yale Divinity School, New Haven, Connecticut; *401, 411, 413, 420, 423.* **Johnny B. Hill,** Assistant Professor of Theology, Louisville Presbyterian Theological Seminary, Louisville, Kentucky; *47, 69.* **Allen Hilton,** Minister of Faith and Learning, Wayzata Community Church, Wayzata, Minnesota; *511.* **Todd M. Hobbie,** Pastor, First Presbyterian Church, Concord, North Carolina; *470.* **John C. Holbert,** Lois Craddock Perkins Professor of Homiletics, Perkins School of Theology, Southern Methodist University, Dallas, Texas; *224, 233.* **David Holmes,** Minister, McDougall United Church, Calgary, Alberta, Canada; *4, 17, 22.* **H. James Hopkins,** Pastor, Lakeshore Avenue Baptist Church, Oakland, California; *326, 327, 336.* **Leah McKell Horton,** Associate Pastor for Adult Ministries, Trinity Presbyterian Church, Atlanta, Georgia; *515, 524.* **Patrick J. Howell,** Professor of Pastoral Theology and Rector of the Jesuit Community, Seattle University, Seattle, Washington; *15, 27.* **Paul Junggap Huh,** Assistant Professor of Worship and Director of Korean American Ministries, Columbia Theological Seminary, Decatur, Georgia; *104, 113.* **Edith M. Humphrey,** William F. Orr Professor of New Testament, Pittsburgh Theological Seminary, Pittsburgh, Pennsylvania; *114, 120.* **Alice W. Hunt,** President, Chicago Theological Seminary, Chicago, Illinois; *251.*

William N. Jackson, Honorably Retired Minister, Presbyterian Church (U.S.A.), Mount Joy, Pennsylvania; *512.* **Cynthia A. Jarvis,** Minister and Head of Staff, The Presbyterian Church of Chestnut Hill, Philadelphia, Pennsylvania; *249, 258, 261.* **Joseph R. Jeter,** Granville and Erline Walker Professor of Homiletics, Brite Divinity School at Texas Christian University, Fort Worth, Texas; *132.* **Pablo A. Jiménez,** Consultant Editor, Chalice Press, and Pastor, Iglesia Cristiana (Discipulos de Cristo), Dorado, Puerto Rico; *512.* **E. Elizabeth Johnson,** J. Davison Philips Professor of New Testament, Columbia Theological Seminary, Decatur, Georgia; *230.* **Jay Emerson Johnson,** Senior Director, Academic Research and Resources, Center for Lesbian and Gay Studies in Religion and Ministry, Pacific School of Religion and

The Graduate Theological Union, Berkeley, California; *488, 497.* **Kristen Deede Johnson,** Associate Director, The CrossRoads Project, and Assistant Professor of Political Science, Hope College, Holland, Michigan; *546.* **Nicole L. Johnson,** Assistant Professor in Religious Studies, Mount Union College, Alliance, Ohio; *217, 219.* **Patrick W. T. Johnson,** Pastor, Frenchtown Presbyterian Church, Frenchtown, New Jersey; *30, 38.* **Susan B. W. Johnson,** Minister, Hyde Park Union Church, Chicago, Illinois; *251.* **Trygve David Johnson,** Hinga-Boersma Dean of the Chapel, Hope College, Holland, Michigan; *220.* **Kirk Byron Jones,** Adjunct Faculty in Ethics, Andover Newton Theological School, Newton Centre, Massachusetts; *432.* **L. Shannon Jung,** Professor of Town and Country Ministry, Saint Paul School of Theology, Kansas City, Missouri; *46, 59.*

Deborah J. Kapp, Edward F. and Phyllis K. Campbell Associate Professor of Urban Ministry, McCormick Theological Seminary, Chicago, Illinois; *176, 179, 188, 197.* **Grace Ji-Sun Kim,** Associate Professor of Doctrinal Theology, Moravian Theological Seminary, Bethlehem, Pennsylvania; *510, 515, 520, 525.* **Jin S. Kim,** Senior Pastor, Church of All Nations, Minneapolis, Minnesota; *432, 439, 441, 448, 450.* **Katie Givens Kime,** Associate Pastor for Adult Ministries, Trinity Presbyterian Church, Atlanta, Georgia; *400, 409, 413.* **Clifton Kirkpatrick,** Visiting Professor of Ecumenical Studies and Global Ministries, Louisville Presbyterian Theological Seminary, Louisville, Kentucky; *402, 403, 405, 412, 414.* **Aaron Klink,** Westbrook Fellow, Program in Theology and Medicine, Duke University, Durham, North Carolina; *33, 42.* **Constance M. Koch, OP,** Dominican Sisters of Hope, Dobbs Ferry, New York; *292, 305.*

Jae Won Lee, Adjunct Professor, The Lutheran School of Theology, Chicago, Illinois; *421.* **Mark B. Lee,** Director of Adult Education, Plymouth Congregational United Church of Christ, Fort Collins, Colorado; *534, 548.* **Kimberly Bracken Long,** Assistant Professor of Worship, Columbia Theological Seminary, Decatur, Georgia; *233.* **Thomas G. Long,** Bandy Professor of Preaching, Candler School of Theology, Emory University, Atlanta, Georgia; *295, 306, 313, 315.* **Mary Elise Lowe,** Assistant Professor, Department of Religion, Augsburg College, Minneapolis, Minnesota; *436.* **Barbara K. Lundblad,** Joe R. Engle Professor of Preaching, Union Theological Seminary, New York, New York; *248, 256.*

W. Eugene March, A. B. Rhodes Professor of Old Testament Emeritus, Louisville Presbyterian Theological Seminary, Louisville, Kentucky; *533.* **Molly T. Marshall,** President and Professor of Theology and Spiritual Formation, Central Baptist Theological Seminary, Shawnee, Kansas; *243, 252.* **Martin E. Marty,** Fairfax M. Cone Distinguished Service Professor Emeritus, University of Chicago, Illinois; *205, 209, 212, 216.* **Peter W. Marty,** Pastor, St. Paul Lutheran Church, Davenport, Iowa; *224, 233.* **David Maxwell,** Executive Editor, Geneva Press and The Thoughtful Christian, Louisville, Kentucky; *398, 399, 407, 408, 413, 416, 417.* **Jennifer M. McBride,** Postdoctoral Fellow, Candler School of Theology, Emory University, Atlanta, Georgia; *530.* **Gordon McClellan,** Pastor, First Presbyterian Church, Corvallis, Oregon; *284, 287.* **John S. McClure,** Charles G. Finney Professor of Homiletics and Chair of Graduate Department of Religion, Vanderbilt Divinity School, Nashville, Tennessee; *269, 273.* **Thomas P. McCreesh,** Associate Professor, Theology Department, Providence College, Providence, Rhode Island; *224, 229.* **Dean McDonald,** Cathedral College of Preachers, Washington, D.C.; *68.* **Donald K. McKim,** Retired Academic Editor, Westminster John Knox Press; *221.* **Marvin A. McMickle,** Professor of Homiletics, Ashland Theological Seminary, Ashland, Ohio; *484, 486, 493, 502.* **Jennifer Powell McNutt,** Assistant Professor of Theology and History of Christianity, Wheaton College, Wheaton, Illinois; *81, 86.* **Allen C. McSween Jr.,** Pastor, Fourth Presbyterian Church, Greenville, South Carolina; *158, 161,*

164. **James McTyre,** Pastor, Lake Hills Presbyterian Church, Knoxville, Tennessee; *172.* **Veronice Miles,** Ruby Pardue and Shelmer D. Blackburn Assistant Professor of Homiletics and Christian Education, Wake Forest University School of Divinity, Winston-Salem, North Carolina; *203, 204, 206, 215, 216.* **Steven D. Miller,** Pastor, Community United Methodist Church, Westcliffe, Colorado; *319, 338, 341.* **Troy A. Miller,** Associate Professor of Bible and Theology, Crichton College, Memphis, Tennessee; *94.* **Stephanie Y. Mitchem,** Professor and Chair, Department of Religious Studies, University of South Carolina, Columbia, South Carolina; *404, 422.* **Randle R. (Rick) Mixon,** Pastor, First Baptist Church, Palo Alto, California; *263, 264, 272, 278, 281, 282, 287.* **Diane Givens Moffett,** Senior Pastor, St. James Presbyterian Church, Greensboro, North Carolina; *320, 339.* **Shawnthea Monroe,** Senior Minister, Plymouth United Church of Christ, Shaker Heights, Ohio; *350, 356, 357, 359, 366.* **Mary Alice Mulligan,** Affiliate Professor of Homiletics and Ethics, Christian Theological Seminary, Indianapolis, Indiana; *318, 332.* **Debra J. Mumford,** Frank H. Caldwell Assistant Professor of Homiletics, Louisville Presbyterian Theological Seminary, Louisville, Kentucky; *329, 337.* **D. Cameron Murchison,** Dean of Faculty, Columbia Theological Seminary, Decatur, Georgia; *231, 391.* **Stephen Butler Murray,** Senior Pastor, The First Baptist Church of Boston, Massachusetts, and College Chaplain and Associate Professor of Religion, Endicott College, Beverly, Massachusetts; *321.*

Andrew Nagy-Benson, Senior Minister, Spring Glen Church, United Church of Christ, Hamden, Connecticut; *77, 82, 91.* **Carmen Nanko-Fernández,** Assistant Professor of Pastoral Ministry; Director, Ecumenical Doctor of Ministry Program, Catholic Theological Union, Chicago, Illinois; *95.* **Frederick Niedner,** Professor of Theology, Department of Theology, Valparaiso University, Valparaiso, Indiana; *181, 190.* **Rodger Y. Nishioka,** Benton Family Associate Professor of Christian Education, Columbia Theological Seminary, Decatur, Georgia; *85.*

Kathleen M. O'Connor, William Marcellus McPheeters Professor of Old Testament, Columbia Theological Seminary, Decatur, Georgia; *41.* **Donald P. Olsen,** Minister, Plymouth Congregational Church, Wichita, Kansas; *178, 187, 196.* **Robert J. Owens,** Professor of Old Testament, General Theological Seminary of the Episcopal Church, New York, New York; *50.*

Earl F. Palmer, Preaching Pastor-in-Residence, National Presbyterian Church, Washington, D.C.; *511, 523.* **Lance Pape,** Assistant Professor of Homiletics, Brite Divinity School, Fort Worth, Texas; *369.* **V. Steven Parrish,** Professor of Old Testament, Memphis Theological Seminary, Memphis, Tennessee; *314.* **Jeff Paschal,** Pastor, First Presbyterian Church, Wooster, Ohio; *238, 242, 246.* **Shannon Michael Pater,** Minister, Central Congregational United Church of Christ, Atlanta, Georgia; *241, 250, 259.* **Stephanie A. Paulsell,** Houghton Professor of the Practice of Ministry Studies, Harvard Divinity School, Cambridge, Massachusetts; *71, 72, 80, 89.* **Amy Plantinga Pauw,** Henry P. Mobley Professor of Doctrinal Theology, Louisville Presbyterian Theological Seminary, Louisville, Kentucky; *205, 213.* **Julie Peeples,** Senior Minister, Congregational United Church of Christ, Greensboro, North Carolina; *427, 431, 440, 445, 449.* **Pheme Perkins,** Professor of New Testament, Theology Department, Boston College, Chestnut Hill, Massachusetts; *159.* **Ronald E. Peters,** President, the Inter-Denominational Theological Center, Atlanta, Georgia; *434, 435, 443.* **Blair Alison Pogue,** Rector, St. Matthew's Episcopal Church, St. Paul, Minnesota; *374, 393, 396.* **Emerson B. Powery,** Professor of Biblical Studies, Messiah College, Grantham, Pennsylvania; *237.* **Luke A. Powery,** Perry and Georgia Engle Assistant Professor of Homiletics, Princeton Theological Seminary, Princeton, New Jersey; *324, 330, 331, 333, 340.* **Andrew Purves,** Professor of Reformed Theology, Pittsburgh Theological Seminary, Pittsburgh, Pennsylvania; *483, 504.*

Melinda A. Quivik, Associate Professor of Christian Assembly, Lutheran Theological Seminary at Philadelphia, Pennsylvania; *299, 308, 314.*

Nancy J. Ramsay, Executive Vice President and Dean, Brite Divinity School, Texas Christian University, Fort Worth, Texas; *268, 276, 279, 288.* **Elizabeth P. Randall,** Cathedral Spiritual Director, St. John's Cathedral, Denver, Colorado; *445.* **Mitchell G. Reddish,** O. L. Walker Professor of Christian Studies and Chair of the Department of Religious Studies, Stetson University, DeLand, Florida; *429.* **Marcia Y. Riggs,** J. Erskine Love Professor of Christian Ethics, Columbia Theological Seminary, Decatur, Georgia; *103, 111.* **John D. Rohrs,** Associate Rector, Christ Episcopal Church, Raleigh, North Carolina; *153, 169.* **John Rollefson,** Pastor, Lutheran Church of the Master, Los Angeles, California; *210.* **Iwan Russell-Jones,** Television Producer, Cardiff, United Kingdom; *423.*

Don E. Saliers, William R. Cannon Professor Emeritus of Theology and Worship, Candler School of Theology, Emory University, Atlanta, Georgia; *29, 35, 41.* **Christian Scharen,** Assistant Professor of Worship and Theology, Luther Seminary, St. Paul, Minnesota; *13.* **David J. Schlafer,** Homiletics Consultant, Author, and Conference Leader, Bethesda, Maryland; *32.* **Clayton J. Schmit,** Arthur DeKruyter/Christ Church Oak Brook Professor of Preaching and Academic Director of the Brehm Center for Worship, Theology, and the Arts, Fuller Theological Seminary, Pasadena, California; *234.* **Timothy F. Sedgwick,** Vice President and Associate Dean of Academic Affairs, The Clinton S. Quin Professor of Christian Ethics, Virginia Theological Seminary, Alexandria, Virginia; *75, 78.* **William L. Self,** Senior Pastor, Johns Creek Baptist Church, Alpharetta, Georgia; *48, 60, 65.* **Donald Senior,** President, Catholic Theological Union, Chicago, Illinois; *250.* **Mary E. Shields,** Pathways to Healing and Ministry, a specialized ministry of the Presbyterian Church (U.S.A.), Columbus, Ohio; *481.* **Elizabeth McGregor Simmons,** Pastor, Davidson College Presbyterian Church, Davidson, North Carolina; *418, 419.* **Richard M. Simpson,** Rector, St. Francis Episcopal Church, Holden, Massachusetts; *105.* **Stephanie Mar Smith,** Independent Scholar, Seattle, Washington; *480, 494, 498.* **Susan Marie Smith,** Assistant Professor of Preaching and Worship, Saint Paul School of Theology, Kansas City, Missouri; *521.* **Ted A. Smith,** Assistant Professor of Ethics and Society, Vanderbilt Divinity School, Nashville, Tennessee; *347, 369.* **Sheldon W. Sorge,** Pastor to Presbytery, Presbytery of Pittsburgh, Presbyterian Church (U.S.A.), Pittsburgh, Pennsylvania; *126, 144.* **Richard E. Spalding,** Chaplain to the College, Williams College, Williamstown, Massachusetts; *495, 501.* **Haywood Spangler,** Rector, St. Bartholomew's Church, Richmond, Virginia; *529, 547, 551.* **Rochelle A. Stackhouse,** Senior Minister, Church of the Redeemer United Church of Christ, New Haven, Connecticut; *441, 450.* **Joy Douglas Strome,** Pastor, Lake View Presbyterian Church, Chicago, Illinois; *240, 242, 251, 257, 260.* **George W. Stroup,** J. B. Green Professor of Theology, Columbia Theological Seminary, Decatur, Georgia; *195.* **Nibs Stroupe,** Pastor, Oakhurst Presbyterian Church, Decatur, Georgia; *296, 301, 310.* **Laird J. Stuart,** Interim President, San Francisco Theological Seminary, San Francisco, California; *178, 184.*

Jessica Tate, Associate Pastor, Fairfax Presbyterian Church, Fairfax, Virginia; *528, 537, 542, 551.* **Tom Tate,** Pastor, Plaza Presbyterian Church, Charlotte, North Carolina; *506.* **Barbara Brown Taylor,** Harry R. Butman Professor of Religion, Piedmont College, Demorest, Georgia; *45, 53, 62, 507.* **Frank A. Thomas,** Senior Servant, Mississippi Boulevard Christian Church, Memphis, Tennessee; *49, 57, 69.* **James W. Thompson,** Robert R. and Kay Onstead Professor of New Testament, Abilene Christian University, Abilene, Texas; *87, 92.* **Robert V. Thompson,** Minister, Lake Street Church, Evanston, Illinois; *269.* **David Toole,** Associate Dean, Duke Divinity School, Durham, North Carolina; *87, 96.* **W. Sibley Towner,** Professor

Emeritus of Biblical Interpretation, Union Presbyterian Seminary, Richmond, Virginia; *104*. **Emilie M. Townes,** Dean, Vanderbilt Divinity School, Nashville, Tennessee; *348, 349, 358, 360, 367*. **Martin G. Townsend,** Bishop Retired, The Diocese of Easton, Springfield, West Virginia; *54, 64*. **Douglas Travis,** Dean and President, Episcopal Theological Seminary of the Southwest, Austin, Texas; *202, 216*. **David G. Trickett,** President and Henry Warren Professor of Ethics and Leadership, The Iliff School of Theology, Denver, Colorado; *302*. **Thomas H. Troeger,** J. Edward and Ruth Cox Lantz Professor of Christian Communication, Yale Divinity School, New Haven, Connecticut; *51, 58, 66*. **Diane Turner-Sharazz,** Director, Course of Study School of Ohio, Methodist Theological School in Ohio, Delaware, Ohio, and Pastor, McKinley United Methodist Church, Dayton, Ohio; *323, 332, 341*.

Edwin Chr. Van Driel, Assistant Professor of Theology, Pittsburgh Theological Seminary, Pittsburgh, Pennsylvania; *121*. **Leanne Van Dyk,** Dean and Vice President of Academic Affairs, Western Theological Seminary, Holland, Michigan; *404, 410, 422*

Carol L. Wade, Canon Precentor, Washington National Cathedral, Washington, D.C.; *3, 8, 26*. **Paul Walaskay,** Professor Emeritus of Biblical Studies, Union Presbyterian Seminary, Richmond, Virginia; *51*. **Richard F. Ward,** Fred B. Craddock Chair in Preaching and Worship, Phillips Theological Seminary, Tulsa, Oklahoma; *77, 95, 463*. **Don Wardlaw,** James G. K. McClure Professor Emeritus of Preaching and Worship, McCormick Theological Seminary, Chicago, Illinois; *194, 196*. **Theodore J. Wardlaw,** President, Austin Presbyterian Theological Seminary, Austin, Texas; *378, 385, 394*. **Carolyn R. Waters,** Senior Pastor, Christ Church, United Methodist Church, Denver, Colorado; *508, 516*. **Jann Cather Weaver,** Associate Professor of Worship, Theology, and the Arts, United Theological Seminary of the Twin Cities, New Brighton, Minnesota; *509, 519*. **Jo Bailey Wells,** Associate Professor of the Practice of Christian Ministry and Bible and Director of Anglican Studies, Duke University Divinity School, Durham, North Carolina; *377*. **Audrey West,** Adjunct Professor of New Testament, Lutheran School of Theology at Chicago, Illinois; *214*. **Barbara G. Wheeler,** Director, Center for the Study of Theological Education, Auburn Theological Seminary, New York, New York; *323, 341*. **John E. White,** Dean of Students, Columbia Theological Seminary, Decatur, Georgia; *247, 255*. **Andrea Wigodsky,** Chaplain, St. Mary's School, Raleigh, North Carolina; *154, 158, 164*. **John Wilkinson,** Pastor, Third Presbyterian Church, Rochester, New York; *485, 486*. **Patrick J. Willson,** Pastor, Williamsburg Presbyterian Church, Williamsburg, Virginia; *159*. **Kevin A. Wilson,** Adjunct Professor of Religion and Theology, Merrimack College, North Andover, Massachusetts; *118, 122*. **Alexander Wimberly,** Minister, McCracken Memorial Presbyterian Church, Belfast, Northern Ireland; *322, 342*. **Karyn L. Wiseman,** Professor of Homiletics, Lutheran Theological Seminary at Philadelphia, Pennsylvania; *545*. **David J. Wood,** Senior Pastor, Glencoe Union Church, Glencoe, Illinois; *36, 39, 42*. **Erica Brown Wood,** Priest-in-Charge, St. Luke's Episcopal Church, Mount Joy, Pennsylvania, and Adjunct Professor, Lancaster Theological Seminary, Lancaster, Pennsylvania; *152*.

Brett Younger, Associate Professor of Preaching, McAfee School of Theology, Atlanta, Georgia; *99, 108, 116*. **Mark E. Yurs,** Pastor, Salem United Church of Christ, Verona, Wisconsin; *7*.

Scripture Index